Environmental Education in the Primary School

PHILIP NEAL and JOY PALMER

BLACKWELL EDUCATION

© Philip Neal, Joy Palmer, 1990
First published 1990

Published by
Basil Blackwell Ltd
108 Cowley Road
Oxford OX4 1JF
UK

British Library Cataloguing in Publication Data
Neal, Philip 1923–
    Environmental education in the primary school. – (Primary matters).
    1. Great Britain. Primary schools. Curriculum subjects :
    Environmental studies. Teaching
    I. Title. II. Palmer, Joy III. Series
    372.3570941

    ISBN 0–631–17055–3
    ISBN 0–631–17056–1 pbk

Typeset in 11/13pt Century Schoolbook
by Photo·graphics, Honiton, Devon.
Printed in Great Britain by Dotesios (Printers) Ltd., Trowbridge.

Contents

Acronyms used in this book

AA	Association of Agriculture
CCI	Cross Curriculum Issue
CEE	Council for Environmental Education
CT	Conservation Trust
DoE	Department of the Environment
DES	Department of Education and Science
EEAA	Environmental Education Advisors Association
FSC	Field Studies Council
HET	Heritage Education Trust
ICCE	International Centre for Conservation Education
IWCC	Interim Whole Curriculum Committee
LMS	Local Management of Schools
MAFF	Ministry of Agriculture, Food and Fisheries
NAEE	National Association for Environmental Education
NAFSO	National Association for Field Study Officers
NAOE	National Association for Outdoor Education
NAUS	National Association for Urban Studies
NCC	Nature Conservancy Council
NCC	National Curriculum Council
NT	National Trust
RSPB	Royal Society for the Protection of Birds
RSPCA	Royal Society for the Prevention of Cruelty to Animals
SAT	Standard Assessment Task
TGAT	Task Group for Assessment and Testing
UNEP	United Nations Environment Programme
WCS	World Conservation Strategy

Acknowledgements

We are grateful to the following individuals who provided us with **case study** materials, and would like to thank their headteachers and pupils for allowing the work to be published.

1 *Local history*
Mrs J F Palmer and Mrs M Bingham, Holland House First School, Sutton Coldfield

2 *The school grounds*
Mrs J Beesley, Merridale Primary School, Wolverhampton

3 *The school grounds*
Mr M Berry, Churchfield CE (C) School, Rugeley

4 *Animals in the classroom* (environmental science)
Mr T Gunn (Headteacher) Witton-le-Wear Primary School, Durham

5 *A historic house* (cooperation between schools and with the LEA)
Mr D Brook (Headteacher) King Charles Primary School, Walsall

6 *The school neighbourhood* (urban study)
Mrs J Beesley, Merridale Primary School, Wolverhampton

7 *A local stream* (use of Field Study Centre)
Mrs A Jones, St George's Junior School, Shrewsbury

8 *Link with local industry/information technology*
Mrs D Tedcastle (Headteacher) Hope Primary School, Shropshire

We would also like to thank the following for photographs:
Mrs J F Palmer (Case study 1); Mr T Gunn (Case study 4); Mr D Brook (Case study 5); Mr E Jackson, Croxteth Park, Liverpool (Butter making and Victorian Christmas); Shropshire Star (Interviewing the village postmistress). All other photographs are by Philip Neal.

We wish to acknowledge the work of members of the Environmental Education Task Group of the Interim Whole Curriculum Committee of the National Curriculum Council. We are pleased to make some of the original consultation documents available to a wider audience; they stand in their own right as useful and important additions to the literature of environmental education.

We would also like to acknowledge the source material provided by many Local Education Authorities, in particular those from whose material we have quoted: Birmingham, Kent, Norfolk, Sheffield, Wiltshire, Wolverhampton.

Source material has been provided by many organisations. We wish to acknowledge that quoted from the:
Council for Environmental Education (with which both authors are closely associated);
Department of Education and Science (including press releases);
National Association for Environmental Education (the authors are executive officers of the NAEE);
Nature Conservancy Council
Schools Council
Scottish Environmental Education Council
United Nations Environment Programme

The UK's response (education section) to the World Conservation Strategy was written by John Baines, the former Director of the CEE. We wish to place on record our appreciation of his contribution to it.

Many other people have been most helpful in the compilation of this book. We would particularly like to mention David Brook, Jackie Donnelly, Tim Gunn and Keith Morrison. Finally we thank our series editors, Leone Burton and Henry Pluckrose.

Primary Matters: Editors' Preface

It is hard to find an acknowledgment of how recent are primary schools whose curriculum and management reflects the particular emotional, social, intellectual and physical needs of young children or of how far they have developed in a very brief time span. Indeed, there are teachers in today's primary schools who remember that in 1949, five years after the famous Butler Education Act, 36% of children of secondary age were still attending schools which also housed children under 11. Those same teachers have seen the development of primary schools through the Plowden era in the 1960s, the building of open-plan schools which aroused such intense international interest in the 1960s and '70s, into the 1980s and the new Act introducing a national curriculum and attainment targets for children of 7 and 11 years.

In the years following the First World War, successive government committees examined the educational needs of adolescents, of boys and girls in the middle years of childhood (7–11) and of children of 'infant and nursery' age. These committees reported between 1926 and 1933; their recommendations, though implemented in a piece-meal fashion, led to a considerable restructuring of schooling in England and Wales. The most profound effect of these changes was the acknowledgment that the primary years were a coherent and essential stage in the educational process, a stage which had distinctive needs and requirements. Prior to this, children had been educated in all-age schools. Unless a child were fortunate enough to be selected at the age of 11 (usually as a successful outcome of academic competition), the school s/he joined at 5 years of age would be the school s/he left at 13. Ninety per cent of the school population attended such schools and it became increasingly obvious that they were failing simultaneously to meet the differing needs of the 5-year-old, the child in the middle years, and of the 13-year-old school leaver. In the late 1930s, primary schools began to develop, with secondary (elementary) schools providing for those children who failed the selective examination. The distinctive categories of secondary education were enshrined in the 1944 Education Act which established a comprehensive tri-partite system of secondary education, but even five years later this was still not fully realised.

It took, therefore, some twenty years from the mid-1930s for primary schools to become generally established and, with the population explosion of the 1950s and '60s, primary school practice underwent many developments as the early years of schooling came to be regarded as an essential phase in the educational process. Experiments were undertaken in teaching and learning methodology in the curriculum, in the organisation of classes (remember vertical or family grouping?), and, as already mentioned, in the architectural style of new schools. The curriculum became richer and more challenging to young children. Enthusiastic support for these changes was found in the report published by the Plowden Committee in 1967.

In contrast to this period, more recently primary education has been subject to critical appraisal and retrenchment. Academics (like Peters and Dearden) and politicians (like Boyson and Cox), as well as Inspectors from local education authorities and Her Majesty's Inspectorate, have focused attention upon the issues and assumptions underlying the work offered by teachers to young children. Are there things which *all* children should learn during their primary years? What constitutes essential knowledge for the primary-aged child? What should be the balance between the teaching of facts, the development of skills, the understanding of the concepts which underlie knowledge, and the processes through which this knowledge is acquired and developed? How effective are different classroom approaches in developing thinking skills, social awareness and responsibility? How can the primary curriculum best address the fundamental technological changes brought about by the microchip? In what ways are social issues such as racism, sexism or disadvantage best addressed? How should the particular insights and experiences of the disabled child be incorporated? How can institutional barriers to the involvement of all interested parties, especially parents, in the education of each child be dismantled? How should religious education be handled within a society which is more and more secular but also no longer made up of only one major faith group?

Questions such as these are not asked in a vacuum. They reflect the anxieties (real and imagined) of parents, academics, politicians, industrialists and, most of all, of the teachers themselves. That such questions are now being asked is, in part, a recognition of how far primary schools have come over the fifty or so years since they were first conceived. In a climate of concern and criticism, it is also easy to forget that British developments in primary education have been the focus of attention, respect and emulation in many other countries.

Indeed, many have argued that it was a freedom from bureaucracy which gave English primary schools their unique character and made possible the kinds of thoughtful experiment which attracted an international reputation. At the same time, others have suggested that piecemeal development has led to idiosyncracy. Hence the current demand for every school to follow a programme reflecting clearly defined national criteria. However, the need for the individual teacher to make choices, ask questions, and influence every child's development continues to be respected and, however centralised the curriculum may become, however much the school programme is evaluated, however regularly children are tested against performance norms, the thoughtful teacher will continue to ask questions about *what* John or Akbar, Mary or Mai-Lin will learn, how they will learn it, what particular needs they have and how their individual interests, attitudes and aptitudes can be accommodated into the daily work of the classroom.

All the books in this series address aspects of these kinds of questions which teachers are asking as part of their concern to establish effective strategies for learning. Part of that concern focuses upon the links between the excitement of learning evidenced by young children, and the need to evaluate and maintain coherence in their experiences. Effective learning is the product of engagement as each and every member of the group struggles to make the learning process her or his own. At the same time, personal learning can still be limited unless it is placed in a broader context so that, for example, subject strands unite into a comprehensible and rational whole. Each author in this series seeks to indicate cross-curricular links, even though the titles indicate particular subject specialisms as starting points, so that the approach unifies rather than divides the child's experience of the curriculum.

As editors of this series, we wish to present to practising primary teachers a range of titles which recognises the complexity of the primary teacher's role. Each book will give shape and purpose to specific curriculum areas, dealing with issues which are particular to that specialism, presenting ideas for interesting and innovative practice in that area but, at the same time, emphasising the unity of the primary experience. Thus each title is set against a broad canvas, that of the primary school as a living and vibrant place in which young children grow and learn.

Leone Burton
Henry Pluckrose

Introduction

This book is published at a time of continuing optimism in the world of environmental education. Indeed the recent past has been something of a landmark era in the development of this area of learning. Of paramount importance has been the recognition of environmental education as a cross-curricular theme of the National Curriculum for schools. In August 1988 the Secretary of State reminded the National Curriculum Council of its responsibility for keeping the *whole* curriculum under review, not just the core and foundation subjects. Among other matters, the NCC was requested to examine the nature of cross-curricular issues – these being 'aspects of learning and teaching that permeate almost all elements within the school curriculum whether they be formal or informal'. As elaborated in Chapter 2 the Interim Whole Curriculum Committee (IWCC) of the NCC identified three 'areas' of cross-curricular issues; dimensions, skills/competencies and themes. Within this framework, environmental education was identified as one of the key themes to be included in the basic curriculum entitlement for every child. As such it should have progression and continuity like all core and foundation subjects, and should in practice permeate the curriculum as a whole. Thus it is clear that schools are intended to regard cross-curricular themes as part of the entitlement of children that goes beyond the core and foundation subjects.

A task group of the IWCC was established to 'produce advice on the nature and scope of Environmental Education and how this subject might be delivered through the core and foundation subjects of the National Curriculum'. Key papers were written and the National Curriculum Council published substantial documentation on the development and management of an overall curriculum framework and the nature and place of cross-curricular themes, dimensions and skills within this.

Environmental education has been well established on the curriculum map of primary schools in England and Wales for three decades. Local authorities, national bodies and individual schools and teachers have done a tremendous amount to promote its importance; the result being some splendid and wide-ranging examples of good practice. Our optimism now lies, however, in the fact that for the first time in our formal education service, it is ensured that there will be a clearly laid down *progression* of an *entitlement* for every child in environmental education.

National developments must be set against a backcloth of dramatically increased public awareness of an interest in environmental matters, and developments within the European Community. The World Conservation Strategy (1980) raised fundamental issues that needed attention. The UK response to this (The Conservation and Development Programme for the UK) emphasised the importance of environmental education, listing many recommendations. In November 1987, Norway's Prime Minister, Mrs Gro Harlem Brundtland, published her United Nations World Commission for the Environment report *Our Common Future*. This argued for sustainable development in the world. Inevitably public education is needed to achieve this end. UK Prime Minister, Mrs Margaret Thatcher backed environmental initiatives in a speech to the Royal Society in September 1988 which was, in no small measure, the trigger for the publication of the DES document *Environmental Education from 5–16*.

The importance of environmental education was also underlined by Mrs Angela Rumbold, UK Minister of State for Education and Science, in a speech to young people on Thursday 27 July 1989 at the London International Science Fortnight.

> Good environmental education, like any good education, must lead pupils and students out and on from their immediate perceptions and experience to a wider understanding. It must develop their capacity to go beyond the anecdotal and the particular. None of that happens by chance. A number of subjects and aspects of the school curriculum deal with matters to do with the interplay between man and his environment. Key among them are geography; science; design and technology and health education. Lesser roles may be played by art, history and drama. In England and Wales we are reforming our education system and bringing in a National Curriculum. That will ensure among other things, that each of those subjects makes its unique contribution and combines with others in providing environmental education in both primary and secondary schools. Of course what is done will vary between subjects and with younger and older children. I am convinced that pupils must first learn about natural phenomena in order to understand complex environmental matters ... Within our own specific education policies and structure, we will promote environmental education in schools and in further and higher education ... The importance of environmental education is that it sensitises us

to the causes and effects of problems of which, for too long, we have been only dimly aware. The environment is our children's future and many already know that. We must encourage them to think positively about it ... what needs to be done to reduce the damage we do to it, what opportunities there are for improving the quality of our surroundings – and to come up with *practical* solutions. THEY SHOULD DRAW ON WHAT THEY LEARN AT SCHOOL ....

A most important motivation to the more positive attitude of the UK government to environmental education was the May 1988 meeting of the Council of the European Community when they agreed: 'on the need to take concrete steps for the promotion of environmental education so that this can be intensified in a comprehensive way throughout the Community'. A Resolution on Environmental Education was adopted to that end, with the following objective and guiding principles:

> The objective of environmental education is to increase the public awareness of the problems in this field, as well as possible solutions, and to lay the foundations for a fully informed and active participation of the individual in the protection of the environment and the prudent and rational use of natural resources. For the achievement of the objectives environmental education should take into account particularly the following guiding principles:
> – the environment as the common heritage of mankind,
> – the common duty of maintaining, protecting and improving the quality of the environment, as a contribution to the protection of human health and the safeguarding of the ecological balance,
> – the need for a prudent and rational utilisation of natural resources,
> – the way in which each individual can, by his own behaviour, particularly as a consumer, contribute to the protection of the environment.
> Journal of the European Communities, 6.7.88

It was resolved that Member States would make every effort to implement certain measures, including

> the promotion of environmental education in all sectors of education ... giving consideration to the basic aims of environmental education when drawing up curricula ...

> ... taking appropriate measures to develop teachers' knowledge of environmental matters in the context of their initial and in-service training ...

No-one can doubt the significance of these national and international developments. Yet perhaps mention should be made of the aims of a certain primary school, not included within the examples of good practice outlined in the pages of this book. These aims contain the following statements:

> To create an atmosphere in which the national interests of the children are stimulated and they are encouraged and given all possible freedom to enjoy their immediate surroundings and to learn from them ...

> to bring children (infants) into contact with the right kinds of practical experiences ... to encourage them to observe, to experiment, to discover and to talk about their experiences in a natural manner.
> In later years (juniors) to keep alive the spirit of wonder and enquiry, to give appropriate scope for activity ... plenty of practical work done in connection with first hand observation ...

These are aims with which any reader would no doubt be pleased to be associated. It may come as something of a surprise, however, to find that they were drawn up in July 1938 for Littledown JMI School, Durham.

In these days of National Curriculum complexities it is, perhaps, impossible to avoid 're-inventing the wheel ...' from time to time. We may often remind ourselves that there is nothing new except what has been forgotten.

At least we rest assured that it is a vital wheel that we are trying to turn, and that all hands are now moving it in the same direction. At last a basic entitlement for every child in the formal education service in environmental education is now laid down. It is our sincere hope that school-based in-service work will give urgent attention to cross-curricular issues, including familiarisation with the location of environmental education as a cross-curricular theme and with the specific documentation concerning the teaching and learning of its particular knowledge, understanding and skills. It is also our hope that in-service education will go beyond this basic minimum and give due attention to a proper location of environmental education in relation to the whole curriculum framework and the *context* of children's learning. Environmental education *must* be viewed as part of a coherent whole – perhaps the basis of it – rather than as an isolated element or 'yet another subject to be added on'. This book is intended to assist in the process of enabling teachers and schools to achieve these ends, resulting in the environmental education of every child in a way that is not only coherent and progressive but is also meaningful and relevant to life in the twenty-first century.

Several case study examples are interspersed in the main body of the text of this book. They have been chosen to illustrate some of the more important starting points for environmental education in the primary school; the range of these starting points is, of course, infinite. They exemplify but a small number, nevertheless we consider that they fairly describe some of the more obvious and important themes. The case studies presented are of differing lengths and focus. It is not our intention to impose a common style or approach – rather to allow the individual nature of each class teacher's work to be apparent in their own individual style. Study 4 is more substantial, outlining not only the content of work that was developed but also some of the theory underpinning the children's learning. Others, by design, offer a much briefer overview of activities that were undertaken by the class concerned. Also it is intentional that some accounts pay greater attention to links with the National Curriculum core subject attainment targets, perhaps leaving room for speculation on the desirability of organising all environmental work around the aim of teaching to specific targets.

Finally it should be mentioned that most of the accounts are preceded by a general introduction to the starting point. That for 'animals in the classroom' is particularly full as it is perhaps a topic of specific complexity. All accounts however are based on that all-important baseline – the involvement of the learners with objects and experiences in their immediate or local environments.

A note on terminology and national legislation

This book covers the United Kingdom, that is, England, Wales, Scotland and Northern Ireland. In each of the constituent countries of the UK there are not only important similarities, but also significant differences where education and educational provision is concerned. Wherever possible the authors have tried to recognise national variations, but inevitably some will have escaped attention. It is hoped that readers will accept this in the spirit intended and apply the points made to suit appropriate national circumstances as required.

It is also hoped that the basic arguments for a considered approach to environmental education will transcend national frontiers and be helpful to others outside the UK.

1 Towards a definition

During the past 30 years there have been many changes in approaches to education in primary schools. The development of environmental study over this time may be regarded not so much as the development of a new subject area but as the development of a philosophy and an approach. This approach is consistent with significant trends that have emerged in this period, which include:

- a move from formal towards informal methods;
- an increasing stress on child-centred as opposed to teacher-directed learning, and on helping children to find things out for themselves;
- the integration of work within a day and within the curriculum as a whole;
- the organisation of work on an individual basis and through assignments for small groups whereby children are encouraged to learn from each other;
- widening the learning and teaching environment to include the whole space of the school so that children are not confined to one classroom for a day's activities;
- the provision and use of a rich range of resources and experiences, both within the school and outside it.

As pointed out in papers presented as part of the United Kingdom delegation's contribution to the UNESCO inter-governmental conference in Tbilisi, USSR, October 1977,[1] the merits of traditional approaches have not been lost sight of, and they persist in varying degree in most schools; but the emergence of environmental studies as an important element of the primary school curriculum must be seen in the setting of these trends and developments.

> To an extent much of the 'content' has always been there, but now the environment is often looked at in a new way and not least as a stimulus to the curiosity and imagination of teacher and pupil alike.
> (UK papers for Tbilisi Conference, 1977[1])

Children need to learn that value judgements and decision making are worthless unless they are established on an understanding of fundamental relationships and principles. Shirley Williams, the then Secretary of State for Education, wrote

> The environment is a key factor in determining the quality of life. A well-founded understanding of the world about us is essential if we are to appreciate our heritage, recognise the international dimension of many environmental problems and plan soundly and imaginatively for the future.
>
> (Foreword to the UK's submission, Tbilisi 1977[1])

What is environmental education?

At this stage it would seem necessary to give brief consideration to the question 'What is environmental education?' and to a justification for the development of the approach and its widespread inclusion in the primary school curriculum, for indeed it seems widely accepted that environmental education should permeate the whole curriculum both inside and outside the school and that every school should have adequate arrangements for planning and implementing a programme of environmental education.

Many and varied attempts have been made to define the term environmental education in particular during the past 20 or so years when the implementation of environmental education has taken on a new urgency in response to critical problems that are becoming apparent in the world. As pointed out by Carson (1978)[2], in the United States of America, many people were independently facing up to problems, particularly after the publication of Rachael Carson's *Silent Spring*[3] in 1962. Worldwide concern of a similar nature intensified and in 1970 the International Union for the Conservation of Nature and Natural Resources called a Conference on environmental education in Nevada. The findings of that conference continue to be a major influence on the development of environmental education. The definition drawn up at the Conference is accepted in Britain by the National Association for Environmental Education and by many other organisations both in the UK and elsewhere.

> Environmental education is the process of recognising values and clarifying concepts in order to develop skills and attitudes necessary to understand and appreciate the inter-relatedness among man, his culture and his biophysical surroundings. Environmental education also entails practice in decision making and self-formulation of a code of behaviour about issues concerning environmental quality.[4]

The development of environmental education in the UK

In 1967 the Plowden Report, *Children and Their Primary Schools,*[5] confirmed the value of using the environment. From that point 'environment' became one of the most widely discussed words in education. Environmental education as a school subject has evolved rapidly, through the efforts of individuals, the campaigns of voluntary organisations and the development of governmental environment policy worldwide.

The National Association for Environmental Education is Britain's main teachers' organisation concerned with Environmental Education. The NAEE promotes environmental education in discussion and activities. National conferences are held regularly, working committees carry out research and outline possible courses and useful activities, and the results of the Association's work and ideas are published regularly in newsletters, journals and booklets.

The national Council for Environmental Education (CEE) was established as an educational charity in 1968 to provide a focus for organisations involved or interested in environmental education. Today its membership consists of some 60 national organisations from the professional, statutory and voluntary sectors. The CEE has three broad goals:

> *Development*: CEE aims to facilitate the development of the theory and practice of environmental education.
> *Promotion*: CEE aims to promote the concept of environmental education and facilitate its application in all spheres of education.
> *Review*: CEE aims to monitor the progress of environmental education and assess its effectiveness.

The international development of environmental education

At an international level there are frequent gatherings and conferences of people working in the field of environmental education leading to a great deal of common understanding of the aims, objectives and approaches to the subject.

Principle 19 enunciated at the United Nations Conference on the Human Environment, held in Stockholm in 1972, stated:

> Education in environmental matters for the younger generation as well as adults, giving due consideration to the underprivileged, is essential
> . . .
>
> (UN Conference on Human Environment, Stockholm 1972)

A year earlier the Ministers' Deputies at a Council of Europe meeting in Strasbourg had adopted a resolution advocating the introduction of the principles of nature conservation into education:

> The principles of ecology and the various forms of practical application embraced by the term 'nature conservation' must be taught in schools continuously at every level ...
>
> (Resolution (71)14 Council of Europe, 1971)

A further resolution was adopted:

> ... to encourage the training of teachers and officers capable of carrying out action both in and out of school, to organise introductory courses on environmental problems for youth leaders ...
>
> (Resolution (71)22 Council of Europe, 1971)

1975 saw the establishment of The Belgrade Charter,[6] prepared at the meeting set up by the new United Nations Environment Programme. This was the first inter-governmental statement on environmental education. It listed the aims, objectives, key concepts and guiding principles of environmental education, as discussed below. This was followed in 1977 by the first inter-governmental Conference on Environmental Education, held in Tbilisi, USSR, and organised by UNESCO. This conference prepared recommendations for the wider application of environmental education in formal and non-formal education. This major event and subsequent publications based on it, continue to provide the framework for the development of environmental education in the world today.

In 1980 the World Conservation Strategy[7] was produced. This is one of the most significant documents concerning conservation and environmental education at a global level ever to be published. The WCS is very significant indeed for those involved in environmental education as it emphasises the need to build support for world conservation through programmes of environmental education. We refer to some of the educational responses by the UK[8] to the World Conservation Strategy in chapters 3 and 6.

From 1986 onwards, work at an international level has continued on preparing supplements to the World Conservation Strategy, dealing with environmental education and ethics and culture among other issues.

1987 marked the tenth anniversary of the first Tbilisi conference and a 'Tbilisi Plus Ten' Conference,[9] jointly organised by UNESCO and UNEP, was held in Moscow. A number of major themes emerged from the deliberations of this event, including the vital importance of environmental education, summed up as follows in an introductory address:

> In the long run nothing significant will happen to reduce local and international threats to the environment unless widespread public awareness is aroused concerning the essential links between environmental quality and the continued satisfaction of human needs. Human action depends upon motivation which depends upon widespread understanding. This is why we feel it is so important that everyone becomes environmentally conscious through proper environmental education.
>
> (Booth 1987)[10]

Objectives for environmental education

In 1988 the Council of the European Community agreed on the need to promote environmental education throughout the Community. Bearing in mind the accepted definition of environmental education as stated at Nevada (see page 2), it follows that its contents should be directed towards certain ends. It is helpful at this stage to consider the brief but comprehensive set of objectives for environmental education set out by UNESCO (1975) at the Belgrade Workshop.[11] These are summarised as follows:

1 To foster clear awareness of and concern about economic, social, political and ecological inter-dependence in urban and rural areas;
2 To provide every person with opportunities to acquire the knowledge, values, attitudes, commitment and skills needed to protect and improve the environment;
3 To create new patterns of behaviour of individuals, groups and society as a whole towards the environment.

In its Statement of Aims (1976 and 1982)[12] the National Association for Environmental Education recognised that 'throughout primary and secondary education, the human environment, both rural and urban, should be regarded as a continuum from the wilderness, through the productive countryside, small settlements and suburbs, to the heart of the inner city'.

As pointed out by the Council for Environmental Education in its overview of Environmental Education,[13] since the environment is all-embracing then it must at some stage be considered in its totality to include aspects which are urban and rural, technological and social, aesthetic and ethical. This overview should be reflected in environmental education. This in itself raises certain problems: either environmental education becomes equated with the whole of education, thus losing its identity; or else, in order to become comprehensible, selected features only are considered. Either way, essential aspects of environmental education may be lost. One way to help overcome this problem is to recognise that an environmental dimension can be found in most aspects of education. Environmental education thus becomes an approach to education which incorporates considerations of the environment rather than being a separate part of education.

It is widely accepted that education related to the environment may take three forms. This was first formalised in the Schools Council's *Project Environment*:[14]

> There are three threads which have contributed to our present ideas and it has become almost commonplace nowadays to characterise these as education either ABOUT, FROM or FOR the environment.
>
> ... education ABOUT the environment seeks to discover the nature of the area under study often through investigatory and discovery approaches; the objectives are chiefly cognitive ones in that the aim is to amass information.
>
> ... In educating FROM the environment, teachers have sought to forward the general education of the child by using the environment as a resource in two main ways; firstly as a medium for enquiry and discovery which may lead to the enhancement of the learning process, the most important aspect being learning how to learn; secondly, as a source of material for realistic activities in language, mathematics, science and craft.
>
> ... To educate FOR the environment ... is education which is environmental in style with emphasis on developing an informed concern for the environment. The objectives go beyond the acquisition of skills and knowledge and require the development of involvement to the extent that values are formed which affect behaviour ... Thus the aim is to develop attitudes and levels of understanding which lead to a personal environmental ethic; that is, to educate pupils so that their actions and influences on collective action will be positively for the benefit of the earthly environment.
>
> > *(Project Environment 1970–73*, Schools Council, 1974)[14]

In 1974 the report[15] by H M Inspectors of Schools (Scotland) recognised that 'A programme of environmental education must disseminate knowledge, encourage understanding and foster attitudes' which reflected the views of *Project Environment*. They went on to say

> It contains empirical, synoptic, aesthetic and ethical elements, none of which can be studied in isolation:
> a)   The Empirical element. This is concerned with those aspects of

the environment which lend themselves to objective observation, measurement and analysis ... the main priority is to ensure that all pupils have as many opportunities as possible of making direct contact with the environment through observation and by measuring, recording, interpreting and discussing what has been observed.

b) The Synoptic element ... pupils need to be made aware of the complex nature of the environment. The aim of synoptic studies is to help pupils to realise the complexity of such issues and to introduce them to the inseparable nature of the various components of an environment and to the inter-relations of these. Method is as important as content in achieving this.

c) The Aesthetic element. Of the many aspects of the environment, perhaps the most important are qualitative rather than quantitative ... The aesthetic elements ... can help a pupil to realise that there is no right or wrong answer in absolute terms to aesthetic questions and that the answer to environmental issues is frequently a compromise.

d) The Ethical element. A programme of environmental education aims at introducing pupils to the idea of personal responsibility for the environment and to the concept of stewardship. It trains pupils to ask if the criteria of proposed actions are based on morally justifiable values.

A few years earlier, the more limited Schools Council *Environmental Studies Project (5–13)*[16] based at Cartrefle College of Education 1967–71 had defined environmental studies as 'an approach, through activities based on a child's physical and social environment, which leads to the progressive development of attitudes and skills required for the observation, recording, interpretation and communication of scientific, historical and geographical data'. The essential innovation of the project is the systematic use of the environment with skill development in mind.

Whatever its form, environmental education cannot be without key educational aims concerned with knowledge and skills as well as attitudes and behaviour. The CEE (1987)[13] summarises these aims as follows:

Knowledge and Skills

i) To develop a coherent body of knowledge about the environment, both built and rural, sufficient to recognise actual and potential problems,

ii) To be able to gather information from or about the environment independently or as part of co-operative activity,

iii) To be able to consider different opinions related to environmental issues and to arrive at a balanced judgement,

iv) To appreciate the ways in which environmental issues are inter-related so that one factor affects others,

v)   To be able to evaluate information about the environment from different sources and to try to resolve environmental problems,

vi)   To understand and to know how to use the mechanisms available in society for bringing about environmental change.

Attitudes and Behaviour

i)   To develop an appreciation of the environment and critical awareness of the natural and built environment,

ii)   To develop an attitude of concern for environmental matters and a wish to improve environmental understanding,

iii) To be critical of one's own environmental attitudes and to take steps to change one's own behaviour and actions,

iv)   To have a desire to participate in initiatives to care for or improve the environment,

v)   To wish to participate in environmental decision making and to make opinions known publicly.

Using these aims as a guide it should be appreciated that environmental education may take many forms and that a wide variety of activities or programmes may be appropriate.

(CEE 1987)[13]

The possibilities for the acquisition of knowledge, concepts, skills and attitudes (DES 1985)[17] promoted by the teaching of environmental education in the primary school have been outlined in many sources. Key contributions to this debate have been made by Her Majesty's Inspectorate. In 1984 in their comments on the aims of environmental studies they stated that the

> Aims of environmental studies are to contribute to the general purposes of primary education, including the attainment of acceptable standards of literacy and numeracy by providing suitable learning contexts and offering relevant opportunities for the application of skills and the formation of positive life-long attitudes to learning.
>
> (DES, 1984)[18]

Two years later, Her Majesty's Inspectorate extended its statement of aims as follows:

> General aims for environmental education include: the need to develop attitudes of care, curiosity and concern for the environment in such a way as to develop a sense of responsibility towards home, school and community; to demonstrate to children the complex inter-relationships between humanity and the environment; and to give pupils the necessary skills to do these things.
>
> (DES 1986)[19]

In their *Environmental Education from 5–16 Curriculum Matters 13* (DES 1989)[20] HMI make it quite clear that they perceive environmental education as a cross-curricular approach to learning:

In exploring and explaining inter-relationships in the environment, environmental education draws on and contributes to, the concepts, skills and knowledge underpinning a range of subjects or areas of learning and experience.

(DES 1989)[20]

Environmental education or environmental studies?

The terms 'environmental education' and 'environmental studies' are both used in the above statements. Within the context of this book, we define and differentiate between the two terms as follows:

1 Environmental education is advocated by the Department of Education and Science as *a process to which the whole curriculum and every subject discipline may contribute.*

Environmental education transcends environmental studies, outdoor pursuits and conservation. Curricular, recreational and social experiences contribute to it. It begins with the investigation of the physical and human local environment, widening and deepening its approach to include the new and the more distant until eventually its concentric framework encompasses international and global scenes.

(Report by HMI Scotland, 1974)[15]

2 Environmental studies is *an approach to learning – that which is concerned with skill development in particular, including the basic skills of literacy and numeracy.*

Environmental Studies is not thought of by the team as a 'subject' with its own body of factual information but as a way of learning through organised enquiry.

(Environmental Studies Project 5–13)[16]

There is currently an active debate in research and writings concerned with environmental studies as to whether it represents an approach to learning or is a discrete subject in its own right. Her Majesty's Inspectorate state that, to a greater or lesser extent, all aspects of the curriculum draw on the environment as a resource.

Local Authority guidelines

It is generally agreed that the aims and content of environmental education should be directed towards certain ends, as recommended in the guidelines of various Local Education Authorities. For example, those of the City of Birmingham Education Department[21] (1986) suggest that first and foremost will be the encouragement of clear thinking, the acquisition of knowledge and the art of utilising this knowledge. Second will be an appreciation of the interrelationships of subjects, derived from an appreciation of the links between individual environmental phenomena and the whole of which they are a part. Third, it is vital that there is a formation of positive attitudes concerning social responsibility, tolerance, initiative and international understanding fostered by stimulating interest in local, national and world affairs, and the growth of accurate, realistic ideas concerning other people; and finally, there will be opportunities for aesthetic awareness.

The Curriculum Statement from Kent[22] (1988) emphasises that environmental education is neither a subject nor a syllabus but rather one function of the whole curriculum. It is recognised that the teaching strategy should contain three elements: the environment as a medium for education using real-life situations; the environment as a subject for investigation; and education for conserving and improving the environment by studying contemporary issues. As far as Kent is concerned 'successful teaching from environmental resources will involve developing the skills of enquiry and exploration; communication skills; self-reliance and the ability to organise work programmes; and building an understanding of place, time, change and relationships'.

Certainly, the keystone of the whole approach is first-hand experience. This is interpreted to include studying the locality and places further afield, also experiences which are school-based such as caring for small animals, growing plants, recording the weather and items of interest in the school grounds; visits to sites and establishments such as farms, nature reserves, parks, museums, buildings of interest and archaeological sites; and finally, meeting and interviewing people who live and work in the community. In many ways the range of themes and concerns that can be covered by the environmental studies approach is complex even to the point of being bewildering. In practice, the organisation of work in schools is often presented in the form of flow diagrams, which indicate the range and extent of investigations which might develop from a given theme. There is a heavy onus on the teacher to plan the work, and upon heads of schools to provide guidelines, and at the same time to retain opportunity for spontaneous development.

At a higher level, many local education authorities have published definitive guidelines in relation to structure, balance and progression and the ordering of academic skills, notably Hertfordshire – in its publication *Environmental Education Guidelines for the Primary and Middle Years* (1978)[23] – and Birmingham, in *Further Developments in the Primary Curriculum Environmental Education* (1980)[24]. These are but two of a wide range of excellent LEA statements. The National Association for Environmental Education's publication *Environmental Education: A Statement of Aims* (Second

Edition[12] 1982) is also a very valuable contribution to the establishment of guidelines for teachers.

All such documents stress the importance of the benefit of investigations into everyday objects and events, and 'real-life' situations that are within the conceptual capacity of the children concerned.

Curriculum statements from the Department of Education and Science

Recent statements from the Department of Education and Science reinforce this view. The document *Curriculum Matters 5–16* (1985) specifically recommends that the curriculum should be relevant in the sense that it is seen by the pupils to meet their present and prospective needs. As environmental studies usually focuses upon the pupils' immediate surroundings and everyday objects and experiences, then it can be argued that it makes a strong contribution to a curriculum that is indeed highly relevant.

The DES publication *Curriculum Matters 5–16* also requires that the primary curriculum must have breadth and balance. Again, adequate breadth may be achieved through environmental education:

> Environmental education which can help pupils to develop an awareness, appreciation and understanding of their surroundings, may be presented through science, history and geography, for example, or can act as a unifying approach for work in and out of school in several subjects and curricular areas.
>
> (DES 1985)[19]

The document goes on to explain further that environmental education can be a feature of all, or at least several, of the areas of learning and experience it outlines, namely 'aesthetic and creative, human and social, literary and linguistic, mathematical, moral, physical, spiritual, scientific and technological'. (DES 1985)[19]

The DES suggests that the choice of themes or topics for environmental education 'should include essential facts and concepts, develop general skills and use pupils' own experience where possible as starting points'. (DES 1985)[19]

Over the years environmental educationalists have emphasised that the real world outside the classroom should not be excluded.

> The environment in which a child lives and with which he has constant interaction is clearly the starting point for education which involves using the familiar world to encourage the development of concepts, skills and attitudes which will be of value later on ... From the first

moment of a child's encounter with the environment, his senses will provide natural means of investigation and the primary task of a first school teacher is to develop this awakening of the senses to the outside world.

(Palmer 1977)[25]

By using the world around them, by learning about their world and by formulating codes of behaviour towards it, pupils are able to pursue the essentials of environmental education and at the same time encompass all that is necessary to become literate and numerate.

(Neal 1982)[26]

Accepting the definition and scope of environmental education as outlined above, it must be seen to have a very close association with the philosophy and practice of an integrated curriculum. Indeed, environmental studies has been strongly supported by some educationalists because of its ability to incorporate many of the areas of learning of the school curriculum.

Primary school environmental education

The document on *Geography 5–16*[27] in the DES *Curriculum Matters* series states that environmental investigations naturally integrate language, mathematics, computer work, art and history. Indeed, in the literature of the five years leading up to the establishment of the National Curriculum, environmental studies is to be regarded to a greater or lesser extent as an approach to inter-disciplinary or integrated enquiry. Certainly with children of a very young age, it is convenient to regard environmental studies, however broadly conceived and practised, as an approach to learning that can be separately identified. It is perhaps useful to reinforce the three categories of interpretation of environmental education, namely:

1 The environment as a medium for education – the use of real life situations as the basis for enquiry learning, particularly with younger children;
2 The environment as a subject for investigation;
3 Education for conserving or improving the environment – the study of topical problems such as conservation, pollution, population, and the attempt to promote a sense of personal responsibility. (UK Tbilisi papers 1977)[1]

The United Kingdom's government paper presented at the Tbilisi Conference concluded that: 'What is beyond doubt is that environmental study and the enthusiasm and commitment it generates, has enhanced the quality of education in primary schools at large.'

As long ago as 1931 the Primary School Report stressed that: 'The curriculum is to be thought of in terms of activity and experience rather than of knowledge to be acquired and facts to be stored'. Since that time educationalists have increasingly realised just how important it is that children's learning should be based on practical experience rather than on rote learning and memorisation of facts. In order that sound and meaningful learning should take place, there must be ample opportunity for direct personal experience of the child's own environment. Such experiences should be planned by teachers with due regard given to the concepts, skills and attitudes they intend children to develop during the primary school years.

Environmental education provides experience of problem solving, decision making and participation, with considerations based on ecological, political, economic, social, aesthetic and ethical aspects. It is also about promoting changes in behaviour that will help to solve existing problems relating to the environment and to avoid the creation of new ones. The ultimate aim of environmental education is for each school leaver to have formulated a responsible attitude towards the sustainable development of Planet Earth, an appreciation of its beauty and an assumption of an environmental ethic. To fulfil this aim, every school should strive to have adequate arrangements for planning and implementing a programme of environmental education. That these arrangements may vary between schools reflects that they must be tailored and modified to the particular needs of individual neighbourhoods and individual children. Physical processes, ecological interaction and human behaviour shape the environment. Environmental education seeks to make young learners aware of these, helping to develop an informed concern for the way the resources of the Earth are used and the quality of life on it, now, and in the future. Indeed, environmental education is essential for what may be considered to be a full education.

2 Environmental education and the National Curriculum: the way forward

The environmental education movement and all those concerned with promotion of this area of learning naturally greeted the Government's *The National Curriculum 5–16*[1] consultation document (1987) with great interest. Various key responses were made to this document by organisations concerned with environmental education, most of them through the Council for Environmental Education, whose consultative processes included the setting up of shadow working groups to the national working parties in Science, Mathematics and English and consultative committees in History, Geography and Technology. The overall CEE submission (1989)[2] identified a number of positive elements in the National Curriculum, yet expressed sincere misgivings. It attempted to draw attention to the possible implications for environmental education of the Government's proposals, and for related and overlapping areas such as development and health education.

The consultation document itself does not include environmental education as a foundation subject. It does however state that:

> successive Secretaries of State have aimed to achieve agreement with their partners in the education service on policies for the school curriculum which will develop the potential of all pupils and equip them for the responsibilities of citizenship and for the challenges of employment in tomorrow's world.

and

> The curriculum should equip pupils with the knowledge, skills and understanding that they need for adult life and employment.
> (DES 1987)[1]

The response of the CEE pointed out that

> Understanding must relate to the issues that underlie what (pupils)

learn, as well as to the processes and structures by which things function. Equally, understanding should be related to the inter-relatedness among humans, their culture and biophysical surroundings and to the concept of using resources sustainably.

(CEE 1987)[2]

The latter part of this document quotes directly the internationally-accepted working definition of environmental education (see page 2). At the time of the publication of the consultative document, it seemed that, from an environmental education point of view, the way forward in terms of interpreting the National Curriculum was to lay strong emphasis on a small number of statements which recognise the 'relevance to and links with pupils' own experiences' (Paragraph 8 iii); which encourage pupils to
'become thinking and informed people' (Paragraph 23);
and which refer to the development of personal qualities (Paragraphs 23 and 68).

Within these almost throw-away statements are the seeds of environmental education and global awareness. Probably the most important statement of the document, however, where environmental education is concerned, is as follows:

In addition, there are a number of subjects on themes such as health education ... which can be taught through other subjects ... It is proposed that such subjects or themes should be taught through the foundation subjects. (Paragraph 18)

This paragraph is vitally important for those who seek to promote environmental education. Since the document fails to mention environmental education directly or, indeed, any of its component parts such as rural science, urban studies, global education, heritage education or development studies, it is on paragraph 18 that hopes must be pinned. This recognition of cross-curricular learning, coupled with the many statements emanating from the DES in the past few years, encourages optimism in environmental circles. In a letter to the NAEE, for example, Minister of State for Education, Angela Rumbold, said 'Imaginative use of the environment beyond the confines of the classroom has much to offer in terms of enhancing pupils' learning experiences' (October 1988)[3].

Quite clearly this interpretation and viewpoint strongly reinforce the important links between integrated and interdisciplinary learning through themes and environmental education. Subjects and themes are seen to have sound reciprocal benefits in terms of understanding and reinforcement. This has always been regarded by many as a central feature of environmental education. The Government here recognises the principle that themes can enhance other subjects at the same time as being taught through them. At this stage in the development of the National Curriculum, those committed to the development of environmental education and deeply believing in its importance remained optimistic that it might be promoted in the ways mentioned above, through close reference to paragraph 18 of the consultation document.

In 1988/89 however, events of great significance in the history of this area of learning transformed its status to that of an officially recognised cross-curricular theme of the National Curriculum. Naturally the news was greeted with tremendous enthusiasm by those promoting environmental education. Without doubt, the recognition of environmental education must be set against a backcloth of increasing public and governmental concern for the environment as emphasised in our introduction with the 1987 United Nations World Commission for the Environmental report *Our Common Future*[4], the resolution on environmental education by the Council of the European Economic Community in May 1988 and the environmental speech by Margaret Thatcher to the Royal Society in September 1988. The publication of the government's booklet in the Curriculum Matters series – *Environmental Education from 5 to 16*[5] (1989) was well timed to follow this resolution, clearly raising the status of the 'subject' at national level and being helpful to schools and Local Education Authorities in their consideration of how best to organise and implement a policy for this area of learning.

Environmental Education and the National Curriculum

As far as the National Curriculum is concerned, the National Curriculum Council has the task of overseeing the deliberations and progress of individual subject working groups.

In August 1988 the Secretary of State reminded the National Curriculum Council of its responsibility for keeping the *whole* curriculum under review as well as the core and foundation subjects. Among other matters, the NCC was requested to examine the nature of cross-curricular issues. In particular, the theme of Personal and Social Education (PSE) was to be studied with emphasis on health education and other related cross-curricular areas. The Interim Whole Curriculum Committee (IWCC) of the National Curriculum Council set about the major task of examining how far cross-curricular issues could be reflected in the Attainment Targets of the core and foundation subjects. The IWCC was requested to produce a report on cross-curricular issues, then to examine these in relation to the four key stages of learning identified within the National Curriculum and finally to set these within a coherent framework for the curriculum as a whole. The accepted definition of cross-curricular issues in the context of National Curriculum developments is 'aspects of learning and teaching that permeate almost all elements within the school curriculum whether they be formal or informal'.

The IWCC identified three 'areas' of cross-curricular issues, namely

1 *Dimensions*, for example, multi-cultural education, personal and social education.
2 *Skills and competencies*, for example, oracy, numeracy, study skills.
3 *Themes*, for example, environmental education and health education. The basic curriculum entitlement for every child identified by the IWCC is the National Curriculum plus Religious Education, with the National Curriculum consisting of three core and seven foundation subjects plus the teaching of cross-curricular issues. The latter must have progression and continuity like all core and foundation subjects. In other words, cross-curricular themes are not an appendage but should be seen as central to the curriculum as a whole.

Within this framework, Personal and Social Education was one of the key areas singled out by the Secretary of State for close examination by the IWCC. From the overarching title of PSE, some major themes were identified for initial exploration;

- Health education
- Environmental education
- Education for citizenship
- Careers and guidance
- Economic and industrial understanding

It is clear that schools are intended to regard these cross-curricular themes as part of the entitlement of children that goes beyond the core and foundation subjects.

Following on from the identification of the five themes within the PSE umbrella, the IWCC established (in 1989) five task groups, one to examine each of the five themes. These groups were briefed to report back to the IWCC, having 'mapped' their theme, identified outcome/entitlement for children aged 5–16 and shown how progression in the teaching and learning of the theme might be achieved throughout the four key stages. A matrix was to be produced for each theme, identifying with the Programmes of Study and Attainment Targets of the core and foundation subjects. The task of the group members was:

> to produce advice on the nature and scope of Environmental Education and how this subject area might be delivered through the core and foundation subjects of the National Curriculum.

A number of key papers were written during the course of the group's deliberations and were later circulated widely for consultation and response. Several open seminars were held to collect and collate the views of the environmental education movement.

The first of these is a statement of proposed 'Entitlement of all children of 5–16 in Environmental Education' as follows:

> It is suggested that the Entitlement should be founded on knowledge, understanding and skills. A brief summary of the Entitlement is given as follows:

> By the age of 16 all pupils should have had educational experiences, which range from local to global in scale, and which enable them to:
> 1   Understand the natural processes that take place in the environment including the ecological principles and relationships that exist.
> 2   Understand that human lives and livelihoods are totally dependent on the processes, relationships and resources that exist in the environment.
> 3   Be aware of the impact of human activities on the environment, including planning and design; to understand the processes by which communities organise themselves, initiate and cope with change; to appreciate that these are affected by personal, economic, technological, social, aesthetic, political, cultural, ethical and spiritual considerations.
> 4   Be competent in a range of skills which help them to appreciate and enjoy, communicate ideas, and participate in the decision-making processes which shape the environment.
> 5   View, evaluate, interpret and experience their surroundings critically so that a balanced appreciation can be reached.
> 6   Have insights into a range of environments and cultures, both past and present, to include an understanding of the ways in which different cultural groups perceive and interact with their environment.
> 7   Understand the conflicts that may arise over environmental issues, particularly in relation to the use of resources, and to consider alternative ways to resolve such conflicts.

8 Be aware of the interdependence of communities and nations and some of the environmental consequences and opportunities of those relationships.

9 Be aware that the current state of the environment has resulted from past decisions and actions and that the future of the environment depends on contemporary actions and decisions to which they make a contribution.

10 Identify their own level of commitment towards the care of the environment.

It is expected that, as part of the entitlement, by the age of 16 years pupils will have had the opportunity to experience their own and other environments at first hand.

Following on from this, the group prepared a 'Suggested Broad Outline Structure' for this entitlement:

This is based on two broad areas which relate to the core and foundation subjects. Each of the two broad areas is further divided into three sub-sections as follows:

1 Knowledge and Understanding
   (a) Knowledge about the Environment at a variety of levels, ranging from local to global.
   (b) Knowledge and understanding of Environmental issues at a variety of levels, ranging from local to global; to include understanding of the different influences, both natural and human, on the issues.
   (c) Knowledge of alternative attitudes and approaches to environmental issues and the value systems underlying such attitudes and approaches.
2 Skills
   (a) Finding out about the environment, either directly through the environment or by using secondary sources.
   (b) Communicating:
      i. Knowledge about the environment.
      ii. Both the pupil's own and alternative attitudes to environmental issues, to include justification for the attitudes or approaches advanced.
   (c) Participation
      i. As part of group decision making
      ii. As part of making a personal response.

The 'Development of Skills' was considered vital and a further paper clarified thinking on the matter:

1. *Definition of skills.*
A skill is a capacity or competence to perform a task. Many of the skills required in undertaking work in Environmental Education are

embodied in other disciplines. Some are common to a range of disciplines whilst others are more subject specific. This paper will argue the case for clustering skills into three groups and then, through an analysis of other curriculum areas, try to determine the main body of skills that are required for work in Environmental Education.

2. *Concept of Skills Model for all subjects.*

It has been found difficult to formulate a simple skills model which could be testable against all areas of the curriculum. All available HMI 5–16 documents plus the core curriculum documents which are currently available have been analysed. It has been possible to create a three-sided model which attempts to cover the main skill areas as defined in the above documents. It was felt important to keep the model as simple as possible in order that the inter-lacing of the elements could be observed in a particular skill development.

3. *Grouping of skills.*

HMI document The Curriculum from 5–16 suggests that skills can be grouped into eight areas. These are, communication, observation, study, problem solving, physical and practical, creative and imaginative, numerical and personal and social. Whilst it would be possible to examine environmental skills in the light of these divisions, it has been decided to attempt a simpler pattern, dividing the skills into three areas but at the same time remaining mindful of the more detailed sub-divisions embodied in the HMI documents.

a) COMMUNICATION – The ability to express ideas either for the sake of the individual or the enlightenment of others.

b) INTELLECTUAL – Skills that are acquired and practised through the process of learning.

c) SOCIAL – Skills that are needed in dealing with the whole range of living and working in groups including the whole area of participation and decision making.

4. *Progression and overlap.*

As with knowledge and understanding there has to be progression in skill development. No one expects a 5-year-old to be able to set down ideas in writing with any degree of sophistication, but the communication skill of writing is as relevant to the 5-year-old as to the 16-year-old. Intellectual skills are also subject to progression, for example moving from concrete to abstract thought and the linking of skills with the development of knowledge and understanding. Also, whilst the skills are identified on three sides of a triangle there are areas of overlap. All communication skills are in part intellectual skills, and social skills demand many elements of intellectual development. For example, developing reading skills is an intellectual activity but through the reading process communication takes place.

5. *Environmental Education and skill development.*

An analysis of the core and foundation subjects indicates that the major groupings relate to intellectual and communication skills. It could however be argued that these are totally irrelevant unless children develop the ability to use skills in situations that enable them to relate to one another and the wider community. A major argument for cross-curricular themes is that they provide a medium through which children can use and develop knowledge, understanding and skills acquired in other subject areas. This cross-fertilisation helps show children the relevance and value of skills which have often been acquired in separate discipline areas.

As a cross-curricular theme, Environmental Education allows children the opportunity to understand the many and varied environmental issues that surround them, how decisions are made about the environment and how people can have the opportunity of participating in the decision-making process.

Work in Environmental Education represents a good opportunity for children to use a whole range of skills in a way which is both relevant to their lives as well as useful to their future as citizens. By stretching children intellectually and creatively, by asking them to communicate ideas and work in a cooperative manner on the environmental issues that face them, it is hoped to produce adults provoked and challenged into making a positive and constructive contribution to the future well-being of the world.

Other papers written during the course of the group's deliberations include 'Knowledge and Understanding in relation to the Environment' and 'The Environmental Context for the Linking of Skills with Knowledge and Understanding' (see Appendices A and B).

The broad structure suggested for providing an environmental education dimension in the National Curriculum reinforces the long-held views of environmental educationalists, including those of the present authors, that the curriculum can be understood to consist of two mutually dependent components. This can be expressed as a matrix with its vertical component corresponding to the core and foundation subjects and its horizontal component to the cross-curricular themes identified for the National Curriculum.

The terms 'profile components' and 'attainment targets' are reserved for use in the context of the core and foundation subjects only. No new profile components or attainment targets have been suggested for environmental education (or indeed any other cross-curricular theme). The structure suggested for environmental education as a cross-curricular theme, may, if thought appropriate, be capable of generalisation and adaptation so that it can be applied (with minor modification of wording) to all the other cross-curricular themes. In this way, some degree of correspondence and similarity may be given to all cross-curricular themes.

Finally, it was agreed that emphasis should be given to knowledge and understanding as well as skills. Although encouraging pupils to form their own well-thought-out attitudes is considered important, this is not considered to be a separate activity unrelated to knowledge, understanding and skills.

Reflecting and reinforcing the work and thoughts of the pioneers for environmental education as detailed earlier, the task group's rationale recognises three distinct but related types of activity:

1 Education *about* the environment, with the purpose of developing knowledge and understanding about values and attitudes.
2 Education *in* or *through* the environment, in which the environment is used as a familiar and relevant resource for educational purposes. In this way a good deal of the knowledge and understanding as well as the skills required by the National Curriculum will be developed by pupils.
3 Education *for* the environment, in which pupils explore their personal response to and relationship with the environment and environmental issues. This includes the elements of human understanding and behaviour necessary for the development of sustainable and caring use of the environment, now and in the future.

There can be no doubt that environmental education is a planned element of the National Curriculum for schools. Set against the backcloth of the resolution of the Council of Ministers of the European Community, it seems certain that as a matter of priority it will be promoted within all schools of the Community.

Attention is now turned to a practical classroom situation, in order to illuminate many of the general issues discussed above, as well as to focus on a particular starting point for sound environmental education. The following subject-based study, in this case history, shows the way in which a topic approach can not only fulfil particular objectives for that subject, but at the same time contribute:

• in a cross-curricular way to environmental education and vice versa;
• to knowledge, understanding and skills in another subject: here it is science.

There can be no doubt that it is possible to lay firm foundations for progressive historical understanding in a child's infant school years. Indeed, such foundations are essential if any measure of real progression to more advanced and sophisticated stages of historical understanding is to be achieved. Published views on the nature of history teaching by HMI have suggested that in a large majority of primary schools the subject is not taught discernibly. Although many interesting projects are studied, these attempt to put equal weight on all areas of learning covered by the contents and have no rigorous guidelines for each component. Progression of understanding both within and between projects is noticeable by its absence. Future curriculum planning should take account of such criticism and go some way towards not only identifying or quantifying the amount of history that is incorporated into a thematic/project approach but also building in scope for progression. No-one would doubt the tremendous value of the project/topic approach to learning in key stages 1 and 2 and the many advantages of integrated learning. The method is not called into question – rather the rigour and planning with which it is executed.

Inevitably the publication of National Curriculum requirements in history aided curriculum development in this area, providing a focus on the body of historical knowledge children should have as well as on historical skills and processes.

As far as environmental education is concerned, the case study described below served to illustrate a fact of fundamental importance, which is that history can contribute to environmental education (and vice versa) in many ways. A sense of chronology, for example, was developed through the study of buildings and building materials in the children's local environment. Active fieldwork was an essential component of the project, leading not only to an accumulation of data and facts, but also to imaginative understanding of, and empathy with, the past approaches which are central to historical study. The local environment provided the essential first-hand experiences so necessary for this. Finally, this detailed study of the children's own environment, including a range of historical evidence, proved to be a very effective way of developing their sense of the relationship and continuity between past and present, helping them to 'find a focus' and a sense of place and identity in their own lives. In these and many other ways, environmental education permeated sound integrated learning, helping to provide a firm foundation for historical understanding.

Case study 1   Images of our school

Holland House First School, Sutton Coldfield

Introduction
Images of our school is an account of a historical project based on the children's immediate environment, undertaken with children of top infant age (6–7 years). The aim was to address the key concepts of **time** and **change**. Two classes in the school followed this integrated topic work for a period of one school term. The project formed the basis for the development of work in environmental studies, with strong links into science, mathematics, language, art, movement and drama. There was considerable emphasis on addressing knowledge, understanding and skills of the core area of science in the National Curriculum.

This account is in two sections:
A An overview of the project and its content, drawing particular attention to its relationship with the core area of science;
B Comments on approaches, organisation and examples of children's work.

A An overview
This project took as its central theme **images through time**, based on the premise that history at infant school level starts 'where the children are' and is concerned first with that which is within their own memory, then working back into the more distant past. It had two distinct yet inter-related parts:
1   Images of today
2   Images of the past
These were linked, with the second naturally following on from the first.

Three key sub-headings (figure 2.1) were addressed in both parts, namely:
a   Childhood (related particularly to schooldays)
b   School buildings
c   Games and activities

Images of today
The starting point was **Childhood today – images of our school day**. Key concepts to be explored were **time**, **order** and **sequence**. This involved an investigation into time itself, that is, sequence of time and duration of time. There was much scope at this stage for

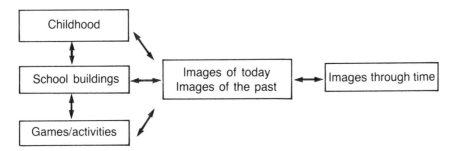

Figure 2.1 *Images through time – three key sub-headings.*

linking with the National Curriculum attainment targets for mathematics. Questions addressed included:

- How long is a minute? an hour? a day? a week? a year?
- Why do we have clocks?
- Do we need time?
- What would happen in a world without time?

This was then related to the school day with discussion of such issues
as:

- Why is it necessary to have order in our school day?
- Why is assembly always at the same time (and lunch, playtime
  etc)?
- Idea of a school timetable
- What do we do in the course of a day at school? (worktime,
  playtime, eating time, story time etc)
- How long do these activities last?

Discussion was then elaborated to include such matters as:

- What is it like to be a schoolchild today?
- What do we wear to school?
- What do we eat at school?
- What do we use at school?
- What do we bring to school?
- What time do we come to school?
- What do we have in our classrooms?
- What games do we play at playtime?
- What does our school look like?
- What is it made of?
- When was it built?
- Why is it made of these building materials?

All these issues and ideas were brought together in discussion and writing, and the key concepts of time order and sequence were gradually linked to that of **change**. The children readily understood the notion that in a year, *we* change, and so do other things around us. As the years go by, a lot changes in our world. Fundamental questions addressed at this stage included:

- Has our school always been like this?
- Have schooldays always been like ours?
- Have children always played the same games and done the same activities?
- How do we find out?

Practical investigations included interviews with people who went to school several or many years ago (bearing in mind that the day before yesterday is historical to infants!) – talking to parents, grandparents, great-grandparents and school staff and visitors. The people interviewed were asked to comment on such matters as:

- What did they wear to school?
- What was their school building like?
- What was a school day like?
- What games did they play?

Images of the past
From this, the second major element of the project unfolded: **Images of the past**, with its three related foci, namely:

a) Schooldays of long ago (particularly Edwardian and Victorian times)
b) The school building
c) Games and activities of long ago

This dimension began with a major field activity, a visit to the original building of the children's present modern school – attended by many of their parents and grandparents. As a whole, which clearly derived from first-hand experiences of the environment, the project related closely to the core and foundation subjects of the National Curriculum in a truly integrated fashion. For the purpose of this account, science has been singled out as an example to demonstrate how this was addressed:

Attainment Target 6 – Types and uses of materials was delivered through an investigation of building materials: Questions addressed included:

- What was the 'old school' built of? What is the modern school built of? (–the walls, doors, roof, windows ...)
- Why have some building materials changed through time?
- Why are some building materials apparently better than others? Can we test this?
- What factors must be considered when choosing them? (expense, durability, weather-proofing, availability etc)
- What experiments can we do to investigate whether certain materials are harder, tougher than others?

Materials in the classroom were also investigated –

- How have these changed since the 'old school' days?
  What is slate? Where does it come from? Why don't we use it now?
- Where does our paper come from? (introducing ideas about con-servation and limited world resources)
- Slate/paper as surfaces – What will mark them? clean them?
- Chalk – What is it? Where does it come from?
- What other materials are there in the classroom? (wooden desks, plastic apparatus, metal scissors, cloth etc)
- Would the Victorian school have had plastic apparatus?
- Did they have wooden desks?
- Group the materials in our school today according to their charac-teristics and origins.

Attainment Target 9 – Earth and atmosphere was approached by looking at:

- What *natural* materials do we find in our school building and in classroom materials – stone, chalk, sand, timber.
- Where have these things come from?
  Key Idea: they have all come from the earth and the earth's resources are limited.
  Weather affects natural materials, e.g. weathering of stone build-ings. Evidence was sought of weathering on the school building which *changes* a building through *time*.

Attainment Target 11 – Electricity and magnetism was delivered by posing questions for investigation such as:

- How is our school heated and lighted?
- Where does the power come from? (leading to the key concept of *energy*)

- Was this power available in Victorian times? (Idea of candle power – sources of heat and light and ideas on how these have changed through historical times.)
- What domestic appliances do we have in school today (kitchen equipment, kettles, projectors etc) In schools of yesterday?
- When was electricity 'invented'?

Attainment Target 12 – The scientific aspects of information technology including micro-electronics was very relevant as it obviously represents one of the key changes since Edwardian/Victorian times. Children in schools today use computers, tape recorders, televisions.

- What are the benefits of these?
- Why do we want to store information?

Attainment Target 13 – Energy was originally brought into the topic in relation to the foods eaten during the day. We need food for energy, so that we can do our schoolwork, run around the playground etc. Methods of preparing foods over the years and the nature and variety of foods eaten were also considered.

- Have schools always had kitchens?
- Did the children's grandparents have lunch at school?
- Kitchens then and now
- Butter-making of old …
- Have our diets changed over the years? (there were no Indian or Chinese take-aways close to the school then!)

From *food* the concept of energy developed by looking at *toys* which move and use energy – clockwork toys from historical times and then to *machines* which need a source of energy in order to work and *power* needed to heat and light the school.

Attainment Target 14 – Sound and music was covered by investigating 'Sounds of our school today' and 'Sounds of yesterday'.

- What musical instruments do we hear and use in the course of a day? Were they to be found in Victorian schools?
- Songs/hymns of Edwardian/Victorian times
- Music of that era
- School bells – from hand to electric

Needless to say Attainment Target 1 was relevant throughout the entire topic as children were actively encouraged to:

Attainment targets – relevant for 5–7 year-olds

	1	2	3	4	5	6	7	8	9	10	11	12	13	14	15	16
Level 1	√					√	√				√					
Level 2	√					√	√		√	√	√	√				
Level 3	√					√	√			√	√	√				

Figure 2.2 *Summary of attainment targets and levels of attainment in science covered within the topic 'Images of our school'.*

- plan;
- carry out;
- interpret results and findings;
- draw inferences;
- communicate exploratory tasks and findings.

B   Approaches, organisation, illustrations of work

From a reading of the project overview, it will be apparent that a great deal of preliminary work centred around class discussion of issues and ideas relating to the concepts of time, order and sequence. As the topic as a whole developed, it involved class-centred discussions followed by a tremendous amount of individual and small group experimentation, investigation and recording. Emphasis throughout was on the children's own spontaneous ideas and discoveries being used as starting points for further practical investigation. For example, one child writes:

Our school looks rotten. It has one floor, a flat roof and lots of windows.

and another:

Our school was built in 1972. It is made of wood, metal and a kind of weather-proof board. I think it is made of cheap materials because they didn't want to spend a lot of money building it. A lot of wood is beginning to rot away.

From comments such as these arose extensive practical investigations, conducted in small groups, into the nature and durability of various building materials, with recorded comments on how and why they have changed through time in the context of the school building (figure 2.3). The topic had two major focal points: 1 A class visit to the original school building; 2 A day in school devoted to role play of life in Victorian times. Both were enormously enjoyed by the children and they formed springboards from which a tremendous amount of learning and excitement derived.

Name Adrian

What has happened to the
building materials used to build the
2 schools?

glass	No Change
Brick	crumbled a bit but still strong
Tiles	Some have been replaced
wood	rotting away
metal	rusting
waterprooffelt	lets in rain
plaastic	is craking

What has caused these things
to happen? the weather :- wind, rain,
Sun, frost, snow

Figure 2.3

1 Class visit
The original school building was replaced by the present 1972 construction. The old building is now a church and the children were
fascinated by its atmosphere and history:

**The first Town School was built in 1825. It had few children.
The toilets were just two holes in the ground. The health must**

have been very bad. In 1876 it closed because of scarlet fever. The little children used slate and sat on benches. Every now and again inspectors came to the school to make sure that everyone was being taught properly. The children in the school had no apparatus. The head decided to do something about it so she fixed some old desks together to make a kind of slide.

The children got caned if they were naughty. Oh and I forgot to tell you, the girls used to have the task of doing rows of sewing or knitting. If they didn't knit the right number of rows, they had to stay in at night. If they did more than the task, they would get a quarter of a penny. They would need four quarters to get a penny. I haven't told you who the girls were doing this work for. Well, it was because there were a lot of poor children in the school and if they came to school regularly they would get some of the clothing the girls used to knit and sew. The girls' uniform was brown dresses with blue and white check pinafores over them and black stockings, boots and a black straw hat with a blue ribbon round it.

The visit offered invaluable insights into social history with much scope for creative writing, art work, health education, mathematics and dramatic role play. First-hand observances were detailed and illuminating:

I knew the steps were very old because they were wearing out and not level.

I noticed that the windows were so high the children couldn't see out.

Combined with field notes, sketches, photographs and tape recording, these provided a sound basis for integrated learning deriving from the children's local environment. The field experiences and follow-up work were recorded in a wide variety of ways. Factual and creative accounts were written and shared, photographs were displayed, sketches drawn and mathematical data pictorially represented. The teachers skilfully encouraged the sharing of opinions and conclusions of investigations by providing wide-ranging opportunities for oral, pictorial and written communication. Classroom walls soon became surfaces of lively and colourful displays of the children's own work in a variety of media. The value of oral communication was not underestimated and the children were actively encouraged to share their thoughts – ranging from discovered facts to personal and reflective opinion, e.g.

Isn't *time* a funny thing Miss? It's a bit like a dream … You can't see it or feel it it's just there …

The definite scientific focus in no way stifled creativity and originality of thought. Indeed they were positively encouraged through open-ended questioning, the posing of problems for investigation and support for original or individual methods of recording.

2 A Victorian day

The second major focal point of the study was a day in school entirely devoted to role play of life in Victorian times. A large amount of preparation and overwhelming support from parents ensured that 'appropriate dress' was worn and every child wholeheartedly entered into the spirit of the occasion (figure 2.4). The atmosphere was authentic and exciting:

For a whole day we pretended we were at school in the olden days. It was great fun. We sang hymns in the hall . . . we played with whip and top . . . we ate some bread and cheese . . . we dressed like children of long ago.

Not only was the spirit of the occasion entered into, so too was the hard work . . . the drill and the abacus mathematics. Once again, recording and communication of the event took place in a variety of innovative ways, including photography and tape recording.

Figure 2.4 *The old blends with the new.*

The combined impact of the fieldwork and role play served to underpin enormous enthusiasm for this topic as a whole. The key concepts of time and change readily unfolded through discussion, activity, investigation and experimentation in a completely natural manner. The children's learning was spontaneous and extensive, deriving from their personal experiences and enthusiasms and leading into an understanding of content of a wide variety of areas of learning.

3 The formulation of a school environmental education policy

The need for all schools to have a curriculum policy for environmental education has always been high on the agenda of environmentalists. Specific reference was given to this in the Conservation and Development Programme for the United Kingdom which was a response to the World Conservation Strategy.[1] Recommendation 1 in the Education section was stated as:

> *Aim*:
> For all schools to have a written environmental education policy with specific reference to living resource issues.
> *Proposals for action*:
> a) All schools should have a written policy for environmental education within the total curriculum policy of the school and the LEA. This should include environmental education objectives, and guidelines on how the school can achieve these objectives. All teachers should be involved in the formulation and implementation of the policy.

This recommendation reinforces our opinion that the environmental education policy will form part of the overall curriculum policy of the school. This will need to reflect the curriculum policy of both national and local governments, as far as the maintained sector is concerned.

Documentation of the National Curriculum is extensive and readily available to schools, together with helpful advice given in the National Curriculum Council's publication *A Framework for the Primary Curriculum*.[2] On the other hand the statements of curriculum policy of each LEA vary in length, content and detail. It is essential that all such relevant material is perused before an attempt is made to establish a school policy document, with special regard paid to the policy of the school's own local council.

In this chapter we will consider the formulation of a school policy for environmental education. As a learning area environmental education can go a very long way towards ensuring that the attainment targets of the core and foundation subjects of the National Curriculum are set within an appropriate context for meaning and understanding. It will draw and build upon the natural experiences of the child.

It may be helpful here to summarise a few of the curriculum statements produced by LEAs, chosen solely for their range of detail and varied approach. Those of the Scottish Environmental Education Council (SEEC) and the United Nations Environment Programme (UNEP) are also relevant.

Some examples of curriculum policy published by LEAs

Sheffield[3]

The curriculum policy statement for Sheffield schools gives an overall indication of what is to be contained in each schools' 'written curriculum portfolio'. A main tenet of the Entitlement Curriculum emphasises that

> All pupils are entitled to a curriculum designed to introduce them to a broad range of educational experience, to make them more aware of the cultural diversity of society, and to foster the skills they need to deal critically and creatively with their world.

Environmental education is highlighted when direction is given to the integration of common courses.

> At appropriate stages throughout their schooling (pupils) should enjoy the opportunity to explore key cross-curricular disciplines such as environmental education ... Schools should take every care to ensure that these elements are not omitted by default.

Under the classification of 'Human and Social' in the Primary Years curriculum the document states that

> Beginning in the immediate circumstances of their lives, children should have opportunity to develop a sense of chronology, to learn to distinguish between fiction and historical fact, and to appreciate that evidence may itself be partial. They should become more aware of aspects of their locality, and, more generally, both of the effects of landscape and climate on patterns of human settlement, communication and transport, and of the ways in which people themselves shape their environment. Children should thus be helped to appreciate the impact of the environment on the quality of people's lives and develop a responsible attitude towards use of the earth's resources. Pupils should become aware, too, of the inter-dependence of people,

and acquire the necessary personal and social skills to form and develop satisfying relationships. From the earliest years their sense of the adult world beyond the school should be fostered, so that they better understand how the economic, social and cultural life of the community is organised and sustained.

The study of science is to be viewed in the light of its interaction with the pupils' environment and they

should be helped to appreciate the role of science in understanding their physical and biological environments and how science may be applied in the solution of real life problems ... Pupils should come to see, too, that there are moral issues on which people may differ with integrity.

Continuity and progression are stressed:

Issues of balance, continuity and progression are especially important when the curriculum is organised on a theme, topic or modular basis. Curriculum integration of this kind requires a clear overall plan for the work, identifying the knowledge, skills, concepts and attitudes to be developed; sufficient coherence across individual activities to provide a meaningful and useful experience for pupils; and agreement among staff that, if topics are repeated in children's school careers, subsequent teaching will build on what has gone before.

The importance of first-hand experience and the use of the neighbourhood as an educational resource receive particular attention.

Children should have the opportunity at all stages, and whenever possible in the primary years, of learning from active, first-hand experiences and the local environment. Relevant experience can sharpen the senses, develop physical abilities, stimulate the imagination, extend the use of language, demand thought and illustrate new concepts. It is a cardinal principle of the curriculum that, where appropriate, work should be centred in children's lives in and out of school, with learning applied to tasks and problems which are real and relevant to them. In this, parents and the community are an important curricular and general education resource. Schools should make the fullest use of the locality and have clear policies for the involvement of parents, the community, and local commerce and industry in children's education.

The statement concludes by placing great emphasis on the ethos of the school, suggesting that it should provide a 'secure environment for personal growth and motivation, (and) some compensation for external deficiencies'.

Norfolk[4]
The overall statement of policy for the curriculum by Norfolk County
Council is presented as a series of principles and an enunciation of
the best of current practice in teaching, learning and assessment. A
separate document gives guidelines for environmental education in
primary schools under the title of 'An agenda for action'. In particular
it draws attention to the fact that the UK's response to the World
Conservation Strategy listed two aims

1   For all schools to have a written environmental education policy
2   To assist with growth of environmental education programmes
    within the existing administration and curriculum structures.

The comprehensive 'Agenda for action' gives clear guidance to
schools in preparing their environmental education policy. A suggested plan of procedure illustrates the text, which suggests that the
school policy shall give clear guidance to staff on each of the following
areas:

1	Aims and objectives	8	Equal opportunities
2	Skills and concepts	9	Cultural diversity
3	Teaching strategies	10	Resources (school-based)
4	Differentiation	11	Resources (local and
5	Assessment		national)
6	Continuity and	12	Links with outside bodies
	progression	13	The school site
7	Cross-curricular links	14	Residential experience
		15	'Field' studies including
			urban studies, visits, farm
			links and consideration of
			safety regulations

Wiltshire[5]
This LEA lays down a broad statement which will be supported in
the future by more detailed guidance on individual subjects and cross-
curricular themes, including examples of good practice. It is also
intended to set curricular targets. One of the general aims of the
authority's view of the curriculum is that pupils must understand the
world in which they live and the inter-dependence of individuals,
groups and nations. They must be encouraged to develop lively,
enquiring minds with the ability to question and argue rationally. The
raising of environmental awareness is emphasised.

> Pupils are entitled to expect an education which is relevant to their individual abilities, experience, interests and present needs and which is clearly of application and value to the world outside the school.

> This implies that the curriculum shall offer:
> (amongst other matters)
> an active practical approach to learning
> a range of appropriate contexts for learning – including those outside the classroom.

Prominence is given to coherence, continuity and progression. The statement points out that at the primary age there is likely to be greater emphasis on an integrated approach. Within this, class teachers will need to ensure that all aspects of their pupils' learning are adequately covered. Whatever the form of organisation, schools must deal effectively with cross-curricular themes in a coherent manner and this includes environmental education.

Kent[6]

Kent County Council has produced a very full Curriculum Statement under the title *Education for life*. We quote from it elsewhere. After setting down the aims of school education it proceeds to discuss the foundations and nature of the curriculum.

In the section on 'Approaches to the Curriculum' the statement deals with environmental education as a separate and important issue which, it emphasises, is multi-disciplinary and which

> provides a particular style of teaching, allowing teachers to extend their work beyond the confines of the classroom into the immediate environment of the pupil, extending gradually from the home and school to the natural and built environments. It offers opportunities for learning experiences from first hand, and in every phase, making the world in which the pupil lives a more relevant place.

Successful teaching from environmental resources will involve:

   i)   Using relevant first-hand resources and experiences from the immediate environment where this is possible and appropriate.

   ii)   Working outside the classroom as a natural extension of the learning environment.

   iii) Developing the skills of enquiry and exploration in both local and contrasting environments.

   iv) Developing communication skills, particularly through discussion and debate, leading towards practice of decision making and value judgement.

   v)   Developing the pupil's self-reliance and ability to organise work programmes in the school and in the field, with an increasing degree of responsibility for their own learning.

vi) Building an understanding of place, time, change and relationship using concrete phenomena that pupils can perceive and relate to.

The investigative approach to learning receives special attention

In adopting an investigative approach to learning, much of the work should arise from pupils' spontaneous interests and from natural curiosity. It should be so structured that pupils gain a progressively deeper understanding of important concepts. Pupils need to meet and grasp certain fundamental ideas if they are to make significant progress. In any particular piece of work teachers need to be clear about which concepts are to be used or developed, in ways appropriate to the age and maturity of the pupils. A carefully organised sequence of teaching is necessary if concept development is to take place and progression ensured from year to year. It is the teacher's responsibility to lead and encourage pupils to:

i) make observations through first-hand activities involving all the senses;

ii) raise questions;

iii) seek and identify patterns, compare and evaluate and record appropriately;

iv) order ideas based on selected observations;

v) design investigations to test the ideas; record and interpret the results and findings;

–thereby developing a perceptive, sensitive use of materials and a responsibility towards their real world.

Scottish Environmental Education Council[7]

In their curriculum guidelines for environmental education the Scottish Environmental Education Council suggests some guiding principles for creating a policy for environmental education.

It is possible to characterise further the approach to environmental education by means of a set of guiding principles. These combine philosophical, pedagogical and organisational considerations, and together they amount to a checklist of essential elements. Environmental education should:

• be a coherent, continuous and progressive lifelong process which should start at the pre-school level and continue through all stages of formal education and beyond. If this idea is to be realised it will require a co-ordinated approach, particularly at school level, based on carefully devised whole-school policies for environmental education sustained by appropriate management and organisational structures.

- be firmly rooted in direct experience. Fieldwork is an indispensable part of environmental education. It should be continuous, focused and progressive, and properly integrated with classroom and other learning experiences. It should provide for a range of experiences in the environment – sensory, aesthetic, contemplative, in addition to empirical study – and use a range of environmental settings, from urban to rural and local to remote. The importance of fieldwork should be reflected in timetable and other institutional arrangements which are flexible enough to accommodate and even encourage work outside the classroom.
- adopt a concentric approach. Environmental education should begin with and be based in the local environment, but should also promote awareness which extends to the regional, national, and global scale. As part of this progression it is important that the learner is led to appreciate and to understand the connections between the wider environment and everyday local actions and needs.
- be essentially interdisciplinary in character. Environmental education cannot be the exclusive preserve of any one subject or group of subjects. Ideally environmental education should pervade the whole curriculum whether it be through existing subjects, by means of curriculum inserts, specialised courses, or through genuinely interdisciplinary programmes of study. Whatever the form of implementation, co-ordination will be essential at school level to ensure a comprehensive and balanced treatment of topics and to avoid unnecessary overlap.
- use an issue-based approach when appropriate and incorporate an approach which involves problem solving where the aim is to identify and define problems and to generate answers and explore possible alternative solutions to real issues at an appropriate level.
- use as wide a variety of teaching and learning approaches as possible. Environmental issues are generally complex and demand such a variety of approaches. These might include class and field-based project work, simulations, role play, action research, use of information and other microtechnology, visits and residential experience.
- be conspicuously pupil centred so that all pupils can make a full contribution to the learning process and develop their own ideas about the environment and their role in it.

United Nations Environment Programme[8]

Developing an Environmental Education Curriculum is an attempt by the United Nations Environment Programme (UNEP) to ensure an effective environmental education curriculum in all schools. Although written within the constraint of trying to 'speak' to a wide variety of nation states and for the whole pupil age range, it parallels much of what has been said in this book.

Curricula are the core of education, no less so of environmental education. It is not enough to tell pupils or students about ecology or make them aware of environmental concerns. An effective curriculum takes them beyond these levels to that of interacting with the environment themselves and assessing their impact. Further, it helps them develop investigative, evaluative and action skills in the interdisciplinary, problem-solving, decision-making process.

UNEP suggests eight specific steps for the development of an environmental education curriculum with an emphasis that they need to be modified to fit the special needs of each school's, region's, or Nation's educational situation. The steps are:

1 Organize a curriculum Core Development Team (CDT) – choose CDT members; establish tasks and timelines for the CDT; collect appropriate resources, e.g. curriculum materials and professional references; identify the constraints upon the curriculum-development effort and plan for their resolution.
2 Identify professional consultants who will serve as a Recommended Support Team (RST) – establish task and timelines; identify liaison procedures to be used between RST and CDT.
3 Develop the EE curriculum's scope and sequence – define curriculum goals; define concepts, skills and attitudes to be incorporated as objectives into the curriculum; assign objective components to appropriate content areas and grade levels.
4 Evaluate the existing school programme with respect to potential EE infusion elements – identify EE objectives which already exist in the present curricula; identify materials in present curricula which could be modified to meet EE objectives; identify deficiencies in present curricula where new materials must be selected or developed to complete the proposed EE scope and sequence.
5 Inventory and evaluate the community/regional resources available for use in the EE curriculum.
6 Prepare the EE curriculum – review and evaluate the materials which have been collected for potential adaptation or adoption; organize writing teams to adapt or develop EE materials needed to complete the curriculum.
7 Develop plans for both pilot and full scale implementation.
8 Develop a comprehensive evaluation programme.

Summary
It is clear from the foregoing examples that the initiation of any school curriculum policy, and this includes that for environmental education, must begin with examination of the local curriculum statement. It may well be that the local advisory service has had experience elsewhere which is helpful to the task in hand – the production of an environmental education policy for an individual school.

The planning and construction of an environmental education policy

A final consideration might be called 'transfer', or the transposition of the environmental knowledge, cognitive skills and attitudes acquired in the classroom to the decision-making processes of the learners throughout their lives. Experience and research have demonstrated that if such transfer is to take place, *it must be taught* – through problem solving in a variety of different, even confusing, situations.

(UNEP/IEEP *Connect* newsletter September 1989)[8]

Whatever the arrangements for cross curricular issues, they should not be left to chance or to individual initiatives; their place needs to be assured through consultation, be consistent with the general framework adopted by the school and be recorded in schemes of work which indicate the progression to be expected.

(*The curriculum from 5–16, Curriculum Matters 2* HMSO)[9]

The fact that every school is unique has been emphasised elsewhere; it is clearly incompatible with this concept to suggest a model environmental education policy for a primary school. What can be done is to put forward some guidelines which could form the basis for the establishment of such a policy. In general they are based on experience gained from several schools in quite different situations. A synthesis of their planning gives rise to some key points which should appear in any policy document.

The school policy for environmental education must be planned to consider the organisation of learning experiences. An overall framework should address the following issues:

- What is our school doing already? (See figures 6.1a and 6.1b)
- What should we do next?
- How is environmental education set in the context of the school curriculum as a whole?
- What are our policies for environmental education?
- What is our common school viewpoint that will give consistent approaches to the implementation and organisation of environmental learning experiences?
- How will time be organised and prioritised?
- Do we have adequate facility for acquisition, storage and distribution of resources?
- How do we ensure environmental curriculum continuity?
- How will pupils be grouped and staff deployed?
- What forms will assessment and record keeping take?

- How shall we monitor and evaluate environmental education in practice?
- How do we achieve a balance between flexibility and the necessary timetable restrictions?

Figure 3.1 indicates the suggestion of the Scottish Environmental Education Council[7] for a framework for the production of a school environmental education policy. It recognises that the school policy on environmental education should contain guidance to staff on each of the following:

Aims and objectives	Differentiation
Skills, concepts, attitudes to be promoted	Resources
	Fieldwork and residential
Content/list of themes	experience
Flow chart for each theme	Use of the school site and the
Assessment and expectations	wider environment
Time allocation	Hidden curriculum
Progression and primary/secondary liaison	

That all of these headings are important matters to be considered is accepted but perhaps some of them are matters for documentation beyond the initial statement of policy. For example, the content list of themes and their flow charts will be ongoing as extra topics are added as seems appropriate.

A policy document may usefully be broken down into eight sections. As much or as little as the school requires may be included under the following headings, conditioned by local choice and, not least, by the existing curriculum statements for the school.

1 Aims
2 Objectives
3 Methods and timing
4 Content (knowledge, understanding, skills and concepts)
5 Resources and the organisation of resources
6 Assessment, record keeping and evaluation
7 The school as an environmental stimulus
8 Other matters

1 and 2 Aims and objectives
These have been discussed for environmental education as a whole. They will be of a similar nature when applied to an individual school. It will be necessary for the objectives to take into account the experience and special needs of individual pupils and to be explicit

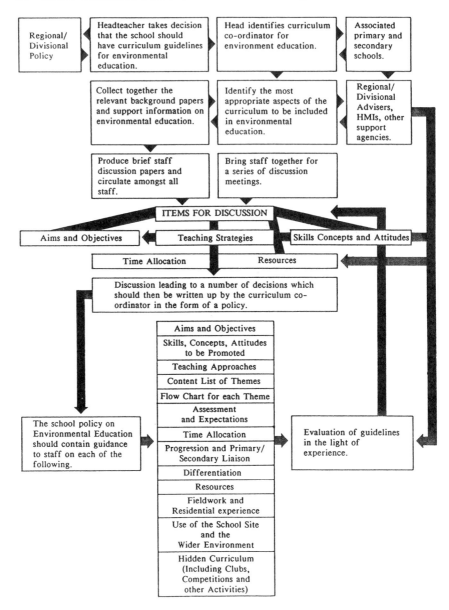

Figure 3.1   *Framework for the production of a school environmental education policy (Scottish Environmental Education Council)*[7].

about the provision for continuity and progression together with equality of opportunity for every pupil. Experience has shown that objectives are often implicitly supportive of an environmental approach but have not been defined clearly enough for the local situation, a fault not confined to environmental matters. Commonly they read thus: 'have a degree of insight into other people's environments, lifestyles and predicaments'.

Contemplation of this leads to the conclusion that the study is limitless, a total impracticality within the working time of school. It is for each school to make positive recommendations in order to limit the scope of environmental work. It may be considered that an environmental policy statement can rest at this point – if the aims and objectives are defined satisfactorily it is then up to the teacher to work out the rest. This inevitably leads to a lack of coherence in a pupil's overall programme of environmental work. Although rigidity needs to be avoided a better-defined structure seems to be essential.

3 Methods and timing

The methods to be employed in the environmental education learning situation are as wide as for any other curriculum area and it is not necessary to draw up detailed lists of ways and means of teaching. The way in which the school day and school year is divided is essentially an individual matter. Our plea is for flexibility so that any timetabling that is necessary is the servant of the learning situation and not the master. This is not the place to go into the many ploys for a flexible approach, but they range from simple cover arrangements to release staff for a special piece of planning, to the complete abandonment of the normal routine for a day or longer. Enough has been said already for it to be apparent that a thematic/topic approach which includes a substantial element of direct experience is favoured. Out-of-the-classroom learning is paramount in this and for all of the reasons given earlier it ought to form the starting point for most environmental work. It is up to the policy document to bring order to what could be *ad hoc* arrangements leading to repetition and omission, with some pupils receiving a high quality of experience whilst others follow tasks of a limited range both in content and in the opportunity to extend their thinking. Attention should be given to sequential learning and progression, as is apparent in some of our case studies. In this context progression is conceived as the acquisition of increasingly difficult concepts and skills, a matter which may involve consideration of the role of environmental education in delivering the National Curriculum.

4 Content

Knowledge, understanding, skills and concepts are all matters of content, precisely what any lists should contain and how comprehensive they should be, has to be a matter for the overall school policy. The environmental education policy statement of content is very much conditioned by the detail of the curriculum statements for the core and foundation subjects. Some will find it helpful to go into great detail, particularly as far as the final years of the primary school are concerned, others will be content with broad statements. It can be argued that the environmental approach is to practise the skills of other learning areas, listed in their policies.

> Because environmental education is to be integrated within all curriculum areas ... it is not possible to specify in detail, environmental education content for all subjects. What is important is that the content of a particular subject is treated in a way that contributes to the aims and outcomes of environmental education. In general, this can be achieved by using the content of a particular curriculum area to develop students' understanding of key environmental concepts and by providing students with learning experiences from the processes and strands of environmental education.[10]

Indisputably the recognition of environmental issues and problems and in particular their local application and relevance are best established in the environmental education policy document.

5 Resources and the organisation of resources

A policy statement is not the place for listing school-based resources but it is not without relevance to indicate the type and variety of aids to environmental learning that are to be accumulated in the school. It is also appropriate to indicate how the archive material of environmental projects will be kept so that it becomes one of the most important of resource items.

It is appropriate to describe the resources that are to be found in the neighbourhood and to give an indication of the most appropriate age level with which to use them. It is essential that an ordered age/ability related list is published so that progression of environmental work in the school is not pre-empted by previous, casual use of a chosen resource.

The school grounds will need to be assessed as to their use for environmental work (see Case studies 2 and 3). A broad indication of the lines along which future developments may take place is appropriate at this point. In particular a development plan will be a signpost to some of the environmental projects to be carried out; for the first few years the conservation element of a balanced environmental approach can be catered for within the school estate itself.

A general indication of the contrasting environments to be experienced by pupils of the school as they pass from entry to secondary transfer, is to be commended as part of the policy content. This will focus attention on the provision of field study centres by the local authority and others. Since residential experience will be desirable by the end of the primary stage, a planned use of distant facilities is essential. This in itself, helps to determine which contrasting local environments will be utilised. This will lead to planned community involvement and some links with local employers.

Nevertheless it is important that the policy document emphasises that individual initiative and the exploitation of opportunity and current events are not to be ignored.

6 Assessment, record keeping and evaluation
It is a case of 'grasping the nettle' where assessment and evaluation of environmental work is concerned. Each school will need to give attention to this, difficult though it may prove to be. Almost certainly a pupil profile system will need to be adopted. What we say in Chapter 5 may assist with this task.

7 The school as an environmental stimulus
The environment is where we are, and where we are for much of the time is 'school'. The importance of a clear policy concerning the quality of the school environment cannot be over-emphasised. It is up to the headteacher to ensure that the fabric of the school is properly maintained and that the entrances are such as to encourage positive feelings. It is up to staff and pupils to see that the school is positive from a living together point of view. Wall spaces and display areas should reflect a busy, high quality work force, which stimulates visitor and occupant alike. The hidden curriculum, that which is not written down but which affects the young learner for all that, is dominated by the school itself – people, buildings and grounds. Appearance and attitude are of paramount importance.

It is difficult to write detail into the policy document but this does not prevent an emphasis being placed on the general point, namely that the school itself must reflect positive environmental stimuli.

8 Other matters
Individual circumstances will dictate other contents of the environmental education policy statement, something which we cannot prescribe, except to observe that consideration of other matters is essential. For example, a church school may need to examine the links that are necessary with the patron church, or a school which caters for pupils with special needs will have certain environmental priorities beyond those of other schools.

Whether or not a school expresses an opinion on the part which environmental education has to play in delivering the national curriculum, is something for each school to consider. Such an approach is possible – it is up to the environmental conviction of the individual headteacher and staff. Indeed, in our opinion, the whole policy document must be built around it!

The following case studies (2 and 3) illustrate the way two schools have made use of the school grounds and developed their estate area.

In recent years there has been a proliferation of nature areas in schools, yet we feel that, in almost every case, better educational use could be made of them. It has become fashionable to have an area of the school grounds set aside as a 'conservation area' in which children may observe and collect mini-beasts, engage in pond-dipping or pursue practical conservation activities. Unfortunately, however, in too many instances, such developments have tremendously enthusiastic beginnings but rapidly deteriorate into sources of conflict with grounds maintenance staff and neighbours or totally unmanaged patches of land which are the losers in constant struggles against vandalism. It is our hope that more positive approaches will prevail in the future – where development of school grounds results in a) an increase in wildlife habitats available in a locality and b) an increase in young learners' involvement in conservation matters and in learning more about the natural world. In order to achieve this, it is essential that school grounds development and maintenance is included as an integral aspect of a school's policy for environmental education and that planned programmes of study exist so that all children and staff in the school are actively engaged in learning experiences which take place within the grounds.

A number of LEAs employ advisory staff who will liaise with schools and help in school grounds/nature area development, giving advice on the practicalities of design and costing as well as on education potential and use. Also, the Nature Conservancy Council (NCC) (see Useful addresses p 220) has always recognised the importance of environmental education. As part of its work the NCC has provided grants to several hundred schools for the creation of nature areas within their grounds. For there to be long-lasting benefit from the use of such areas, the NCC argues, environmental education must be seen as having a cross-curricular role, as an essential approach to education as a whole.

> The ideal school grounds should benefit the children by stimulating their imagination, promoting observation and enquiry, and integrating many strands of education. They should also enhance the appearance of the school site. Achievement of this ideal may be rare but, if this is the aim, there will always be great educational and community benefits from the planning, establishment and long-term use of the nature areas.[11]

This Nature Conservancy Council report will no doubt be of interest to readers considering school grounds development. It identifies a number of primary schools which exemplify the educational use of nature areas in a variety of ways. Likewise, the following two case studies demonstrate that the development of nature areas within school grounds is a very worthwhile objective, if it is firmly linked to overall curriculum development.

Case studies 2 and 3 Natural and garden areas in school grounds

Introduction
Many schools use time, money and volunteer labour to develop natural and garden areas on their estate. Others have such a resource provided by the LEA. The Nature Conservancy Council and other organisations encourage such activities with cash grants and advice. But then what happens?

Those involved originally pass through the school so that personal pride in achievement no longer applies. Staff change, other projects become the interest of the moment. In too few cases is the use to be made of the developed areas built into the curriculum as a subject or cross-curricular resource asset.

Two schools, both in urban settings, have taken a more positive approach to the areas developed on their grounds. From the start the projects were seen to fall into three parts:

1 Setting up
2 Follow-up utilisation
3 Maintenance and extension

Some examples of the uses made by the schools are described below:

Case study 2 Use of the school nature area

Merridale School, Wolverhampton

1 The seasons (5/6-year-olds)
2 Providing for the physically handicapped (2nd year juniors)
3 Uses made of garden (3rd year juniors)

1 The Seasons
This was an ongoing topic with 5/6-year-olds. It consisted of regular walks through the natural area in order to observe, discuss and record

Figure 3.2

matters of seasonal interest. At the same time the pupils were learning how to conduct themselves on environmental study excursions within the safe confines of the school grounds. Back in the classroom their observations were translated into a variety of illustrated written work (see figures 3.2 and 3.3) and through class discussion the pattern of seasonal change was discovered.

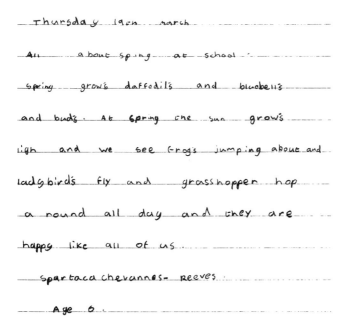

Thursday 19th march

When we went for a walk
in the School grounds we saw
Some buds. They were Pretty
little buds. I dipped my finger
into the Peat bog and there
was some green Stuff and it was
moss

Lorna Banks Age 5

Thursday 19th march

All about spring at school
Spring grows daffodils and bluebells
and buds. At Spring the sun grows
ligh and we see frogs jumping about and
ladybirds fly and grasshopper hop
a round all day and they are
happy like all of us.
Spartaca chevannes- Reeves.
Age 6.

Figure 3.3

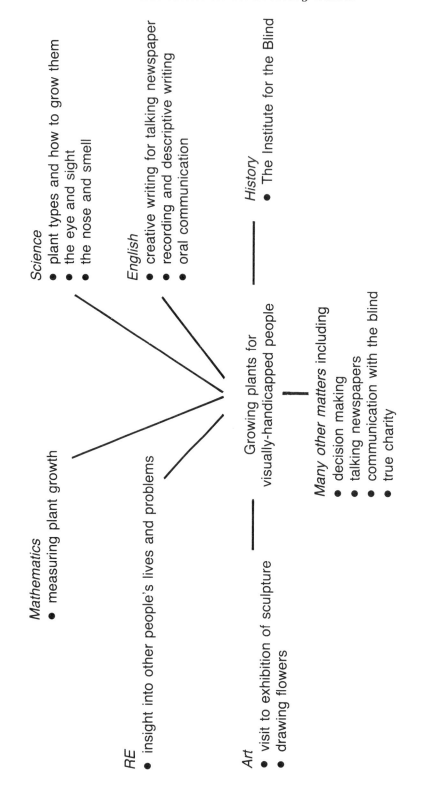

Science
- plant types and how to grow them
- the eye and sight
- the nose and smell

English
- creative writing for talking newspaper
- recording and descriptive writing
- oral communication

History
- The Institute for the Blind

Mathematics
- measuring plant growth

RE
- insight into other people's lives and problems

Growing plants for
visually-handicapped people

Many other matters including
- decision making
- talking newspapers
- communication with the blind
- true charity

Art
- visit to exhibition of sculpture
- drawing flowers

Figure 3.4 *Curriculum aspects of a project on growing plants for visually-handicapped people.*

2 Providing for the physically handicapped

This was a project by 2nd year juniors concerned to help sight-impaired people enjoy a garden. This was to be achieved by selecting scented flowers and herbs and by learning how to grow them. At the culmination of the project it was planned to hand over the plants to local visually-handicapped people, or to plant them in their gardens or window boxes. The project involved:

a   A visit from representatives of the Institute for the Blind to increase the children's awareness of sight handicap.
b   A visit by the class to the Institute for the Blind to see the facilities provided, meet some of the people involved, look at the aids for the visually handicapped and record a programme about the project for the Talking Newspaper.
c   A visit to the local garden nursery to discover suitable plants and how they are grown.
d   Learning some of the skills of plant husbandry.
e   Looking at an exhibition of sculpture for visually-handicapped people.
f   Measuring plant growth.
g   Meeting the people who received the plants.
h   Taking and planting the herbs and flowers at the homes of the handicapped.

The cross-curricular nature of this environmental project is shown in figure 3.4.

3 The use made of a garden

This was an investigative study by 3rd year juniors into the ways in which people use their own gardens and those provided by public and other organisations. The study was approached in three stages:

a)   The use made of the pupil's own garden.
b)   The use made of the school garden.
c)   Looking at some of the open spaces in the neighbourhood and the use made of them by the general public.

Some of the activities which arose from this study included

● measuring and recording to scale
● communicating ideas about garden use
● creating a sensory trail (see figure 3.5)
● design of gardens with the use of colour, pattern, shape
● relation of design to surround

This trail is about four of your senses we will be asking you to, Look, Listen, Smell, touch. We will be taking you to the wild area first go a cross the infant playground to blue marker (1).

(1) You will see a tree by blue marker (1). What is the tree called how big is it, is it bigger than you or smaller than you. Look up what can you see do a rubbing of a tree.

(2) Take the path what blue marker (2) is.

(3) Carry on and you will see a blue marker (3) There is a tree there what is it called Listen for sounds.

(4) Then you will see a blue marker number (4) and there will be some plants and leaves there what are they called.

(5) There will be a blue marker number (5). There is a tree by it what is it called

(6) Then you will see a blue marker (6) by two trees go thought the two trees and can you see anything. On both sides what are they called, Look, Listen what can you hear

(7) There will be a blue marker (7) what can you see in front of it.

Figure 3.5 *Instruction notes for a school nature trail, written by a 10-year-old pupil*.*

- use of plant catalogues
- discussion with a landscape architect
- assessment of access, paths, fences, gates, shelter, seats, services and safety.

One of the advantages of this environmental study was that it gave rise to an investigation into a number of environmental issues pertinent to both the neighbourhood and the country as a whole. It increased the environmental awareness of the young learners in a quite dramatic way.

---

*A further project for a group of 10/11-year-olds was to create two nature trails:
1 A sensory trail for children between 6 and 8 years of age. The written guide to this is reproduced above.
2 A more formal trail using plant and animal identification for older children and adults.

When the trails were open to visitors some of the pupils who designed the route were guides and acted as trail markers rather than provide permanent markers susceptible to interference or vandalism. In any case the children did not think that markers enhanced the area.

A series of related activities were set up which included:

- an area set aside for plant and insect identification, equipped with books and magnifying glasses;
- a selection of games and puzzles made by children based on the trail;
- a computer programme devised by the pupils to assist tree identification using leaves.

Case study 3   Use of the school nature area

Churchfield Junior School, Rugeley

1   The way in which the creation of a school natural area is used in the day-to-day activities of the various classes of the school.
2   The use of the nature area is planned into the curriculum work of the school, is ongoing and cross curricular.

Age range 8–11

Churchfield School uses the outside area (figure 3.6) throughout the school year. Much of the day-to-day work makes use of the pond, bird table, wildflower bank, log pile and other features without a direct project investigation. For example, most children try pond-dipping at some time during the year and a vast amount of cross-curricular environmental work evolves, included in which are model making, descriptive writing, tallying, movement related to creatures, ways of identification, art work, habitat study and many more. The trees, too, provide a never-ending source of stimulation. One particular investigation compared the oak and the plane as hosts for various forms of life. From this the pupils realised that, though every tree is an important part of the natural world, some provide a much richer habitat than others. It follows from this that the destruction of one type of tree may have a far greater impact than the felling of another.

The natural and the cultivated harvest from the school grounds makes a focus for religious education and encourages children's charitable instincts. The Autumn Harvest Festival not only stimulates this aspect of the curriculum but the commercial evaluation of the crop produced brings in mathematical and economic considerations.

The Chequerboard Garden (figure 3.7), a familiar sight in many primary schools, is planted every year with a wide variety of flower seeds. Throughout the year the young learners observe the growth, pattern and colour of the individual plants. All of this is translated into the classroom as direct science or used to provide innumerable opportunities for descriptive and creative writing, drama, art and craft, mathematics and so on across the whole of the curriculum range.

One interesting feature of the outdoor 'classroom' is the Chase Plot. The school is located on the edge of Cannock Chase. A close working relationship has been built up with the local Forestry Commission personnel. They provide seeds, seedlings and small plants of the numerous varieties which grow naturally in the Chase, for the children to plant in the Chase Plot. In any one year these include holly, oak,

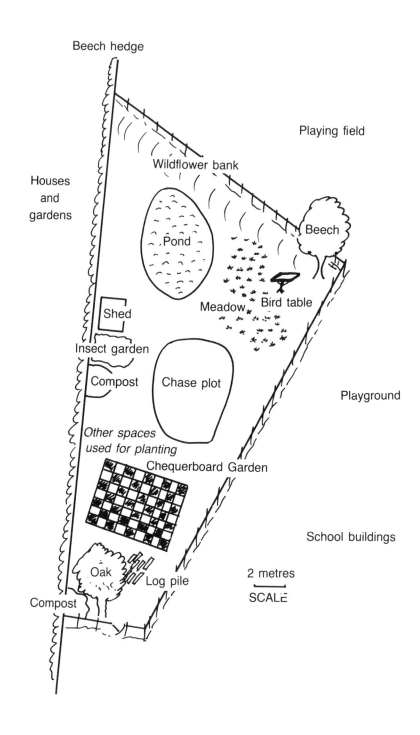

Figure 3.6   *The Outside Resources Area at Churchfield School, Rugeley.*

Figure 3.7 *The Chequerboard Garden at Churchfield School.*

heather, bilberry and hazel, all indigenous to the area. This heightens the youngsters' awareness of the plant life of the forest and provides them with a local pride and responsibility for the welfare of the Chase. The Chase has its darker side so that 'along the way' the natural and the criminal dangers of the forest area can be emphasised throughout the primary years. The plants which are grown on in the plot are transferred to permanent sites in the Chase when appropriate. One particular highlight was the school's participation in National Wild Flower Week when all pupils were invited to plant wild flowers in the Chase.

The work which makes use of the school estate is so varied and ongoing that it is impossible to record it all here. One or two examples of particular environmental projects will give some idea of what takes place.

1 A Topic on Flight with 7- to 9-year olds
The outside area was used to investigate seed dispersal as part of the wider topic under consideration. Opportunities arose for many cross-curricular links, with children writing descriptive passages, sketching, tallying numbers of seeds per seed head, measuring the distances travelled by the seeds and so on. Observation of the birds in the area provided an insight into the problems of how a body that is heavier than air can stay aloft. The local environment provided the basic material for consideration of flight and air travel generally.

2 Birds, their food preferences and feeding habits
Two classes, both 9- to 11-year-olds, studied two aspects of bird
behaviour. The first group looked at food preferences through a
careful experiment with different foods. This was carried out over
the winter period and it brought home to the children the need for a
proper control in any scientific experiment. The other group designed
different types of feeders from milk cartons to see which design was
the most popular. It was found that some birds had a colour preference. (This was done by putting bread on paper of various tints, and
by dying the bread itself to see if this linked in with the paper
preferences established by meticulous observation.)

3 The life cycle of the ladybird
Pupils are allowed free access to the natural areas and cultivated
garden, provided that it is for 'serious' study and not for play. As a
result many chance discoveries ensue. One was the find of a raft of
ladybird eggs. As a result the whole class of 3rd and 4th year juniors
became involved in an environmental project on ladybirds. Some of
the activities included:

● design of containers to house the eggs and act as observation
  chambers
● observation of the emergence of larvae and the rest of the life
  cycle
● model making of life stages of the ladybird
● creative and descriptive writing, including poetry
● use of the classroom computer
● design and use of 'ladybird dominoes'
● measurement, timing, tallying
● creation of ladybird display
● reading books in the *Ladybird* series
● finding out about the Pestalozzi Homes (they use the ladybird
  logo)

4 Cats – an environmental problem
Local cats disturbed the outdoor area in all sorts of ways well known
to gardeners. One group of 7- to 8-year-olds brought Design and
Technology into their work by devising an array of plant protectors
with the specific objective of countering the daily invasion of cats
from the bordering housing estate. In order to do this it was necessary
for pupils to learn something of feline habits, not least by home
observation of their own pets. This is a good example of the way
that minor local issues bring young people face to face with the

complexities and involved inter-relationships of any environmental problem.

5 Creation of a herb plot

A class of 7- to 8-year-olds had the task of adding another dimension to the outdoor area. They were to create a herb garden. This was mainly a technological exercise and involved design of the plot, calculation of the number of bricks and the amount of cement, sand and gravel needed, a search of the Yellow Pages and other local directories, receipt of estimates from local merchants and the follow up order. This was accompanied by the preparations for building and then the construction itself.

Later, when they are one year on in their school career, the children will become involved in the selection of herbs and their planting. Later still this will lead to an investigation into the use of herbs and their varied properties, smells and tastes. Progression and sequential learning in reality.

These examples are but a fraction of all of the environmental activities that arise from purposeful use of a natural and a cultivated area. It does not have to be large to be effective.

4 Approaches and starting points

Approaches

In practice, inclusion of environmental education in the primary school curriculum has traditionally occurred (prior to the advent of the National Curriculum) in time devoted to environmental studies, within a very broad understanding of the term. It has been fitted in after due time has been allocated for meeting children's needs in the core curriculum areas of language, mathematics and science, and for a range of practical and creative activities. Terms such as 'topic work', 'project work', 'local studies' and 'integrated studies' are often taken as being synonymous with environmental studies – as there is usually a strong environmental element in them. The subject areas of history, geography and science have always had close links within this environmental studies work, which may occupy anything from one or two hours a week to a far greater proportion of the timetable, when studies will be used as a vehicle for the development of the more 'basic' skills across the whole curriculum.

Within the framework of the National Curriculum, there would seem little need for this approach to change. It is the view of the national working groups that separate subject areas contribute to environmental education and, in a reciprocating way, environmental education contributes to the subject areas. Consequently, it is not expected that environmental education should appear as a subject on the school timetable. However, understanding of the processes and issues which this area of learning seeks to promote should not be left to chance or to individual initiative and should properly constitute part of the planned curriculum.

It is essential that an entitlement for all children in environmental education is formulated and then matched to the core and foundation subjects. This can be achieved with reference to agreed core subject material. Much of the content can be delivered through the attainment targets of the subject areas within an overarching and cross-referenced structure. The importance of relating environmental education to other cross-curricular themes as well as to the core and foundation subjects must not be overlooked. In this way it is possible to adopt an integrated approach which allows for a coherent programme of personal and social education within the curriculum.

No single acceptable teaching methodology for environmental education is recommended. It is considered that a variety of approaches should be utilised. However, task-based learning derived from children's spontaneous and direct experiences and investigations of their surroundings should always be encouraged, rather than merely 'presenting them' with information. Ideally a school will implement an overall and co-ordinated approach to methodology and organisation of practical investigations and fieldwork. Indeed, a matter which cannot be overemphasised is that co-ordination of the curriculum within each school, with carefully-structured policies, is essential if environmental education is to be effectively delivered across the curriculum. This matter is dealt with in depth in Chapter 6.

Other essential issues related to approaches and starting points are progression and assessment. The former must be achieved through planned programmes of study which are devised to allow for the fact that environmental education will be included in the core and foundation subjects and other cross-curricular areas. It is necessary to identify and construct levels of achievement for the relevant knowledge and understanding so that pupils at the four main reporting stages can demonstrate the appropriate assessment objectives. It is recognised that skills progression may not follow a similar sequential pattern of development to that of knowledge and understanding, it is essential, however, that skills progression is included in the construction of programmes of work.

As far as assessment is concerned, the specification of statutory attainment targets as the basis for pupil assessment is clearly a matter for the Secretary of State, advised by the subject working groups and the NCC. The report of the task group for environmental education recommends that in formulating or reviewing attainment targets, working groups and the NCC should have regard to the following objectives for environmental education:

1 **Knowledge and understanding**: to include knowledge and understanding of alternative attitudes and approaches to environmental issues and the value systems underlying them;
2 **Skills and abilities**: to include the ability to receive ideas about issues and to communicate views and attitudes to others.

Objectives for assessment should focus on the quality of decision making about environmental issues and include evidence of broad and critical understanding of the variety of interacting elements that constitute such issues. They should also make reference to evidence of critical understanding of, and tolerance of, different attitudes to issues. Pupil records should be maintained which provide a profile of experiences and attainments. Whilst it is inevitable that close reference will be made to recommendations outlined in the report of the Task Group on Assessment and Testing (TGAT) it is also important to consider that

> Perhaps in some cases innovatory methods of assessment will be developed appropriate to such aspects of environmental education as awareness skills, or the formation of values and attitudes and these used in conjunction with more established approaches.
>
> (Unpublished Environmental Education Task Group paper, 1989)[1]

Further advice on assessment and record keeping will be found in Chapter 5.

There can be no better way of demonstrating an interpretation of this theory into practice than by reference to examples of good practice, deriving from a number of different starting points. To these we later turn our attention. First, however, perhaps some reflection on the present situation is required.

It is the view of a very large number of teachers that the advent and implementation of the National Curriculum brings with it a move towards more traditional, subject-oriented learning and away from integration of subject matter and cross-curricular approaches. Hopefully this view will not be reflected in practice. Indeed, legislation allows for freedom of interpretation of programmes of study and certainly does not impose specific approaches to organisation or teaching methodologies. Rather than a strait-jacket of subject boundaries, perhaps we actually have an *opportunity* within a *framework* to promote a sound and well-researched entitlement of environmental education which is of fundamental importance to young learners and to our world.

The organisation of learning experiences, especially in the early years phase of education, is clearly not entirely in discrete subject 'parcels'. *Good* primary practice includes the development of work around themes and topics; above all, it builds on the natural experiences of children – their interactions with their environment – and the knowledge, understanding, skills and attitudes that they automatically bring from these experiences and interactions to a learning situation. In other words, learning takes place in a *context* and approaches to curriculum organisation should take account of this. The curriculum as a whole needs unifying elements and this is where cross-curricular dimensions, skills and themes have a vital role to play. Perhaps it is over-optimistic to view cross-curricular issues as the pinnacle of learning, with attainment targets of the core and foundation subjects being subordinate to and interwoven with them. Certainly it must *not* be our view that cross-curricular matters are on the periphery of the National Curriculum or are an appendage to it. An area such as environmental education can go a very long way towards ensuring that the attainment targets of the core and foundation subjects are within an appropriate context for meaning and understanding, drawing and building upon the natural experiences of the child.

The most effective way of demonstrating how theoretical principles such as integration, progression and assessment can be translated into practice is by reference to exemplary material. As seen already there are case studies interspersed in the text which document environmental education work with this end in mind. All derive from a different starting point and illustrate differing aspects of schools' approaches to development of work in this area.

Case study 4 details at length a typical primary school project involving, in the main, though not exclusively, the scientific aspects of environmental education. This project eventually involved every child in the school and encompassed other curriculum areas. It emphasises the need for constant monitoring, assessment and evaluation of the topic approach, something which has too often been lacking from environmental projects in the past. The study of animals in the classroom is one of particular complexity.

The Curriculum document *Science 5–16* (DES 1988)[2] assures us that by the end of their primary school years, children should have

- had opportunities to observe, first hand, a variety of animals and plant life over a period of time in which they take responsibility for the care of these living things
- observed closely their local natural environment to detect seasonal changes, including day length, weather and change in plants and animals and relate these changes to the passage of time
- explored and investigated a range of different localities and the ways in which plants and animals are suited to their location
- explored the ways in which plant and animal behaviour and the life cycles are influenced by daily and seasonal changes
- had opportunity to develop skills in identifying locally occurring species of plants and animals
- investigated some aspects of feeding, support, movement and behaviour in relation to themselves and other animals

- been introduced to basic ideas about the process of breathing, circulation, growth and reproduction
- explored and investigated the similarities and differences between accessible plants and animals.

Science from 5–16[2] states that: 'Over a period of time children should take responsibility for the care of living things, maintaining their welfare by knowing about their needs and understanding the care required'.

The reader of DES curriculum documents can therefore be in no doubt that the introduction of animals into school classrooms is to be encouraged. Indeed, the present authors believe that this is excellent practice from which sound environmental work can develop. Nevertheless, the whole question of animals in schools is controversial and complex, and no book advocating such practice would be complete without paying due regard to some of the major issues and considerations involved. Points that must be considered by anyone thinking of introducing animal life in any of its myriad forms into a school classroom include:

1   The maintenance and welfare of the animals themselves, including weekends and holidays.
2   The educational potential, that is, what benefits will the children derive from the presence of animal life?
3   The safety of the children – from disease and injury.
4   Suitable varieties of animals to keep.
5   Animals that should never be kept in or introduced into classrooms.
6   The law.

It is not within the scope of this book to examine in depth each of the above points relating to the keeping of animals. Other excellent publications documented in the bibliography consider the pros and cons of the matter and the fundamental issues of health, safety and legal requirements. Most Local Education Authorities have official guidelines and policy relating to the keeping of animals **and all schools are advised to consult local advisers, DES regulations and other legislation on the subject**. The following table summarises the main species of vertebrate creatures which are generally considered suitable for keeping in primary schools.

Whilst undoubtedly worthwhile, vertebrate creatures tend to be very demanding of both time and space. Very few may be kept within the four walls of a classroom. Birds certainly require a spacious aviary rather than a classroom cage and most vertebrates need outdoor

		Requirements
Mammals (small)	mice, rats, Mongolian gerbils, rabbits, guinea pigs	indoor housing access to outdoors
Mammals (large)	farm animals such as goats, sheep, pigs, cattle	outdoor housing large time investment
Birds	chickens, ducks, geese, finches, canaries	outdoor housing aviary
Amphibians (native)	frogs, newts, toads, (*not* protected species)	for temporary keeping only
Amphibians (non-native)	salamanders, axolotls	large vivarium
Reptiles	garter snake	large vivarium
Fish	various – consider freshwater, marine, temperate, tropical	large aquarium

Figure 4.1 *Vertebrate animals which are suitable for schools.*

accommodation. All native species, for example frogs and newts, should be kept on a temporary basis only and must be returned to their natural habitat. This gives a splendid opportunity for children to take part in and understand the importance of conservation of wildlife.

In comparison with members of the vertebrate world, invertebrates are a vast and enormously valuable classroom resource. They are, on the whole, easier to keep than mammals, birds, amphibians, reptiles and fish, they are less expensive to house and to feed and they offer tremendous potential for educational investigations as a result of their wide range of body shapes, habits and ways of life. Invertebrates can be kept relatively easily for up to a term, or even longer. Native varieties should always be returned to their natural habitat at the conclusion of a period of study. Non-native varieties may be kept for considerably longer, depending on their life cycle and natural span. Examples of suitable varieties include stick insects (Indian or Australian), earthworms, woodlice, slugs, snails, giant cockroaches, giant millipedes, locusts and fresh water invertebrates. A golden rule to remember is that invertebrates are animals. They should never be exposed to stressful situations and should always be treated with as much care and respect as vertebrates.

Case study 4   Invertebrates

Witton-Le-Wear Primary School, Co Durham

The programme of study
A study of invertebrate land animals carried out at Witton-Le-Wear Primary School, as part of the school programme in the scientific aspects of environmental education.

The school
Witton-Le-Wear Primary School is a small rural school catering for 70 pupils between the ages of four and eleven.

The project was conducted by the headteacher who teaches a class of mixed-age (eight to eleven years) junior children on a half time basis, sharing the class with a part-time teacher. This class is the subject of the programme of study.

Scientific/environmental aims of the school
The broad aims of the environmental/science teaching at the school can most concisely be expressed with reference to the Schools Council '5–13' series of books with the following aims for our children:

- to develop an enquiring mind and a scientific approach to problems
- to develop interests, attitudes and aesthetic awareness
- to observe, explore and order observations
- to develop basic concepts and logical thinking
- to pose questions and devise experiments or investigations to answer them
- to acquire knowledge and learn skills
- to communicate
- to appreciate patterns and relationships
- to interpret findings critically.

In addition to gearing our teaching towards these broad aims we must also ensure that it meets the needs and abilities of the particular children involved, especially those with special educational needs, and learning difficulties.

Whilst the above encompasses a concise statement of broad scientific aims for any primary school, as with other subject areas our educational aims should now satisfy the requirements of the National

Curriculum as well as meeting the needs of the particular pupils involved.

The children

The children used for my programme of study were my class of 24 juniors, consisting of seven 2nd years (8 to 9 years old), ten 3rd years (9 to 10 years old) and seven 4th years (10 to 11 years old). The group comprised seven girls and 17 boys. I chose to carry out the study with the whole class group for various reasons:

1 I knew all the children very well, having a detailed knowledge of their skills and abilities.
2 I wanted as many children as possible to experience the work in question and felt it would be unfair if part of the class undertook the study and part did not.
3 I wanted the children to encompass as wide an ability range as possible.
4 The topic chosen was perfectly practical to carry out with a full class and indeed actually needed several groups of children to make it fully viable.
5 I was fortunate to have access to ample resources in terms of equipment and books.

I was able to use both our school-based resources and also those loaned by local Higher Education establishments. In addition much of the study was perfectly feasible using everyday items of equipment such as glass jars, plastic trays, tape-measures, stop-watches etc. In terms of ability the children ranged from a slightly below average eight-year-old to an extremely bright eleven-year-old, ensuring that the programme of study was going to be an invigorating challenge!

Choice of topic

A variety of factors influenced my choice of topic for this programme of work with the children in school:

1 It should form an integral part of the children's environmental/science work in school and be relevant to the overall plan of work for the year.
2 It should be of a largely practical nature and be feasible in terms of resources and preparation.
3 It should be interesting and motivating to the children and offer them as many new experiences as possible.
4 It should be valuable in terms of using skills already possessed, developing new skills and gaining concepts and showing real progression.

5　It should be scientifically sound and relate to at least one attainment target in the National Curriculum.

6　As it was to be carried out during the Summer Term it should, where possible, involve the use of the whole school environment, working outside as well as in the classroom.

7　As it is our school policy to involve parents with their children's work it was important to choose a topic which would allow for pupils to do research, gathering of specimens and other activities at home.

8　It should be an area of study in which I felt confident and enthusiastic and would thus be more readily able to motivate the children.

As a result I decided upon the topic of invertebrate land animals which could be found within the school and grounds, with particular reference to their behaviour. My 'pupil learning objectives' for this topic were:

- for the pupils to gain various important concepts relating to invertebrates, their behaviour and their habitats e.g. the avoidance of dessication;
- for the pupils, working co-operatively in groups, jointly to discuss and develop ideas for testing hypotheses;
- for the pupils, having developed ideas to test a hypothesis, to put these ideas into practice by setting up an experiment to test them;
- in carrying out these experiments, for the pupils to observe carefully, note movements, changes, reactions etc. and to report accurately on what was discovered.
- for the children to develop the concept that different invertebrates would be found in, and would prefer, differing habitats and living conditions;
- for the pupils to understand that various invertebrate body structures are adapted to these differing environments;
- for the children, by careful observation, recording and discussion to discover certain specific behavioural factors about invertebrates such as:
  How does a spider move its legs?
  How does a slug breathe?
  How does a snail move? How fast can it move?
- for the learning gained from this programme of study to be of direct relevance to the National Curriculum attainment targets;
- for the children to develop the concept that there is a vast variety of life on earth and that a wide variety of invertebrate life can be discovered in their immediate school environment;
- to ensure that the programme of study incorporated real pro-

gression so that each child, whatever stage of learning he or she was at before the programme of study, had gained meaningful concepts and knowledge to further their learning by the end of the topic. The plan was to implement a process of assessment at various stages throughout the topic to ascertain that progression in learning was taking place (see Chapter 5).

- for the children to become familiar with, and proficient in using a variety of equipment;
- for the children to discover things for themselves, both as individuals and in groups, and for their learning to be meaningful and to motivate a desire to learn more.

The preparation

As preparation for the programme of study I discussed with the whole class the work, what it involved and how they could help to prepare for the topic. I found the children to be highly motivated for a variety of reasons:

1 I was able to amass a large amount of equipment, some unfamiliar to the children – this immediately provoked curiosity and enthusiasm.
2 We were enjoying the start of a particularly fine, warm summer and the children looked forward to doing a large part of their studies outdoors.
3 I explained to the children that during this programme of study they would be expected to demonstrate a high degree of 'self-responsibility' and co-operation: forming their own work groups, often working without direct supervision, forming hypotheses, devising experiments, observing, reporting results etc. I also explained that I would help and guide them but wherever possible would not give direct answers, rather encouraging them to find things out. They were most enthusiastic about this; they were aware of this method of working as it is the ethos of our environmental and other science teaching in school.

The pre-test

The class concerned with the programme of study had an extremely wide range of ability, but as I taught them regularly I was well able to assess at which sort of level to aim the pre-test. In addition, the preliminary discussion had given me an idea as to the children's knowledge or otherwise of the concepts involved.

I felt that the pre-test would be of most value to me if it was not too complicated and I therefore decided to limit it to the two basic concepts of 'What is an invertebrate?' and 'Where do invertebrates live?'. Within these concepts I also aimed to test the children's knowledge of some of the attributes related to invertebrates, such as body parts of insects and spiders, numbers of legs, specific habitats etc. The pre-test was also designed within the context of National Curriculum Attainment Target 2 (the variety of life).

The results of the pre-test were most informative and enabled me to guide children of differing abilities into different learning situations so as to ensure progression. It was also of interest to note that the results did not always reflect the child's general academic abilities. Whilst the generally able children tended to score well on the pre-test, some of the less able children also scored well, even though they had some difficulty writing down their answers. This indicated a generally high level of knowledge concerning what an invertebrate is and what animals are invertebrates. However, the results were somewhat more 'patchy' when it came to rather more specific attributes such as the number of legs an insect has or the names of its body parts. Thus the pre-test revealed in the children a generally sound basic knowledge of the concepts of what an invertebrate is and where various kinds of invertebrates live while showing at the same time that there was considerable scope for learning.

The grouping of the pupils
This programme of study actually benefited from being carried out by several groups as there were many different activities to be covered. The fact that there were 24 children in three different year groups might at first have been considered a difficulty but was actually an advantage as it enabled a natural progression of difficulty to be built into the programme of study. I grouped the children in six groups of four, as far as possible in their year groups with mixed ability ranges within their year groups. The groups comprised:

1 group of 4th year juniors (year 6)
2 groups of 3rd year juniors (year 5)
1 group of mixed 3rd and 4th year juniors
1 group of mixed 2nd and 3rd year juniors
1 group of 2nd year juniors (year 4)
All children came under key stage 2 of the National Curriculum.

As I knew all the children in the class very well I could have grouped them according to my estimate of their ability and thus have made it rather easier to plan the progression into the programme of study. However, I felt that the less able children in each year group would be motivated and helped by the more able ones and as the work progressed this proved to be the case. Furthermore the children whom I would have considered 'average' or less able academically in fact often proved extremely able at some of the more practical elements of the work. As far as possible girls and boys were mixed but as the class consisted of 17 boys and 7 girls there were two groups which were all boys.

Preparing the classroom
In line with our school policy of group teaching and our encouragement of discovery learning, the classroom needed little reorganization to accommodate this programme of study. Also, as this project encompassed many key areas of the curriculum I decided to spend four to six weeks concentrating entirely on this work. The children stayed in their project groups for the whole of that time, these groups being different in most cases from their normal work groups. A display area was set up at one end of the classroom, with a full range of collecting and observing equipment for the children to select and use themselves. This science equipment necessary for a project such as this does not need to be too sophisticated but I would list the following as very important to the success of the work:

Plastic tanks
Plastic trays
Collecting jars with lids
Pooters
'Magnispectors' and 'minispectors'
'Bugboxes'
Hand lenses (×6)
Table-top lens (×10)
Timeclock
Stopwatch
Thermometers
Tape recorder

In addition, I made available to the children a whole range of books, identification charts and general classroom equipment including scissors, sticky tape, clingfilm, card, paper and various art and construction materials. Space was also made available for the vivaria which were set up by the children to keep the invertebrates which each group had collected. The children had free access to all the books and equipment at all times during the programme of study.

The practical study – Collecting the invertebrates
The general consensus was that three main habitat areas would be examined. These were:

1   In hedges, trees and shrubs;
2   Under rocks, turf and soil;
3   In cracks and crevices in the path, walls and playground.

We toured the school grounds as a class to discover what the children considered to be suitable collection areas. No collection was done at this stage but it was hoped that it would save time the following week when the work was to begin in earnest. As we examined each habitat area I asked the children to sketch it and also to consider how they might actually catch and collect any invertebrates they found, bearing in mind that different habitats would require different collection methods. Following further class discussion to finalise collecting methods, I allocated two groups to each of the three types of habitat to ensure that the full range of collection sites was covered

1 *Hedges, trees and shrubs*
The groups collecting from these habitats soon discovered that the easiest method of finding invertebrates would be to shake the plant and cause the animals to fall out. Any invertebrates gathered were placed in collecting jars for later observation and identification in the classroom. Animals gathered from these habitats included aphids, caterpillars, and spiders as well as slugs and snails from the base of the hedgerow.

2 *Under rocks, turf and soil*
These groups were simply involved in searching underneath rocks, stones and a pile of turf left by the school groundsmen. In addition to collecting jars etc they were equipped with trowels with which to dig into the soil of the school garden area. They also put in place two 'delayed action' collecting methods consisting of a jam jar pitfall trap at ground level and an upturned half grapefruit skin placed in the grass at the bottom of the hedge. Both these 'traps' were inspected twice daily for a week and a variety of invertebrates were caught, notably beetles in the pitfall trap and ants on the grapefruit skin. When questioned as to why the pitfall trap had caught only beetles, the children thought that spiders, slugs and snails would be able to climb out and that flying insects would be able to fly out. They also thought that the ants were attracted to the grapefruit skin by its smell and taste. The children searched with care and the rocks and turf were replaced after collecting to preserve the habitat. These habitats produced a variety of invertebrates including beetles, woodlice, centipedes, millipedes and earthworms.

3 *Cracks and crevices*

These groups used a large paved area on the south side of the school as well as cracks on the edge of the playground and crevices in the brickwork of the building as their collection area. These habitats yielded ants, spiders, woodlice, centipedes, millipedes and small beetles.

While the children were searching the various habitat areas, I worked with each group in turn, discussing their work with them, putting relevant questions and – especially with the younger children – offering guidance where needed. I noted responses and made certain contributions or asked questions in group conversations. For example, a group of 3rd and 4th year junior children who had observed a spider moving across the paving slabs near the wall of the infant classroom:

GEMMA **We've found a hopping spider.**

ME **Why do you call it that Gemma?**

GEMMA **Because it moves fast and hops a lot.**

ME **How far can it hop?**

GEMMA (after observation) **About 2 cm I think.**

ME **Can you describe it to me Gemma?**

GEMMA **He's like black with white on the back and a white outline.**

LINDSAY **Look, he's climbed $\frac{1}{2}$ m up the wall.**

ME **How does he manage to climb the wall?**

GEMMA **He's got sticky stuff on his feet.**

JONATHAN **Is it the same stuff as the web?**

NICKY **I think he puts his feet in the bumps in the wall.**
(The spider runs further up the wall as Lindsay goes closer.)

ME **Why did he run up the wall when Lindsay went close?**

LINDSAY **He's got eyes in the back of his head?**

ME **Why do you think he likes the path and the wall?**
(It was a warm sunny day and the wall faces south.)

GEMMA **He likes warmthness (sic) and sunshine.**

ME **Why?**

GEMMA **Because he's got cold blood.**

LINDSAY **When it's wet he goes in a corner.**

A second group, consisting of 2nd and 3rd year juniors had discovered a woodlouse.

ADRIAN **Look what I've found.**

ME **It's a crustacean and it's got bent tentacles. It's probably got eight legs.**

MARK **It must be a spider then.**

ADRIAN **It's not – spiders aren't crustaceans.**

ADRIAN **His body's in columns – he has two pincer things right at the back. He has a hard shell. He has white legs and a grey shell and eyes and a head.**

NICKY **He curls himself up when he's attacked.**

LEE **I can see his mouth.**

ME **Can you count his legs?**

ADRIAN **He has seven down each side.**

NICKY **That's fourteen altogether.**

ME **What does that mean?**

NICKY **That he's not an insect.**

ADRIAN **It's a crustacean, I said so.**

JONATHAN **What's a crustacean?**

NICKY **It means it's got a shell.**

JONATHAN **Does that mean a snail's a crustacean?**

ADRIAN **He has hairs on his legs.**

NICKY **Aren't they for feeling?**

DANIEL **He has like an armadillo shell.**

ADRIAN **Shall I put him in the snail jar?**

ME **What do you think he eats?**

ADRIAN **Rotten wood.**

The practical study – designing and setting up habitats

The invertebrates were brought into the classroom for identification, if possible, and sorting. A whole range of books and identification charts were available to the children. I had previously told the children that we were going to keep the invertebrates for up to six weeks and asked them how we would set about doing that, bearing in mind the needs of the animals involved. The children were quick to point out that the animals would need a place to live which resembled as closely as possible the habitat from which they had been taken. I was pleased that a few of the older children came up with word 'habitat' without any prompting from me. I also introduced them to the word 'vivarium' and these were the words used from then on to describe the animals' temporary living quarters. In fact the children seemed to positively enjoy using the more scientific words. Once we had discovered the 'real-life' habitat of each of the types of invertebrate collected I asked each group to sort their animals and classify them according to the animal 'families', e.g. snails and slugs, beetles, centipedes and millipedes, ants, woodlice, caterpillars and spiders. The children decided that each of these types of invertebrate would need separate habitats with the exception of the millipedes, centipedes and woodlice which could all live together, as could the slugs and snails. I had planned that each group be involved with one type of habitat and be responsible for looking after it. However, it was not intended that this should limit each group to working with one 'family' of animals, indeed it was hoped that every child would experience most of the invertebrates during the programme of study.

Designing the vivaria
Using the knowledge gained 'in the field' as well as books and other materials, each group was asked to discuss the plan for their vivarium, sketch it and draw up a list of materials needed, again bearing in mind the requirements of the animals involved.

Building the vivaria
Having planned and designed their vivarium, each group was allowed to gather any materials they wished from the school grounds as well as using a range of materials in the classroom including plastic tanks, trays, polystyrene, clingfilm, sticky tape, jars, yoghurt pots etc. The groups then set about constructing their vivaria while I questioned and offered guidance where appropriate.

(National Curriculum Science Attainment Target 1)

Ant vivarium
This was designed and set up by a group of 2nd year juniors who used a plastic aquarium and a variety of sticks, rocks and dry leaves. They decided that ants like dry conditions and so for the bottom of the tank they used dry sand 'begged' from the infant class. The top of the tank was sealed with clingfilm to prevent the ants escaping.

Slug and snail vivarium
A group of 3rd year juniors designed and built the slug and snail habitat, again using a plastic tank. They seemed very aware that it was most important for slugs and snails not to dry out and so covered the bottom of the tank with soil which they moistened. They then

placed damp grass, dead leaves and a rock into the tank. Once again the top was sealed with clingfilm to prevent the animals escaping.

Caterpillar vivarium
A second group of 3rd year juniors designed and set up a habitat for the caterpillars which had been collected. After discussion, one of the children had suggested that while collecting the caterpillars it would be useful to note what type of plant they were living on and to ensure that there was a supply of that plant in the vivarium. The children placed a layer of damp soil in the bottom of the tank and a variety of plant material on which they had hypothesised that the caterpillars might live. These included sycamore, hawthorn, grass and nettles. Again the top of the tank was sealed with clingfilm.

Beetle vivarium
A mixed group of 2nd and 3rd year juniors designed and constructed a habitat for the various species of beetle which had been collected. The children placed a layer of damp soil on the bottom of the tank, together with dead leaves, twigs, and a large rock and a piece of polystyrene. The rock was propped up at one end with a broken piece of roof tile, as they had observed beetles crawling under stones and wanted to make this possible in the habitat they had constructed.

Centipede, millipede and woodlouse vivarium
This was designed and constructed by a mixed group of 3rd and 4th year juniors who decided to use a shallow plastic tray instead of a tank, since these invertebrates would not require a tall container as they lived at or below ground level. The children placed damp soil in the tray and put a broken piece of roof tile on top of the soil, together with a piece of rotten wood and some dead leaves. They too explained that, having observed centipedes, millipedes and woodlice crawling underneath stones etc they should provide similar facilities in their artificial habitat. The top of the tray was sealed with clingfilm to prevent the animals escaping.

Spider vivarium
The habitat for the various spiders collected was designed and set up by a group of 4th year juniors. Following group discussion, they had decided that spiders preferred dry conditions, together with things on which they could climb and fasten silk threads to anchor webs. The children selected a plastic tank and covered the bottom with a variety of rocks and stones, together with dry leaves and a variety of twigs placed vertically, wedged between the rocks. One member of the group had observed a spider in a crack in the wall

and discovered a broken building brick with small round holes in it which he felt would be ideal for those spiders and so this was placed in the tank. I introduced to the children the idea of the prey/predator situation which could possibly occur among the different species of spider in the vivarium. The group agreed to observe the situation closely but did not feel it would be a great problem as all of their spiders appeared to be of a similar size. Once again, the top of the tank was sealed with clingfilm which the children felt was especially important in this case as they had observed that spiders were particularly agile and fast moving.

I was extremely pleased with the thought, care and effort that all the children had put into designing and building each habitat. In each case valuable work had been done towards National Curriculum Science Attainment Targets 1 and 2. Skills used by the children included observing, hypothesising, communicating and classifying.

The practical study – caring for the invertebrates
The children were aware that the animals would need more than a suitable habitat, requiring food, water, air and also moisture for those animals which favoured damp habitats as well as warmth for those which preferred warmer conditions. I asked the children to place these needs in order of priority. Nearly all the children put air as the first priority, followed by food, water, then conditions. The only exception to this order of priority was the answer given by the group of 3rd year juniors who had designed and built the vivarium for slugs and snails. They thought that, after air, keeping a moist environment would be the most important thing for these animals. When I asked them why, they thought it was because the slugs and snails used up a lot of water when they made their trails of slime. Of the other groups, none seemed quite sure why they thought food was more important than water. They were also intrigued and quite surprised when I told them that a spider, for example, could survive for several weeks without food but would die within days if it had no water. The children then set about placing water containers in each vivarium and after group discussions decided on a shallow container to prevent the animals falling in and drowning. One group discovered that the lids of the collecting jars were ideal for this purpose.

I had noticed that, when sealing the top of each tank with clingfilm every group had made numerous air holes in the cover and seemed very concerned that there should be sufficient oxygen for the animals. After some class discussion I suggested that perhaps one or two small holes would be adequate, especially as they would be removing the covers frequently. Again some of the children seemed a little surprised that the invertebrates could survive with such a relatively small amount of air.

There were few problems when it came to food as most of the invertebrates were collected from their feeding sites and samples of those materials were placed in the artificial habitat. However, the group of 2nd year juniors who set up the ant vivarium were unsure of what the ants would eat. One of the children suggested the ants might like something sweet so after 'begging' a spoonful of syrup from the school kitchen they placed it in the ants' vivarium and were delighted when the ants were attracted to it immediately. The group who had set up the slug and snail vivarium decided that in addition to their diet of grass and leaves, the animals might enjoy a scooped out half grapefruit and so this was placed in the tank.

The children displayed great enthusiasm in caring for the invertebrates, often coming into school earlier than usual and also bringing parents to see their work. This contributed towards National Curriculum Science Attainment Targets 1 and 2 and even at this early stage of the work children were developing a caring attitude.

The tests
It was important that each group of children should become familiar with the invertebrates with which they were working, before conducting any specific tests or experiments. I decided, therefore, to allow the children ample time to carry out observations; initially of a general nature but later on rather more specifically and scientifically. Each group chose which invertebrates they wished to observe and I encouraged the children to discuss the animals and to help each other with their observations. The first problem to overcome was that of restraining the animals in order to carry out detailed observations. The children had free access to all the equipment and most groups soon discovered that the 'magnispectors' were ideal for holding the animals. However it was also discovered that even slugs and snails could be surprisingly agile if not kept in place with the lid and there were several 'escapes' before the children decided that observation was perfectly practical with the lid on and indeed that the 'magnispector' lid actually assisted observation as it consisted of a magnifying lens.

Initially I asked the children to observe their animal closely, making notes if they wished, and then to record what they saw by drawing it in as much detail as possible. I ensured progression in this activity by asking the older children to produce more detailed drawings from a number of angles and also to draw the animals to scale, stating the magnification on their drawing. The children carried out this initial observation work extremely conscientiously and I was particularly pleased that a 4th year junior with severe learning difficulties in reading and written language was totally absorbed with this work and asked one of the other children in his group to help him look up the scientific name for a snail.

Progress from the initial observations and drawing from specimens I asked the children to carry out some rather more scientifically specific observations, from which I hoped they would form hypotheses and draw inferences (National Curriculum Science Attainment Target 1). Again I tried to ensure progression within the different age groups of children by allocating tasks of varying difficulty and complexity. With the younger children, I guided their observation with certain questions, such as:

Where is its mouth?
How does it feed?
How long is it?
Where are its eyes?
How does it move? etc

I asked the older children to discuss in their groups what detailed observations they could make of the animals and which, if any, of these observations could be measured. Some of the ideas they came up with included studying movement, measuring body parts, weighing and listing special characteristics and comparisons. The two pieces of work (figures 4.2 and 4.3), show an interesting contrast following the observation of a harvestman spider by two different children. Figure 4.2 more general observation – was by an average ability nine year old. Figure 4.3 more detailed observation – was by a very able eleven year old. I encouraged the children at all levels to hypothesise and draw inferences, an example being a 2nd year junior who studied the movement of a snail. He decided that the slime was not there just to lubricate but had other functions as well. (National Curriculum Attainment Target 1.)

Once children had become familiar with the invertebrates through observation, handling, drawing, measuring etc, I gave them the opportunity to plan and carry out a series of behaviour studies and tests. I planned progression into the work by encouraging the older children to carry out more complex tests involving more variables which required more accurate and involved recording. I was keen for the children to suggest their own ideas and, after group discussion, allowed some of the older children to plan and construct their own tests. I was interested to see what would happen if the children had a 'free hand' and so I allowed a group of 4th year juniors to design

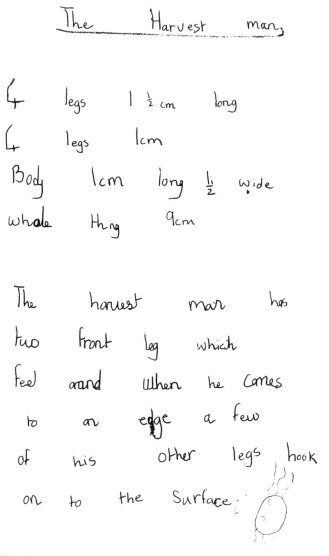

The Harvest man.

4   legs   1 ½ cm   long
4   legs   1cm
Body   1cm   long ½ wide
whole   thing   9cm

The   harvest   man   has
two   front   leg   which
feel   arand   when   he   comes
to   an   edge   a   few
of   his   other   legs   hook
on   to   the   surface.

Janet Heaton

Figure 4.2

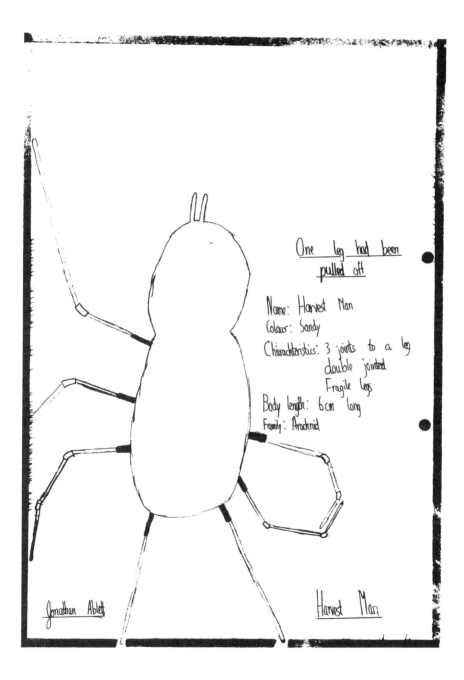

Figure 4.3

and construct their own test without guidance. They very much enjoyed this activity and there was a great deal of useful group co-operation but the results were not conclusive as they built a rather complex 'maze' to test the direction-finding ability of a ground beetle. They were somewhat frustrated when the beetle simply climbed over the edges of the maze instead of choosing one of the intended routes. The group had planned well, including options for the beetle of light/dark, damp/dry and rough/smooth but without teacher guidance they had included too many variables and made the test too complex, perhaps imagining the beetle to perceive things as they did. After the inconclusive results I pointed out the shortcomings of the test and asked them what they thought they could do to make a test more valid. They quickly decided that it would be more effective to test one set of conditions at a time, e.g. the beetle's preference for light or dark. Having allowed the children freedom to work on their own ideas, I allocated a behaviour test to each group as I wanted to:

- ensure progression;
- ensure several types of test were undertaken;
- collate results;
- apply various systems of recording;
  and, most importantly,
- ensure the work included aspects of relevance to various National Curriculum Attainment Targets.

The tests carried out were as follows:

Weighing
This was undertaken by two groups, one of 3rd years and one of 4th year juniors. The younger children were able to select a range of maths and science equipment and set about weighing some of the larger invertebrates such as slugs and snails. They also devised ways of finding the difference in weight between animals. I asked the older group if they could devise a way of accurately weighing one of the smaller invertebrates. They suggested weighing several and dividing by the number present, an exercise some of them had carried out in mathematics the week before. This was carried out successfully and I asked if there was any way we could weigh one small animal with equipment we had in school. They came up with a rather impressive Meccano micro-balance (figure 4.4). They calibrated it without assistance from me to 1/10gram and used it successfully to weigh several of the small invertebrates.

Snail/slug timing

Groups of 2nd year and 3rd year juniors devised ways of timing the speed of movement and the breathing rate of slugs and snails. To start with the invertebrates were simply timed along a set distance; first on the table-top but after trial and error in guided lanes, using rules as dividing strips to ensure easy measurement.

After timing single animals, later experiments involved comparisons of various slugs and snails. This was not always successful as some of the animals had their own ideas; one inquisitive snail even climbed out to inspect the time clock! The timing of breathing rates was done

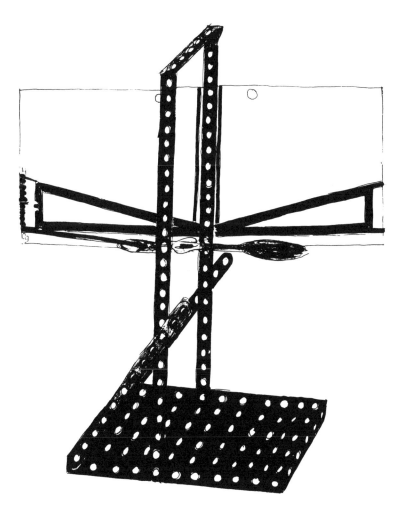

Figure 4.4 *The pupils designed and constructed a Meccano micro-balance to weigh small invertebrates.*

using an electronic stopwatch for greater accuracy and all results were recorded (figure 4.5).

Light/dark

A group of 2nd year juniors devised a simple experiment to test a spider's preference for light and dark. The group agreed that care should be taken in placing the test tray to avoid, for example, direct sunlight which may cause a 'rogue' variable by perhaps attracting the animal to warmth, which in this experiment was not being measured. The result of this test was not as the children had predicted. They expected the spider to scuttle under the dark card, whereas it appeared to have a definite preference for the light. One of the group suggested that this was because it was a diurnal spider.

Colour preference

A group of 3rd year juniors carried out a test to discover if caterpillars had a colour preference for their environment. They had discovered the caterpillars on oak leaves and predicted that they would prefer green as it meant food and a safe place to live. After several trials this appeared to be the case.

Rough/smooth

A group of 3rd and 4th year juniors had observed a violet ground beetle in the vivarium and noted that it could easily climb the vertical sides of a brick but was unable to scale the sides of the plastic tank. I suggested they devise an experiment to prove this and also to

	Breathing time in Seconds	Weight in grams	Descriptive Point	Colour	Length in Cm
Slug1	23:60	10	Tiger marks on his back.	Brown body Black Stripes	15½
Slug2	22:90	2	Plain colour	Brown body	5
Slug3	32:38	9	Small and fat	Black body	4
Slug4	23:39	8	Small and fat	Black body	5

Lee Dawson

Figure 4.5   *One pupil's descriptive record of slug observations.*

discover just how slippery a vertical surface must be before the beetle is unable to climb it. They first constructed a simple one-variable contrast test by dividing a plastic tray into two sections; one end with a 'rough' sugar paper surface and the other left as plain plastic. After tests on these surfaces they later went on to vary the roughness and smoothness of each surface as well as the angle of slope, recording the actions of the beetle each time. The tests were also carried out with other invertebrates such as woodlice and while the group were not too surprised at the results, they were quite impressed with the ability of the animals to cling to relatively slippery vertical surfaces.

Damp/dry
The group of 3rd year juniors who had constructed the slug and snail vivarium were well aware of these animals' need to conserve moisture. They decided to build a test to discover whether the animals would readily sense a damp or dry environment and if they would respond quickly by showing a distinct preference. After several tests the children were able to observe that the slugs and snails moved around the dry side for some time before finally preferring the damp conditions.

Hot/cold
One of the 3rd year juniors had observed that some of the invertebrates, such as beetles and spiders, seemed to enjoy basking in the sunshine, others, such as slugs, snails, centipedes and woodlice, preferred to hide away in the shade. John devised a warm/cold preference test for the animals and decided that the only safe way to create warm conditions was to use hot water. He was also aware of the need to have identical conditions apart from the one variable which was the temperature. He constructed the test using two identical storage tins; one filled with warm water, the other with cold. He carried out the test with several different kinds of invertebrate and recorded the results in the form of writing, tick boxes and a bar chart. The results were not entirely as John expected as the snail showed a distinct preference for the warm side, which rather surprised him.

'A step in the dark'
Over several nights the children placed sooty paper outside the classroom hoping that the tracks of various invertebrates might be recorded. Unfortunately this experiment was singularly unsuccessful which disappointed the children but did teach them the valuable point that experiments do not always work as you want them to.

	1	2	3	4	5	6	7	8	9	10	11	12	13	14
English	√	√	√	√	√									
Mathematics	√	√	√	√				√	√			√	√	√
Science	√	√	√	√		√								

Figure 4.6   *Summary of attainment targets in the core subjects of the National Curriculum – addressed at levels appropriate to the study of invertebrates.*

More success was gained in plotting the tracks of a snail, the results of which showed that snails do anything but travel in straight lines.

Record-keeping
Great emphasis was placed on careful and accurate recording throughout the programme of study and the children were encouraged to record in a number of different ways (National Curriculum Science Attainment Target 1) (figure 4.6). Much recording work was done in written form, accompanied by drawings from observation at frequent opportunities. With teacher guidance the children also devised their own recording systems using tick-boxes, comparison charts, bar charts and a computer database.

I also kept records throughout the programme of study by recording conversations within groups (both written and on tape) and also by constantly monitoring the progress of each group and modifying or extending the work where appropriate. At the end of the programme of study I drew up a chart to show which of the National Curriculum core subject attainment targets had been addressed by the work.

Cross-curricular links
Every child in the school became involved with the project in one way or another and the junior children working on the project took great pleasure in showing the younger children their work. Many parents also became involved. As the project progressed it became clear that as well as environmental science, many other important curricular areas were covered including:

Mathematics
The mathematics in particular was used in problem-solving situations, such as 'How can we design and build a test for ...?' as well as in the measurement of distance, time, speed, weight and area.

English (language)
Much language work, both oral and written, was done in reporting and recording and also in the form of creative writing. In addition the children discovered that there are a surprising number of poems and stories about invertebrates in commercially published books.

Art/craft
The children were enthusiastic about producing artwork, especially as they wanted the classroom to look interesting for parents' evening. The children developed three-dimensional models and some of these were very successful, a good example being the model woodlouse produced by a 3rd year junior girl.

Information technology
Much use was made of the computer during this project, not only in printing out children's written work using 'FOLIO' but also in using software related to the programme of study. A particularly useful programme was 'Microbug' which involved the children in building up their own databases from the results of their tests.

Design/technology
The children were involved in design/technology at several stages during the programme of study, particularly when designing and constructing the vivaria in which to keep the invertebrates, in planning and constructing the tests and also in designing and making equipment for use in the tests. An example of this is the micro-balance developed by some of the older pupils (see figure 4.4 on page 83).

Music
As ours is a small village school we are in a good position to involve all our pupils in any major project. Our infant teacher discovered a lively song called 'Eeny Meeny Minibeasts' which we used with the whole school. The children provided the accompaniment with keyboards and other musical instruments and the whole school involvement was much enjoyed by everyone.

The post-test and evaluation
I had constantly monitored and assessed the children's performance throughout the study and decided not to include a formal written post-test at the end of the work, but to carry out the post-test orally for two main reasons. First, by continuous oral assessment I already had a very good idea of what the children had learnt; second, oral assessment will be a very important aspect of the forthcoming national assessment programme. Towards the end of the project I

asked each child while they were working to tell me about something they knew at the end of the work which they did not know when they had started. Their answers were most encouraging and ranged from learning what an invertebrate is to finding out how many joints there are in a spider's leg or how to make a micro-balance. Above all the children told me that they had thoroughly enjoyed this programme of practical environmental science, as indeed I had too.

5 Assessment and record keeping

The national framework

Any assessment in environmental education must take account of the broad national framework for assessment and testing. This framework entails three inter-related components, namely:

1 Attainment targets for knowledge, skills and understanding, expressed in up to ten levels in the core and foundation subjects, as a basis for assessing and reporting on pupils' performance.
2 A combination of 'external' and 'internal' assessment. The external task is by means of nationally prescribed Standard Assessment Tasks (SATs); the internal task is assessment by teachers themselves.
3 The use of assessment results and outcomes both 'formatively' to help teaching and inform decision making about the next stages of a pupil's learning and also 'summatively' to provide information to parents and other interested parties about children's progress.

As we reported earlier it is recommended that the following objectives for environmental education should be borne in mind:

1 **Knowledge and understanding**; to include knowledge and understanding of alternative attitudes and approaches to environmental issues and the value systems underlying them.
2 **Skills and abilities**; to include the ability to receive ideas about issues and to communicate views and attitudes to others.

In the discussion on the approaches to environmental education we have suggested that the objectives for assessment should focus on the quality of decision making about environmental issues. Although the national framework will need to be considered it is worth repeating the idea that innovatory methods of environmental assessment will need to be developed in relation to awareness skills and the formation of values and attitudes.

The following stages and major considerations will no doubt be helpful as a checklist in assessment for the National Curriculum.

(Checklist from Keith Morrison, 1989, *Assessment, Environmental Education and the National Curriculum*)[1]

In approaching planned assessments
1 It is necessary to plan with assessment in mind, to make teaching tasks assessment tasks.
2 Assessment will have to involve a whole-school approach as it affects whole-school curriculum planning.
3 Assessment in the national curriculum will require more open-ended, task-based teaching which carefully selects which tasks will and will not have ceilings put upon them for assessment purposes.
4 There will be a need to continue to assess children very early on in their school careers in order to put down a series of markers for future reference.

In designing specific tasks
5 Decide when/how often to make formal assessments – the timing of the assessments.
6 Decide how to acquire information for the assessment so that it provides valid evidence for what is being assessed (the methods of assessment).
7 Planning will have to take account of the weightings of the profile components.
8 Decide whether to set assessment tasks which cover attainment targets or profile components.
9 Decide whether each assessment task will cover more than one attainment target and/or more than one curriculum area.
10 Decide whether a particular attainment target has to be assessed by more than one assessment task.
11 Decide whether to assess for only one level per task or more than one level per task.
12 Be very focused in the assessments and the assessment tasks.
13 Decide how to achieve reliability and validity.
14 Decide if the tasks are to be individual or group tasks. If they are group tasks plan how to allow for group dynamics. On what criteria will the children be grouped?
15 Decide which parts of the assessment have to be done *in situ* and which parts can be done with the children not present – e.g. using their written work.
16 Design checklists etc for observations, oral questioning, listening to children's discussions etc to be done whilst the children are present.
17 Plan how to organise children/staff to free the teacher to make assessments *in situ*.
18 Decide whether it is appropriate to put time constraints on tasks.

19 Consider readability levels of tasks – avoid blocking the assessment purpose of the task by difficulty in presentation.
20 When planning the setting of tasks for assessment consider three modes – presentation, operation, response.
21 Decide whether to allow children to repeat the same task at a later date if they were unsuccessful first time.
22 Decide how to allow for teacher intervention in the assessment.
23 Assess and record processes and products – skills and outcomes.
24 Trial and pilot proposed assessments.

In handling assessment evidence
25 Practise sampling strategies – how to fairly sample children/their work/their activities/the inputs/the outcomes.
26 There should be internal moderation meetings before going to external moderation meetings.
27 When carrying out assessments it is necessary to exclude age and effort, you only assess on the evidence.
28 Be clear on the criteria you are using to judge/assess from the information acquired.

In reporting
29 Decide how to mark the tasks/attainment levels – e.g. 'achieved', 'nearly achieved', 'not achieved'.
30 Decide whether to keep an individual or group record.
31 Decide how to comment on background variables for the purposes of reporting – NB no adjustment of scores is allowed.
32 Decide how to build ongoing assessments into less frequent formal records.
33 Decide the most parsimonious ways of presenting/recording formal assessments which still make the records and assessments valid and comprehensible.
34 Rich assessments offer more than aggregations of scores into a crude index, they must be formative and forward looking rather than a summative retrospective on performance.

In a record keeping system
35 Create a folder for each child to accompany them through the school, the folder to contain assessments other than those for the National Curriculum.
36 There is more to be assessed than that which is required by the National Curriculum – the national curriculum does not seek to assess certain aspects of the child which are important.

Without doubt the last of these considerations is very relevant to monitoring work in environmental education and reinforces the plea that innovatory methods of assessment should be developed that are appropriate for aspects of this area of learning since

The approach to Environmental Education should be such that it promotes interpretation in more than physical and biological terms but also in sociological, economic, political, technical, aesthetic, ethical and spiritual terms. There should be an emphasis on decision-making from a position of knowledge and understanding.

(Environmental Education Task Group)[2]

It is essential that assessment in environmental education reflects this view.

The assessment of skills

(The authors acknowledge that this section is an abstraction from the NAEE occasional paper 12 'Assessing Skills Progression in Environmental Studies Curricula' written by Keith Morrison 1989)[3]

It is necessary to recognise at the outset that the assessment of the acquisition of skills by young learners must be guided by their particular needs and not by any political expediency. If the individual development of skills is taken to be the basic criterion it will follow that standard assessments based on uniform curricula cannot be made ... Every teacher will need to see skill development through each child's eyes and to assess them in relation to the individual. If it is accepted that every pupil develops skills in their own individual and unique way it means that uniform plans of development are out of place ... the assessment of skill development has to be tailored to fit the individual.

This might lead us to believe that teacher intuition will be the fundamental guide. This is not so, for the conclusion to be reached is that there is a middle course between silence and too fine detail and it is possible to put forward general criteria which fit the pupil's personal profile. It is this notion of 'profiling' of skills which needs to replace the isolationist approach where skill development is separated into component parts and from them produce a catalogue of skills' assessment.

Assessment viewed in this way entails a careful diagnosis of the tasks being performed. Is the task
- *A practice task?*
- *A revision task?*
- *An incremental task (needing new knowledge to be learned)?*
- *An application task?*

If this approach is used, a better match of the task and the skills can be made for each pupil.

It is self-evident that progression in skill acquisition will be of importance when making an assessment. Both 'progression' and 'skills' are terms which are used loosely. It is important to respect the inherent ambiguities in each of them. Progression can be viewed merely in terms of the passing of time, a matter of sequence. Alternatively it can be perceived as requiring the understanding of increasingly difficult matter – that is a qualitative as well as a quantitative change.

Progression in the acquisition of skills will have to recognise that:

a) children will progress accumulating a quantity of skills;
b) progress may be brought about by the synthesis of several skills;
c) qualitative behaviour changes may be evidence of progression;
d) the application of higher order skills may be evidence of progression;
e) progression may be seen through the application of a skill in increasingly complex situations;
f) the achieved level of concepts and knowledge will condition the level of skill performance.

This being said about progression, what of skills? They are either of abstraction or of application – that is at a simple level they may refer to semi-automatic responses as a result of practice or to intellectual processes arising from memorised facts. On a higher plane, skills may result from complex thought processes. While some skills are developed through rote practice others require understanding. Some skills may be specific to particular areas of learning, other are cross-curricular. Observation and problem solving would be two examples of the latter. These skills are relevant to the integrated curriculum approach of the primary years. The danger of this approach is to equate observation in science with observation in art or problem solving in mathematics with problem solving in other subjects. The solution to this dilemma may lie in recognising a middle ground between curriculum-specific skills and those which cross the subject boundaries. It is to suggest that certain areas of learning will put greater emphasis on some skills than others.

From these general considerations emerge certain principles or criteria for skills assessment:

1 The assessment of skill progression must be within the context of a task and not free standing
2 Skills must be related to curriculum areas
3 Curriculum areas will emphasise clusters of skills
4 Skills must be assessed in combination
5 Assessments are best recorded in profiles
6 Skill development is best viewed through the child's eyes
7 Improvements in skills will need to relate to the strategies used to improve their development
8 The demand level of a skill may be matched to the demand level of a task
9 Progression will need to focus on processes and outcome
10 Classifying skills may seem useful but may be dangerous
11 Too fine a detail for skills may be dangerous
12 Skill development must be viewed qualitatively as well as quantitatively

13 Diagnostic assessment is desirable which is at variance with a standardised approach to skill assessment

14 A set of criteria is a better basis for skills assessment than a long list of skills.

The assessment of progression in skills development where environmental work is concerned, will by virtue of its wide range, prove to be extensive. Nevertheless it is possible to recognise six main areas of skills which relate to the environmental curriculum area but which are not its sole preserve.

They are

1 Communication skills
2 Problem solving skills
3 Investigation skills
4 Study skills
5 Practical skills
6 Personal and social skills

To construct a profile of skills several factors will need to be considered

A   A selection of higher order and lower order skills
B   The context, content and concept through which the skill is developed
C   The recognition that environmental work draws on a variety of teaching methods
D   Room for comment on the emphasis of the skill – whether the skill involves simple awareness or a more complex application
E   The notion of levels of skills (see figure 5.1 *Descriptors of levels of a child's skill performance*).

It is now possible to create a matrix which will highlight areas of environmental skills and allow comments on skill progression to be entered in the profile where appropriate. Such a matrix is shown in figure 5.2. This particular matrix may be too detailed for general use so that a profile sheet which retains the essential elements of skill areas and skill descriptors is given in figure 5.3.

These suggestions for profiles of skill assessment in relation to content and concepts seems to offer a more personalised form of assessment than that given by norm referenced testing or age related indicators of performance. The completion of such matrices by the teacher would be as a result of discussion, observation and assessment of the pupil and with the pupil. Such a system will be expensive of time and may be difficult to operate with very young children. It is both a practical possibility and a viable procedure with older junior pupils. It is not the sort of procedure which endears itself to standardised testers but it will encourage relevant and differentiated curricular in the primary school, particularly appropriate to an environmental education approach.

Skills	Level one	Level two	Level three
Quality of level of skill	Basic	Intermediate	Complex
Quantity of skills	Few	Moderate	Many
Order of skills Skill handling	Awareness Receiving (low order)	Understanding Interpreting Critically interpreting (medium order)	Production and creation (high order)
Speed	Hesitant	Slow but secure	Fast and secure
Precision	Inaccurate	Accurate across a limited range	Highly accurate
Appropriateness of selection	Occasionally appropriate or teacher selected	Usually appropriate, teacher and child input	Consistently appropriate, child-chosen
Range of application	Very limited	Moderate range	Wide range, and in complex combinations
Degree of child autonomy	Teacher directed	Independent choice and teacher selection	Autonomous, child-directed

Figure 5.1 *Descriptors of levels of a child's skill performance.*

Skill area	Quantity of skills	Order of skills	Speed	Precision	Appropriateness of selection	Range of application	Degree of autonomy
Communication	many intermediate few	applying interpreting receiving	immediate methodical hesitant	high limited inaccurate	independent assisted dependent	complex widening limited	total partial negligible
Problem-solving	many intermediate few	applying interpreting receiving	immediate methodical hesitant	high limited inaccurate	independent assisted dependent	complex widening limited	total partial negligible
Investigation	many intermediate few	applying interpreting receiving	immediate methodical hesitant	high limited inaccurate	independent assisted dependent	complex widening limited	total partial negligible
Study skills	many intermediate few	applying interpreting receiving	immediate methodical hesitant	high limited inaccurate	independent assisted dependent	complex widening limited	total partial negligible
Practical	many intermediate few	applying interpreting receiving	immediate methodical hesitant	high limited inaccurate	independent assisted dependent	complex widening limited	total partial negligible
Personal and social	many intermediate few	applying interpreting receiving	immediate methodical hesitant	high limited inaccurate	independent assisted dependent	complex widening limited	total partial negligible

Figure 5.2　*General profile sheet for skill assessment.*

Skill area	Skill performance (Enter level – 1, 2, 3)						
	Quantity of skills	Order of skills	Speed of skills	Precision	Appropriateness of selection	Range of application	Degree of autonomy

Communication eg
  literacy
  numeracy
  listening
  speaking
  graphicacy
  – maps
  – charts
  – graphs
  – diagrams							

Problem solving eg
  analysis
  synthesis
  designing
  making
  experimenting
  hypothesizing
  inferring
  evaluating
  inducing
  deducing							

Investigation eg
  raising
    questions
  classification
  identification
  using data-
    gathering
    tools
  evaluating							

Study skills eg
  data accessing
  data processing
  data presenting
  referencing
  evaluating
  analysis
  selection							

Practical eg
  use of
    equipment
  field-sketching
  observation
  collecting
  recognition							

Personal and social eg
  participation
  initiative
  cooperation
  responsibility
  self-control
  reliability
  leadership
  caring for
    environment							

Figure 5.3 *An environmental profile for skill assessment in topic work.*

The environmental study – a consideration of assessment processes

It follows that an important part of the preparation for any environmental project is a consideration of the assessment processes which will pertain to the study. This is well exemplified by the consideration for assessment which preceded Case Study 4 on page 66.

(We are indebted to Tim Gunn, Headteacher, Witton-le-Wear School, County Durham for this example of which he was project leader).

A good teacher has always assessed their pupils' progress closely to ensure accurate matching of tasks to ability and also to maintain progression and development and the National Curriculum confirms this approach. Science and environmental work has always been difficult to assess in the classroom due to the complex inter-relation of the concepts, knowledge, skills and attitudes which form their backbone. To identify accurately the attainment of a child in science, especially in practical activities, it is essential for the teacher to observe and sometimes participate in the experience with the child and also to allow time for discussion to determine the extent to which the work in question has been understood. It will also be necessary from time to time to use tests or special tasks as 'monitoring instruments'. In terms of the National Curriculum the Standard Assessment Tasks fit into this category.

The main function of assessment must be in diagnosing pupils' capabilities thus enabling the teacher to match closely work to the children's ability. However, any system of assessment must be 'user friendly' and not so cumbersome or time consuming that it deters teachers from making full and relevant use of it. Much valuable assessment can be carried out by the teacher while working with the children in a class, group or individual situation. However, it is of great importance that the teacher enters the discussion at the right point and also listens when appropriate. Asking the right sort of question is also vital, both in terms of developing the pupils' scientific knowledge and in assessing accurately the ability level of the children involved.

The following is an extract from the County of Avon *Primary Science Guidelines*:

> When children are experimenting, setting up hypotheses (be they of the simplest order), discovering scientific truths for themselves they frequently talk freely and easily, particularly if they are working in small groups ... The teacher may well join in the discussion, introduc-

ing correct technical terms for the children to use, and so to understand. At this time too, the teacher's skilled use of questions is important to draw children into clarifying their thoughts by putting them into words.

Questions from the teacher
Closed-ended questions have their use as tests of learnt material, but they do little or nothing to encourage thought or learning. Open-ended questions however are very different.

Closed-ended questions have only one acceptable answer.

1   Yes/no.
2   A simple fact.
3   Regurgitation of something already said.
4   Repetition of facts previously learned.

Open-ended questions do not have a pre-determined answer. They make the pupils think and come to their own conclusions. The answers to open-ended questions could include:

1   Description from observation or a personal interpretation.
2   Reflective response to an experience.
3   Interpretation.
4   Observations leading to a hypothesis.
5   Exploratory talk helping pupils to clarify their experiences.
6   Decision.

It is of great importance in environmental and other sciences to allow as many open-ended questions as possible, thus giving the chance for the child to develop an enquiring mind.

The sort of questions we should try to develop a habit of asking could include:
What do you think ...?
What would happen if ...?
Why do you think ...?
How could you tell if ...?
How could you test ...?
Is it a fair test if ...?
Why would you find ...?
What would you do if ...?

I have attempted to use the above approach during my programme of study with the children to assess the progress both of individuals and of the whole group at various intervals during the course of the work.

100

Skill Development

Assessment grade	Communication (spoken)	Communication (written)	Observation	Solution of problems	Co-operation with other pupils	Graphicacy	Perseverance	Research ability	Self-analysis
A	Able to state views clearly	Descriptions are always clearly stated. Good sentence construction, spelling etc	Has an abundant curiosity & is constantly noticing items of interest. Is accurate in detail	Tries & usually succeeds in mastering problems of appropriate difficulty	Gets on well with others & is always helpful	Can produce good graphic representations of statistical results. Has acceptable artistic skills	Always tries hard & persists to completion of any task	Can use most research material independently	Recognises the good & the bad in own work. Accepts criticism & tries to put such into practice
B	Views can be understood but the active help of the listener is required	With some help can produce a useful description of a task. English skills are acceptable	Notices the obvious but lacks discrimination & detail. Has a healthy curiosity	Tries but usually needs some help towards the correct solution	Has occasional lapses but usually works well with others	With guidance can produce useful graphic results	Tries hard for a while but needs encouragement at regular intervals	Able to use most research skills with some guidance	Knows that certain standards are required & is aware when these are not attained
C	Unable to state views clearly	Unable to produce a meaningful piece of descriptive writing. Poor use of English	Rarely notices anything without guidance. Lacks curiosity – easily distracted	Always needs help	Unhelpful & finds it difficult to co-operate	Unable to produce any graphic illustration without help	Gives up easily	Unable to follow any line of research however basic without help	Careless & unable to assess weaknesses or easily accept criticism

Figure 5.4a *Example of a graticule of assessment for skill development in topic work.*

Record keeping

Records are an essential component of any ongoing assessment/evaluation task. Documentation may comprise a wide range of written material including test results, pupil profile sheets, reports, notes or diaries of casual observations. When structured and comprehensive, records will be a valuable aid to illumination of pupils' progress and subsequent decision-making. In the framework of the national curriculum, record keeping will be essential in all areas of learning, not least the cross-curricular themes. The prepared documents will serve a variety of purposes, notably:

1 They will inform planning for the permeation of environmental education (or any other theme) across the statutory subjects.
2 They will record achievement of individual learners, and help with an understanding of development of the relevant knowledge, skills and attitudes.
3 They will aid the process of comparing one learner's progress with that of others.
4 They will illuminate the achievement of teachers.
5 They will help to ensure that the whole curriculum is being covered.
6 They will aid the implementation of learning experiences/schemes of work in environmental education that demonstrate adequate coherence and progression.
7 They will supply information – to accompany pupils on transfer from one teacher to another or from one stage or school to another.
8 They will help to diagnose pupil needs, strengths and weaknesses.
9 They will supply information for parents and other interested parties eg supporting welfare services.

There is a wealth of types of records that may be kept: class records, summary of content records, individual learner record sheets, pupils' own profiles, samples of children's work, the list and possible combinations of these is infinite.

The examples (figures 5.4 and 5.5) relate to skill development and were evolved within primary schools; they have been 'tried and tested' and are but two ideas from good practice that readers may find useful to consider.

A number of the more recent books on the assessment and evaluation of environmental and other topic work are cited in the Bibliography and will be found useful for further consultation in order to create schemes suitable for the individual circumstances of a school.

Skill development

School title:

Name:

Date of birth:

1 Communication –
  spoken
2 Communication –
  written
3 Observation
4 Solution of
  problems
5 Co-operation

6 Graphicacy
7 Perseverance
8 Research ability
9 Self-analysis

	1	2	3	4	5	6	7	8	9	Teacher
Year 1 date										
Topic 1										
Topic 2										
Year 2 date										
Topic 3										
Topic 4										
Year 3 date										
Topic 5										
Topic 6										
Year 4 date										
Topic 7										

Figure 5.4b *Record sheet to be used in association with assessment graticule.*

Name _____   Year _____

School _____   Age _____

Teacher _____   Date of Birth _____

Date of Record _____

Skill development and attitude (tick in relevant column)

Skill   low ability ⟶ competent

Communication – with peers						
– with teacher						
Observation						
Classification						
Measurement						
Recording						
Interpretation of data						
Application of data						
Research – spoken word						
– written word						
Comprehension – spoken word						
– written word						
Investigation						
Prediction						

Attitude

Co-operation						
Critical ability						
Curiosity						
Perseverance						

Topics undertaken   Date   Teacher

	Date	Teacher
1		
2		
3		
4		

Figure 5.5 *Example of a record of skill and attitude development in environmental topic work.*

6 Co-ordination, communication and co-operation

The corollary to matters cross-curricular is that someone in every school must be in a position to co-ordinate what takes place in the school as a whole, in the individual classes and in subject areas. Nothing which transcends the boundaries of the core and foundation subjects of the National Curriculum, could emphasise this dictum more than environmental education. It is also of vital importance that the co-ordination is backed up with an organised formal system of communication between the teachers involved and that an informal and happy working atmosphere is established which leads to the genuine and willing co-operation of people pursuing a common goal.

The inevitable conclusion of this is that each school shall have a co-ordinator for environmental education, someone rather more than a teacher with 'responsibility for Environmental Studies'. The UK's response to the World Conservation Strategy[1] proposed that:

> Each school should designate responsibility to a member of staff for planning, co-ordination and oversight of environmental education perhaps as part of an overall responsibility for introducing related topics such as 'Third World Issues', 'world peace' and 'population' across the curriculum. Without adequate co-ordination, there is a danger that certain topics and issues covered by more than one teacher will not be complementary.
>
> (Recommendation 2)

Ideally the co-ordinator needs to be someone of seniority by virtue of experience and salary recognition. Inevitably the nature of the school must be a prime consideration in that the size of many schools in the 5–11 age range dictates that the headteacher will need to perform the role of Environmental Education co-ordinator. Where the school is larger it is desirable that someone else is the chosen co-ordinator. Commitment and enthusiasm are almost certainly more important than rank. The need to stimulate, coerce, persuade, facilitate, innovate, synthesise and analyse will mean that above all the co-ordinator must be tactful, understanding and particularly appreciate that the fount of wisdom does not spring from just one source – her/himself. It is vital, as with any other special allocation of responsibility in a school, that the member of staff designated to be the co-ordinator for environmental education, shall have a precisely specified description of what the headteacher expects her/him to do in the task of overall planning and fostering co-ordination and co-operation between staff.

Yet every school situation will be different. Indeed, the same school will be different at various times, reflecting the changes in staff and staffing levels, the number and abilities of the pupils, the views of parents and governors, the nature of the LEA and its officers, the local political structure and Government ideology. The way by which curriculum development is carried out will reflect the way the school is run from the top. If the headteacher believes in an 'open' and participatory organisation the task of the designated co-ordinator will be different from that of one who has to operate under an autocratic regime. Both organisational methods can work to produce a dynamic school, mirroring the personality and philosophy of the headteacher. However the open style is probably more conducive to cross-curricular planning and co-ordination.

Evidence from HM inspectors is that where objectives have been defined closely and where co-operation and co-ordination across subject boundaries has been conscientiously and consciously carried out the standards achieved in environmental education can be very high indeed. This can also be seen by parent, governor, LEA official, councillor or any other visitor passing through the school, for the coherence and the inter-relationship of work on display in corridor and classroom will indicate co-operation and controlled activity in aspects of the curriculum both environmental and non-environmental.

The task of the co-ordinator

The task of the co-ordinator must be to facilitate the implementation of the school's policy for environmental education. In order to do this the school must have such a policy; one may need to be established before any overview can take place. This can be a daunting task if the headteacher is not convinced of its necessity and if the rest of the staff are anticipating extra work on top of the full load carried already. If a senior teacher is fulfilling the role of environmental education co-ordinator then the task of establishing such a policy is considerably eased. This book (Chapter 3) and various other documents, notably the DES *Environmental Education 5–16*[2] and documentation emerging from the National Curriculum Council, will aid this task and give general guidance, but two points need to be made:

1 Every school is unique, the environmental education policy must be constructed to deal with the particular circumstance.
2 There is considerable merit to be gained from establishing the policy through staff consultation and discussion. Personal involvement in the planning aids future co-operation and communication between those who will be using the environmental approach.

It may well be that the headteacher both wishes, and is the best person, to guide the policy-making group and that the future co-ordinator will act as planning group rapporteur or will emerge as the natural co-ordinator as a result of the working party activity.

How to co-ordinate
The co-ordinator must recognise that there are several stages in establishing thriving environmental education in a school. The first involves the setting up of a policy for environmental education. The second is the implementation of that policy and the third is the continuation of that policy after the initial enthusiasm has waned, various alterations and adaptations to the National Curriculum have taken place and staff changes have occurred. Finally there is the continual assessment of success and the need to stimulate fresh ideas and reinforce resource availability. Much of the suggested guidance is applicable at one or more of these stages, some of them are on-going throughout. For example, one continuing task is to stand back from the day-to-day scene of activity, to look and to listen. To become so embroiled in the detail is often to miss appreciating fundamental and major factors affecting progress. It is as important to observe and reflect on the 'culture' of the school during the time when everything seems to be established and proceeding well, as it is to give considerable thought to it before an environmental education policy is even contemplated. A living school has a habit of altering its tone because of staff changes, political pressures, external interruptions (break-in, fire, rebuilding, extension, alteration) and variations in pupil numbers.

Three other dictums should be borne in mind:

1 Perceived success will show other staff the advantage of environmental work better than hundreds of pages of documentation.
2 There is nothing more suffocating to enthusiasm than excess paper work.
3 A deliberate slow process of concentration on one part of inno-

vation at a time is more likely to achieve the required goal than a broad rush along several fronts.

Throughout, the co-ordinator should aim to produce a minimum of paper work. There will need to be a brief initial discussion document; like the parliamentary green papers it has to be a clear statement of intent; it:

- will contain the philosophy of the proposed innovation and not the content, skills or methods to be employed in the classroom;
- should be a clearly-stated stimulator and not something where various interpretations may lead to destructive forces gathering against it;
- must encourage the idea that the project is a team effort and that it is not a case of throwing overboard existing practice but rather a way of building on current work by extending it, with little extra workload, to develop a greater environmental emphasis;
- must be a document which avoids the notion that what has gone before is of no consequence and that which is to come is the revelation of the only truth;
- will point out that small changes in current practice will result in the desired result in a painless way – it is a case of transferring teaching skills rather than the implementation of new ones.
- must be clearly relevant to the implementation of the National Curriculum.

As well as drafting a discussion document it may be useful to involve individual teachers by requesting their co-operation in completing a matrix which shows just what each individual is contributing environmentally in their own classroom. Such a survey not only shows what is happening, it also shows the gaps that need to be filled (see figures 6.1a and 6.1b).

Timing
Content is one thing, timing of what happens is another. Again, re-timing of current practice may give greater relevance to environmental understanding. This last point re-emphasises the fact that many minor changes may well have a more lasting effect than an attempt at one major curriculum change. The size and complexity of the school will determine how full such a survey shall be. It needs to be right so that time is not wasted in unnecessary detail nor is it necessary to go back afterwards for further information. In fact one of the first co-operative tasks is to compile the matrix and/or questionnaire. Perhaps the most simple is a grid construction with topics listed.

TOPIC/THEME:

AGE:

TEACHER:

Learning Areas	Environmental		Natural			Created			Locations				Resources					LEA Input		Other
	Matters	Issues	Plants	Insects	Animals	Buildings	Commu-nication	People	In school	School estate	Locality	Distant	Books	Visual	Audio	Charts Maps	Museums Centres	Libraries	Advisory	Organis-ations
Speaking & Listening																				
Reading																				
Writing																				
Mathematics																				
Science																				
Art																				
Design & Technology																				
Music																				
PE																				
Geography																				
History																				
RE																				

(English grouping spans Speaking & Listening, Reading, Writing)

Figure 6.1a *An investigatory matrix for assessing the contribution of environmental education to present teaching prior to policy making – the answer to 'What are we doing now?'*

TOPIC/THEME   AGE: TEACHER:

Learning Areas	Environmental Matters		Natural			Created			Locations				Resources				LEA Input			Other
	Matters	Issues	Plants	Insects	Animals	Buildings	Communication	People	In school	School estate	Locality	Distant	Books	Visual	Audio	Charts Maps	Museums Centres	Libraries	Advisory	Organisations
Speaking & Listening		Discussion on deforestation						Role play lumberjack						WWF video Rainforest						Visit from forester
Reading								Robin Hood					Tree recognition Forests					Books on Trees		
Writing	The importance of trees								Wooden objects											
Mathematics			Trees per hectare								Tree census in park									
Science			Photo-synthesis The tree	Dutch Elm disease	Monkeys & Apes					Study of Oak tree		Visit to tree nursery				What is a tree?				
Art			Bark rubbing																	
Design & Technology			Growing trees from seed			Log hut models	Paper making												Tree planting	
Music		Musical Yanamamo WWF													Songs about trees					
PE																				
Geography			Amazon rain forest				Logging & St Lawrence	Amazon Indians								Forest locations				
History							Wooden sailing ships										Wooden artefacts			
RE			Cedars of Lebanon		Noah's Ark															

Figure 6.1b *An investigatory matrix, this time using the topic 'trees'. Note that this indicates environmental work carried out before a policy on environmental education was adopted. It is not a matrix to show what could be included in a topic on trees.*

When staff are drawn together to talk about the discussion document and the matrix procedure the very important matter of clarifying the aims and objectives of environmental education in the specific school will emerge. Nothing will hinder the work of the co-ordinator more than the fact that even one of the teachers is not fully aware of such targets. Teachers who have missed a meeting will need to be briefed on their return, so as to avoid needless repetition later. It should be possible to ensure coherent environmental education without detracting from the specific objectives of individual teachers or the core and foundation subjects, and without creating too much pressure on individuals. It is important, however, that each person has the opportunity to discuss and investigate various approaches, methods of teaching and subject content, as become applicable to an environmental policy.

Co-ordination – the individual

It is essential that the co-ordinator is a person who sees her/his role as a teacher in broad terms. It is unlikely that the blinkered specialist will be able to break out from the constraints of the subject approach. Although this is less of a problem in the primary phase nevertheless it does occur. As an individual the co-ordinator must be

- able to relate to people;
- sympathetic to their ideas and ideology;
- a good listener;
- the sort of person who will lead by example.

It is hoped that the co-ordinator will be a person with a high environmental consciousness and her/his general classroom management will reflect this in various ways – for example, an economical approach to the use of paper and the provision of a collecting box for used paper for recycling. All cross-curricular matters ought to be of interest to the co-ordinator and he or she will be willing to attend courses, represent the school on outside committees and play a major part in out-of-school activities of all varieties. It has already been emphasised that the person for the job is one who can successfully lead a major school project. Whatever stances are adopted they must be tailored to the individual school situation, but most certainly the ideologies of other members of staff must not be denigrated. The co-ordinator who desires co-operation must be co-operative in the first place.

The co-ordinator will need to compromise, adapt and co-operate to avoid difficulties which may arise. With a well-motivated staff the path towards successfully achieving the ultimate aims and objectives for environmental education should be smooth. Inevitably, setbacks will occur to the fulfilment of such aims. If individual targets are set they can be viewed as tactics within the main strategy of the complete integration of an environmental approach across the curriculum. Good generals know that it is overall success which matters, even if minor setbacks occur along the way.

Co-ordination – the tasks

It is obvious that curriculum guidelines will need to be produced eventually – but this is not an immediate task of the co-ordinator (at least, not to produce them for public consumption). The real task is to create the right atmosphere for change. It is, for instance, necessary to recognise potential areas of resistance and either to break this in a pleasant way or to work with it as a recognised constraint. Enthusiasm is the keynote to success, but this must not lead to lack of tact towards colleagues or a failure to consider their other activities.

Assuming that the environmental education policy has been established, the co-ordinator will need to give attention to many tasks. These may be divided into several groups:

Teacher appreciation
Pupil involvement
Pressures on the school curriculum
Methods/approaches/assessment
Environmental issues
Beyond the school
Resources
In-service training
Record keeping

Teacher appreciation

Appreciation is a two-way process – from the co-ordinator to the teacher and from the teacher to the co-ordinator. Within this dictum are encapsulated both the hazards and the easy paths to the successful implementation of an environmental education policy. Unless the ideology and philosophy of the environmental approach have been completely explored, clearly stated and thoroughly disseminated, teachers may be confused. An incomplete appreciation of the aims and objectives may lead to frustration with only a partial or inappropriate response. In order to appreciate a 'new' non-traditional curriculum demand, motivation must be kept high.

Genuine innovation does not happen unless a personal commitment to ensuring success is built into each individual. Experience has shown, almost invariably, that staff members will take on extra tasks if they are seen to be realistic and valuable. Rejection will come only if the demand for change is too fast and too unrealistic. Some cynics may claim that the aims and advantages of a fresh approach have less influence on the individual than the ultimate effect on their workload and work routine. It is up to the co-ordinator to ensure that teacher co-operation does not break down into these adversarial components and that no established role in the school situation is a bar to progress. It is vital for the co-ordinator to recognise the overt and the covert structure of the school, and the state of development and attitude of the personnel.

It is necessary to work alongside the individual teacher in the class situation, to recognise the particular expertise that s/he possesses and to exploit it to the best advantage. It is difficult not to overburden the willing horse. It is essential that the co-ordinator is aware of the total school commitment of the teacher and takes care not to make extra demands such that other important areas of the school organisation suffer.

In view of these comments the tasks to be highlighted are to:

- ensure that all teachers appreciate the basic environmental entitlement of every child, of whatever age or ability;
- be quite clear that the aims and objectives for environmental education in the school are understood by all staff;
- evaluate the special talents and interests of each teacher and build on them;
- create a programme of active participation and involvement of all staff in the policy;
- advise teachers on differing methods of environmental approaches and assessment and establish which is best for their particular current needs;
- sound the staff waters to discover the 'shallows and the rapids' which may restrict a full and willing participation and work to remove or reduce these restrictions.
- co-operate with other staff initiatives, even if they are of little personal interest – 'quid pro quo'!

Summary

1 Teacher willingness to participate is paramount.
2 Real and permanent change is only possible with the teacher in the classroom.
3 Planning will depend on the expertise and experience of the staff here and now – this changes, and the policy must not become a 'tablet of stone'.

Pupil involvement

The natural curiosity and interest of primary school children has been emphasised and it is this which makes an environmental approach both relevant and exciting to the young learners. They may be apathetic, bored or even hostile to some of the basic elements of learning. Using the environment as a stimulus may provide an acceptable alternative. It is very important not to underestimate the potential of even the very young to tackle complex environmental issues, providing they are presented to them as an understandable package. Many activities, both in and out of school time, can be undertaken by primary school children at a level which rivals research at a 'higher' level. One has only to recall the Acid Drops Project of the Field Studies Council and WATCH to recognise the truth of this statement. One great advantage of a school is that it has many potential researchers on its roll. The astute co-ordinator will exploit this to advantage, particularly in building up an environmental resource library.

Tasks to be recognised are to:

* examine the scheme of environmental work to ensure that there is no direct relationship between the age of the pupil and the triviality of the pursuit;
* create a programme of active involvement and participation of children in environmental activities, particularly conservation activities;
* establish a newspaper/magazine reading panel leading to a collection of clippings on environmental issues (local, national and global) and a filing system using pupil participation.

Pressures on the school curriculum

In the context of delivering the National Curriculum it may be considered that there is already enough pressure on the school day and the activities within an individual classroom. It is the co-ordinator's prime task to ensure that environmental education does not lead to excessive extra pressure. It certainly has to dovetail with the fabric of other activities within the school. This involves content, resources and time. The skill of the co-ordinator will be severely tested where the overall curriculum of the school is involved.

Tasks that emerge are to:

* ensure that whatever schemes are developed do not increase pressure on the curriculum excessively;
* determine the restrictions placed upon environmental activity by

the timetable and the allocation of space and resources (eg part-time staff, swimming and games commitments, assemblies, school meals, other use of the hall, INSET programme, holidays and special events);

- examine the established school curricula and recognise programmes of study in the core and foundation subjects and other cross-curricular themes;
- be aware of common skills across learning areas and co-ordinate strategies for dealing with them;
- relate, where possible, each piece of individual subject work to the environmental education curriculum as a whole;
- ensure that individual projects of the curriculum which draw on periodic issues/statistics are placed in the context of on-going research (eg school weather station) and that full records are kept for future use;
- recognise that there are other cross-curricular areas which need to be planned into the school menu and which demand support. Exclusivity for environmental education must be rejected.

Methods/approaches/assessment

One of the main tasks of the co-ordinator, after the environmental policy for the school has been agreed, will be to indicate to staff the ways by which environmental education can be approached, the methods for teaching and learning which can be employed and the way in which assessment of progress can be made. Much of this may be linked in with a thematic or topic approach which, though in common use, may need to be better structured to achieve the objectives set out in the policy statement. Certainly time will need to be given to guidance on out-of-classroom work both in the school estate and away from it. Close attention will need to be given to national reports such as those of the National Curriculum working parties and TGAT. The first task suggested below may well be the most crucial of all the steps taken by the co-ordinator, for much of what has been 'preached' will be revealed to the public gaze.

Tasks to be identified are to:

- prepare to lead the first 'across the school' environmental project;
- define the patterns of content to be studied and environments to be investigated at different stages and different times in the young learner's progress through the school;
- formulate a policy for drawing on the experience of all out-of-school activity and not only that pursued for direct environmental purposes eg day trip to a zoo, outing to France, visit to a local factory;

- ensure that teachers realise that work outside school needs as much consideration of aims and objectives as classroom work and that it must be part of a planned experience;
- set up a system whereby teachers not involved in an out-of-school activity are aware of what is planned so that they may request some special attention to be given to the opportunity to further their 'specialist' area;
- be aware of award schemes, competitions, exhibitions, and other opportunities with an environmental content in which pupils or classes may participate;
- plan contributions to the themes and content of school assemblies;
- help staff to formulate and carry out assessment procedures;
- devise evaluation methods using the experiences and ideas of other staff, especially those responsible for other curriculum areas.

Evaluation should be of environmental awareness as well as of factual knowledge and skill development.

Environmental issues
Much of the work of environmental education will be associated with the many environmental issues which beset the world at present. These range from the well-publicised, such as starvation in parts of Africa, to the lesser-known profile of the exploitation of remote parts of the planet, such as Antarctica. A balance must be kept and up-to-date information made available for teaching purposes. It is important to relate the worldwide issues to the problems of the neighbourhood so as to satisfy the environmental dictum 'think globally, act locally'. This will imply some form of enquiry-based learning. After an issue has been recognised, either directly introduced by the teacher or arising from the particular interest of the children, it will be necessary to assess the initial awareness of the individual and the class. This will involve questioning the values they place on the issue at the outset and what are the range of views held, both by the young learners and by society in general. A list of pertinent questions needs to be followed for each 'issue':

- Who and what is involved?
- What are the reasons for these views? The reasons given (the cognitive level)? The beliefs held (the affective level)?
- What are the implications of these views?
- Are these views (or values) supported by evidence?
- Which are the most powerful views?
- With which value does the pupil identify?
- What is the pupil's prediction of how the issue might be resolved?

- What will be the consequences of this resolution?
- Will it create another problem?
  Finally:
- How might each pupil try to sort out the issue?
- How would the majority of the class resolve the issue?
- Would the class or an individual like to find out more or become involved in some way (eg join a local action group)?

In order to achieve a result the co-ordinator will need to recognise certain tasks. He or she needs to:

- recognise current environmental issues and, with staff consultation, prioritise their relative importance within the school's programme of environmental work;
- establish the relevance of such issues to the school neighbourhood;
- recognise that certain aspects of environmental awareness have particular relevance to the individual school eg traffic noise and exhaust pollution, litter from the local supermarket, lack of play facilities;
- deliberately integrate the cognitive and the affective domains within studies of issues and problems.

Beyond the school

The Local Education Authority, people and agencies in the neighbourhood and national organisations are all available for professional exploitation in the cause of furthering the environmental policy. Someone in the local advisory service will have responsibility for environmental work, regrettably, these days, added to other responsibilities. Within the school neighbourhood it may well be that interesting individuals are the best resource for environmental work: further afield many organisations promote environmental opportunities – these are listed later. These considerations lead to further tasks for the co-ordinator. He or she needs to:

- contact the LEA adviser with responsibility for environmental education;
- investigate the provision for environmental work in local teacher and environmental study centres;
- involve parents, councillors, governors, industrialists, local experts and all of those who contribute to the 'environmental' side of community life. Establish local contacts;
- establish links with local environmental groups and, preferably, become involved;

- establish links with national organisations. If possible become a school member eg with RSPB, CEE, NAEE, AA;
- encourage out-of-school individual study and research, for example by establishing a WATCH group;
- make links with local secondary schools. In particular discuss out-of-school vists and agree a list of primary school venues and secondary school venues so that over-use does not occur;
- co-operate with local teacher-training establishments;
- remember to warn local people if the school embarks on a project which may include surveys or disturbance.

Resources
Resource material for environmental education abounds with the 'environment' itself, the greatest resource of all. For the co-ordinator it will be necessary to assess the potential of the locality with environmental learning in mind. The other task is to bring together the mass of material available, much of it free, from outside organisations. The main tasks are to:

- keep up-to-date with and publicise television and radio programmes. Arrange to make video recordings (within the restrictions of copyright);
- arrange to display the regular in-coming items produced by such bodies as the RSPB, CEE, NAEE, WWF etc. Some items, for instance the newsletters of the CEE, the journal of the NAEE and the Civic Trusts newsheet, need to be properly displayed in staff common rooms;
- begin a picture and wallchart library, investing in storage and display units;
- build up a special 'open-ended' resource section of videos, pictures etc which enable pupils to establish their own individual attitudes and evaluations;
- establish good relationships with the local library and teachers' centre for resource loans;
- investigate the usefulness of simulation exercises and games in environmental matters, especially those which stimulate value judgements and the heightening of attitude awareness. Tape recording in sound or video of news events, such as a major oil spillage, can be useful source material to stimulate classroom discussion.

In-service training
Numerous surveys have shown that few teachers involved with environmental education have had any formal training for this curriculum area. In particular they lack confidence to make the best use

of out-of-the-classroom studies. It is essential that the co-ordinator attempts to rectify these omissions.

Again the education section of the UK's response to the World Conservation Strategy[1] recognised this problem. Its fourth recommendation says:

a)   All institutions should have a written policy for environmental education. Training courses at colleges and departments of education should provide an opportunity for students to become familiar with the nature, aims and objectives, and methods of environmental education. A common course for all students may be the most appropriate way of achieving this.

b)   Opportunities for in-service training by LEAs should be increased. While financial restrictions may limit the number of teachers given time off to attend long courses, short courses can be arranged at little cost or inconvenience to the authorities.

The important tasks are to:

- ensure that all courses, seminars and the like involving environmental matters are brought to the attention of the staff.
- plan school-based training in environmental work for the statutory INSET days;
- convince the local adviser and the local teachers' centre of the necessity to organise environmental courses;
- ensure that staff who do attend such courses and seminars report back for the benefit of others;
- investigate the possibility of the nearest higher education establishment running an appropriate diploma or degree course involving environmental education.

Record keeping
Pupil records of environmental understanding and school records of work accomplished need to be kept for assessment and reference purposes. As with any other area of learning, progress is necessary and needs to be recorded in a standardised way. It is essential, too, that project and other work in environmental education is detailed so that similar events in the future can benefit from past experience. The co-ordinator needs to:

- set up a system of recording pupil progress in environmental matters, probably through a pupil profile system;
- establish a reference system which records thematic and other work in the environment. In particular note the useful contacts made, the times when they were used (in order to prevent over-

exploitation of one person or corporate body) and any fruitless avenues explored. The successes and the failures need to be recorded with ideas for the improvement of the project or possible extensions next time.

The system adopted does not need to be sophisticated. One school has made use of a simple storage system of box files, clearly catalogued (figure 6.2). The success of this is due entirely to the fact that every member of staff conscientiously puts their completed project into 'store' when it is completed. This involves selecting the most appropriate examples of pupil work, colour transparencies and other photographic material, audio and video tapes, base maps and plans, worksheets, questionnaires, instructions and many other documents. Where outside bodies have been involved contact names and addresses, help received and an assessment of their usefulness is recorded. The outline details of the project are entered on the school computer system. Oversize items are stored in a map chest. It is the responsibility of the individual to initiate new boxes as and when required, and it is the responsibility of the environmental co-ordinator to check the system regularly and to make cross-references as appropriate. The justification for the extra work involved is the knowledge

Figure 6.2 *An efficient, accessible and simple storage system for records of work done on environmental themes.*

that time and effort will be saved in the future with the experience of others helping to cut down on personal endeavour. Nevertheless, talking to the project leader is invaluable.

Communication

The co-ordinator must consider communication within the school and communication with outside individuals and institutions. In all cases communication is a two-way process.

Communication within the school
Consideration of a good system of communication within a school does not apply solely to environmental education. It may well be that an efficient system is already established and environmental work is but to be added to it. Nevertheless the successful co-ordinator must give her/his own personal attention to it. If environmental education is not understood because of a breakdown in communication, a policy might just as well remain on the shelf. It is true that much sound communication may take place through the chance (or apparent 'chance') meeting in the staffroom between individuals or small groups. Reliance on this is not good enough and a structured system is needed other than the formal staff meeting. Ideally a structure needs to be established so that exchanges of information and ideas are easy and part of the ongoing school day. It is not necessary to detail here the many ways by which groups of teachers may be enabled to meet together within the timetabled schedule. It is even possible, with a large enough school, to arrange special working lunches apart from the interruptions of the school meal. Staff attitudes to their use of time when they are not in front of a class vary considerably. Without doubt the task of the co-ordinator is easiest in a school where professional considerations outweigh personal ones. Enough emphasis cannot be placed on the two-way process. The co-ordinator must encourage teachers to report back their successes and failures as well as passing on to them the necessary information concerning environmental work.

Content is one thing that will bear heavily on the co-ordinator but perhaps of greater importance to the success of environmental education is teaching style and method. Staff discussions about these are essential at regular intervals. The trap of holding a meeting because it is scheduled but without the agenda to occupy the time must be avoided. There must be a system which enables the co-ordinator to bring to the attention of the staff opportunities for environmental work which arise by chance. A reminder that over-enthusiasm can be smothering is perhaps appropriate at this point.

Communication outside the school
It follows from some of the previous suggestions for tasks that involve institutions outside the school that regular communication will be necessary. This is taken for granted. What is perhaps less obvious is the need to communicate in order to exchange ideas, exploit common resources to the full and bring some sort of planned order to the use of local sites. This will need to be done with both primary and secondary schools within the same LEA.

In one education authority an ideal situation occurs. Each primary school has a designated co-ordinator for environmental education. Once a term, and more often for special occasions such as World Environment Day, the co-ordinators meet under the auspices of the local adviser. One task is for them to allocate particular neighbour-hoods to particular schools. For example, supermarkets in the area may well be 'allocated' so that the same complex does not have several school parties carrying out surveys within days of each other. The problem of over-exploitation leads to bad public relations. This is not only a problem involving fellow primaries but extends to the secondary sector as well. Three different school groups, at the same railway station at the same time, each accosting hurrying passengers concerning their travel habits, leads to unnecessary discord. It is also extremely irritating for secondary colleagues to find that all local or near-distant sites have been exploited, often in a superficial way, which has taken away from that place the excitement of a new experience. It is a simple task to draw up a list of possible outdoor 'field work' sites and to agree mutually their use amongst all the primary schools feeding into local secondary schools. The very act of co-operation may lead on to exciting project work.

Communication (and co-operation) with the local secondary school can be carried much further. Many liaison schemes designed to facilitate ease of transfer from primary to secondary involve some exchange teaching. One splendid idea which not only helps to over-come the trauma of transfer but furthers environmental work, is to follow a co-operative two year or two term project. This can be started in the final year or final term in the primary school and be completed in the first year or first term in the secondary school. The planned project will need to consist of well-defined and mainly self-contained parts so that primary pupils who do not transfer locally are not left with a part completion and those of the new secondary intake from other areas are not lacking in the project foundation. It is the overall theme which is important and will provide environmental continuity to the benefit of all concerned. The many other benefits of real co-operation and curriculum planning between primary and secondary must be obvious to all.

It is worthwhile, too, to set up a communication link with the nearest teacher training establishment; co-operation with environmental work can be to the mutual benefit of school and college. The college or university may welcome the opportunity to involve students in training in school projects. Such involvement will lead to additional supervisors and additional technical aids. The school can provide the invaluable student/pupil contact which is an essential feature of initial training courses. One aspect of communication which is underplayed is the passing on of examples of good practice by presenting articles for publication in local newsletters to schools, where they exist, and to national journals whose editors are always seeking such items. It is to be hoped that the individual school co-ordinator will not have to take the initiative in all of these matters. Encouraging communication between schools is properly the job of the local advisory service and links between primary and secondary ought to be part of the normal liaison procedures. So much depends on individual headteachers and their co-operation one with the other.

What follows is an example of a cross-curricular study which was based on a local historic house. It had the added interest of acting as the preliminary work in creating an environmental resource for other schools. It exemplifies the communication, co-ordination and co-operation which can be achieved between schools, with the LEA, its adviser and ancillary services, and with a national organisation. The project involved two urban schools, one primary and one junior. The lengthy process of preparing resource material for use by other schools was started in the knowledge that they, in turn, will be able to pass on what is learned to help others and to protect the environmental heritage.

In the United Kingdom we have an enormously rich heritage of country estates, castles, ancient monuments, large houses, parks and other features. These contain a wealth of material for environmental education. There are several questions to be asked before using any examples of our national heritage for educational purposes:

- Why am I considering taking a school party to this particular place?
- What resources are available at, and what folklore is connected with, the site?
- How can these resources be brought into the normal school

curriculum and work routine?
- What are the educational possibilities?
- What facilities are provided, and what arrangements are made by site owners for school parties?
- What is the view of the LEA and their rules on the conduct of parties out of school?
- What are the various types of activities that can be carried out at the site?
- Are there other interested staff members who may find the results of the visit useful?

Any school excursion should be a rewarding experience for the child – none more so than a visit to a historic site. It ought to be a creative adventure, contributing not only to a particular aspect of the child's educational progress, but generally to his/her personal development. The historic house can make a great contribution to aesthetic appreciation and to a greater understanding of and empathy with the past. Objective study may accompany subjective feeling for the place itself and those that have traversed its history. Each individual has a responsibility for our national heritage and each visit should contribute to the growing child's envolving role as a member of society.

It is unfortunate, therefore, that a visit by schools to the type of site included in our national heritage is often associated with the 'summer outing'. Without doubt the time, effort and indeed money spent in organising such visits ought to be better used when set within the context of planned educational/environmental study – as we see documented on the following pages.

Case Study 5
A role play and historical re-enactment project based on a National Trust property

King Charles School, Walsall and Hathersage Junior School, Walsall

Introduction
The project was designed to assist pupils (age range 7–10) to place events in sequence, use evidence, make emphatic judgements and use historical concepts and ideas. It also aims to further the English skills of participants, enabling them: to locate information, observe, listen and record, translate information, analyse and synthesise, recall information and communicate what was found.

Starting point

Use of a local historic house for a Living History re-enactment. Mosely Old Hall (figure 6.3) is famous for its part in the escape of King Charles II after the Battle of Worcester. It now belongs to the National Trust. The staff on site make 'Living History' sessions available to school groups from Walsall and other local authorities. They also assist those who wish to create a role play situation based on historical times and not the particular event of Charles' escape. Figure 7.3 shows a typical programme.

Figure 6.3   *Moseley Old Hall, Wolverhampton.*

General aims

1 To give purpose to learning.
2 To involve children in understanding the implications of actions, level thinking, decision taking, and effective communication; to pose problems which emphasise common concerns by comparing and contrasting concepts, values and beliefs.
3 To provide a way for teachers not only to focus learning on a task, but also to motivate children to do that task, form connections, solve problems and empathise.
4 To enable teachers to plan a logical progression in children's learning.

Preliminary considerations and the project outline

History is a part of environmental education; it is about people and how they lived. Children live in a world of instant communication, electricity, cars and a thousand other things that the people who lived in Moseley Old Hall soon after it was built could never have imagined. Similarly, it is almost as difficult for those alive today to

Figure 6.4 *Moseley 'time machine' – an interesting attempt to link the children through time with the Civil War period. Circle A contains photographs of the children in the present – at home, at school, at the shops. Circle B shows them in costume at Moseley. The interlock, C, pictures children preparing costumes etc.*

imagine the lives of the Whitgreave family and their household in the years during and after the Civil War (see figure 6.4). When the children visited the house they spent a day 'living' in the remote world of the 17th century, which helped them to imagine what life was like then. Two patterns of use of the Hall were attempted:

1   The King's Flight
2   Restoration Day

There was a very high level of input from the Trust's staff and volunteers, teachers from both schools and Walsall Metropolitan Borough Education Department, especially the Music Service.

Details of the Living History Days
King's Flight
The King's Flight was re-enacted by three classes of lower junior children from the Primary School. The children were of mixed ability

Figure 6.5 *'Foot soldiers' with 'pikes' follow their captain (the headmaster) into Moseley Old Hall.*

and in classes from 34 to 36. As well as the large class size they had the disadvantage of only operating as classes during the afternoon, which restricted the time available to class teachers for preparatory and follow-up work. The children were divided into three groups, the King's party, Parliamentary soldiers and Servants. The King's party explored their part of the story, toured the house and then worked out their part in the subsequent dramatisation. The Parliamentary soldiers had a small part in the story but toured the house, sketched etc. After the first day pike drill (figure 6.5) was added to give them a fuller day – not least in terms of experience. Servants cooked appropriate food and drink, toured the house, learnt dances – they were busy! All of the children then met together in the barn where the story was told to them by 'Samuel Pepys'.

Restoration Day
Restoration Day was re-enacted by the Junior School. Four classes took part, two third year, two fourth year. They were of mixed ability and ranged from 21 to 27 in number. They were welcomed to the Hall with the news that they had arrived on Restoration Day. As a result they had to prepare entertainment, make food for the feast and look around the Hall. The children were divided into three groups. Group 1 performed a masque, toured the Hall and prepared a fruit

punch. Group 2 toured the Hall, cooked 'jumbles' and prepared a dance. Group 3 cooked gingerbread and marzipan, sang and played percussion and toured the house. The final session brought together all the groups and they then 'celebrated' the Restoration. On the last three occasions two 'minstrels' from the Music Service were present all day and played an integral part in these activities. During the final session they were joined by three others.

Programme outline
The programme outline for teachers participating in the project was detailed as follows both for the King's Flight and for Restoration Day.

The King's Flight

The day at Moseley will centre around the story of the King's escape as told by 'Samuel Pepys'. The account will need to be written in the style of Pepys but specifically for the purpose. The children will need to be told a part of the story written from the angle of the group concerned at first and at the end of the day they can act out the story as Pepys told it.

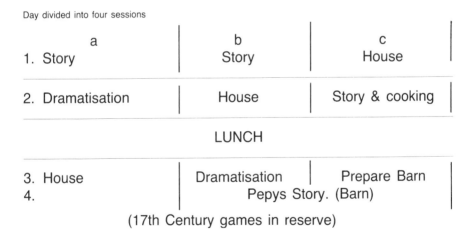

Day divided into four sessions

a	b	c
1. Story	Story	House
2. Dramatisation	House	Story & cooking
LUNCH		
3. House	Dramatisation	Prepare Barn
4.	Pepys Story. (Barn)	

(17th Century games in reserve)

a. Parliamentarian Sympathisers
Classes will before visiting the Hall be told about the story of Charles' escape, and this group will know about the New Model Army and the views of the Parliamentary cause.

On arrival they will change into suitable clothing, and then be told that after the victory at the Battle of Worcester they are to help to hunt out the Traitor Charles Stuart.

They will interview Humphrey Penderel about White Ladies at the local Military Headquarters.

On the afternoon of Monday the 8th of September they arrive at Moseley and interview Thomas Whitgreave outside the open front door. Later they interview the blacksmith.

If there is time then the children may sketch, draw a plan of the garden, listen to the taped presentation and play 17th Century games for children which could include:

Frog in the Middle;
Jingling;
Barley Break;
Drop Glove;
Puss in the Corner;
Fox and Geese.

b. Kings supporters
After hearing the story this group act out their roles in the house, so far as possible, as they go around.
King arrives at Moseley in the middle of the night accompanied by John and Richard Penderel and Francis Yates. Whitgreave waiting in the orchard fails to recognise the King. Charles shown hiding place. Feet bathed by Huddlestone and given food. Went to bed for the remainder of the night. Richard Penderel and Francis Yates sent back to Boscobel.

Mrs. Whitgreave meets the King. Huddlestone's pupils excused lessons to watch for troops. Charles looks out of the window to see his defeated troops going by. Mrs. Whitgreave helps troops by dressing wounds etc.

During the night Colonel Lane collects Wilmot. Whitgreave and Huddlestone keep watch. Charles sleeps fully dressed on the bed. Night passes peacefully.

Huddlestone talks to King in the morning, Whitgreave with mother in the kitchen. In the afternoon the King lay down on the bed to rest. Whitgreave watching at window saw a neighbour run in, maid shouted warning that soliders were coming.

Whitgreave secures King in hiding place, opens all the doors and walks outside to meet the soliders. Whitgreave accused of being at Worcester and told that he would have to accompany soldiers. Whitgreave explained that he had been ill and so was not at Worcester, neighbours confirmed this. Whitgreave stood outside the Hall until soldiers left. After a time King let out of hiding place.

Late afternoon John Penderel brought message to say that the King would go to Bentley that night. Midnight Colonel Lane arrived. Charles said goodbye to Mrs Whitgreave who gave him delicacies and said prayers. Huddlestone gave the King a cloak to wear and the King left.

c. Servants
The servants have a marginal role in the key story. All except the kitchen maid, a Catholic, were sent on a variety of errands to get away from the house. The kitchen maid shouted a warning, that the soldiers were coming, upstairs to the family.

Because the servants were excluded from any knowledge of the King's presence they could re-enact their daily chores.

Cooking. If the 'servants' make food then they have a part to play in the final dramatisation.

Could include: Marzipan Bacon
                 Fruit Drink
                 Gingerbread
                 Gumballs
                 or Oatcakes

In addition children could make tussie mussies, pomanders etc.

If there is time then the children will sketch, draw a plan of the garden, listen to the taped presentation etc.

Preparing the barn
Cleaning, polishing, sweeping and arranging the Barn for the final telling of Pepys' story. The servants serve the food to the assembled audience at the dramatisation.

If the servants have time to spare they can practise a game e.g. Jingling and then demonstrate it to the other groups in the final dramatisation and ask the others to participate.

Restoration day

The day at Moseley will centre around 'Restoration Day'
After arrival the children change into period costume and then go into the main barn.

Children welcomed by Thomas Whitgreave and told that it is the day of the King's restoration and the whole house is to celebrate – there will be a feast. Will they help?

Three groups: one group go round Hall;

one group to devise entertainment;
one group to make food.

Day divided into four sessions.

a	b	c
1. Hall	Food	Entertainment
2. Entertainment	Hall	Food

LUNCH

3. Food	Entertainment	Hall

4. Then come together in the Barn for the feast, sharing food and entertainment.

(17th Century games in reserve).

Hall
The children to be shown around the Hall.

Entertainment
Entertainment will include dancing, music and games.

A suitable dance is Argeers – the music service have pre-recorded the music for it. A song has been written for Lillibulero.

'Here's a Health Unto His Majesty', etc. will need to be learnt before-hand (the recorders etc. will provide the accompaniment). A poem has been written for a Masque. We need to prepare a tape from the pre-recorded material.

Music has been prepared by the Walsall Music Service, who have been very supportive. They have agreed to be present during the trial days and will work with some children to prepare and present suitable music for the 'Entertainment'.

Group a will learn the dance.
Group b will perform the masque.
Group c will sing (with percussion?). They can attempt juggling, acrobatics etc.

Any group with time to spare can practise a game e.g. Jingling and then demonstrate it to the other groups in the final 'feast' and ask the others to participate. We need to take tape recorders etc.

Games for children to learn could include:

Frog in the middle;
Jingling;
Barley Break;
Drop Glove;
Puss in the Corner;
Fox and Geese.

Food
Simple 17th Century recipes with the emphasis on sweetmeats which do not need cooking.

They might include: Group a: Marzipan Bacon
Fruit Drink
Group b: Gingerbread
Group c: Gumballs
or Oatcakes

Depending on time then the children will play games, sketch, draw a plan of the garden, etc.

Follow-up work
The children did much of their work for the summer term around the project. It gave purpose to their learning and kept their interest. They needed to talk and to listen; to read for a variety of purposes; to write in different ways for different audiences. Their enthusiasm and their new understanding of the 'reality' of the seventeenth century made it possible for them to begin to appreciate a period in history, to identify with what happened to the people in it and to look on them as real personalities.

Work produced by the children was shared with their parents and other children and formed part of a display of work at both schools. Subsequently it was displayed at Moseley for general visitors to see.

Evaluation of project

King Charles' Flight
The group activities worked well, especially in their modified form – reached after the first experiences. On the third occasion the story was told by a teacher; this made it easier for the children to understand, and it could be more easily repeated by other schools. The dramatisation needed to be an inherent part of the day – not bolted on at the end! For the next trial, resource material has been prepared with a simpler version of the story.

Restoration Day

This version worked easily although there is a need to pose more problems for the children to solve about their activities during the day. For all of the children differences between the contemporary world and the seventeenth century were easy to see, the similarities were brought home by direct experience and the work in the classroom afterwards.

General

If you want to arrange an easy environmental education project do not try Living History! Teachers must be prepared to participate in activities (figure 6.6) and 'live in the past' – as well as asking the children to do so. The staff from both schools had pursued environmental studies and topic work as their institutional GRIST priorities during the year and were ready to apply the ideas they had discussed in planning a project for the children in their classes. In this way it was possible to give a reason for learning for teachers as well! The planning time put in by staff of both schools and a variety of advisers will not be repeated but it can be used to give an advantage to subsequent schools. Such schools will need to take part in an INSET

Figure 6.6   *'Teachers must be prepared to participate in activities – 'live the part' – as well as ask the children to do so.'*

package designed to outline the opportunities and help with planning. The work pursued by the children before and after their visit is clearly the responsibility of the class teacher, who will also need to ensure that other accompanying adults are prepared for their part. First attempts were a success both in the light of experience with the children and an analysis of their work. For some of the pupils an interest was kindled which will last for the rest of their lives. All of the children were eager to discuss what they had done and what it meant and their learning was facilitated by their interest which gave a new purpose to their work.

It was found that much of the content of the national curriculum can be delivered in primary schools in this way, through an integrated topic approach. The real world does not exist in convenient boxes divided along conventional subject boundaries – real problems range across disciplines and specialities and their solution requires a con-comitant range of response. The problems of the 17th century are a distorted reflection of some of the issues of the 20th century. Con-fronting the former enabled the young learners to appreciate some of the environmental issues of the present time.

Integrated environmental study places considerable demands on tea-chers. They must, therefore, be very clear in their planning of the curriculum balance to achieve their aims and what the children have learned.

This project also demonstrated that children can use a historic prop-erty (where, in this case, everything in sight was 300 years old) in a responsible way without damage to the fabric.

7 Out of the classroom

Beyond the classroom lies the laboratory for environmental education. It is not necessarily a place far away, expensive to reach, which requires extensive organisation and units of school time. The site may be within the school building itself, more usually in the school grounds and often within the local neighbourhood. These locations, all within walking distance, should provide the first regular and progressive out-of-the-classroom experiences, with the distant special environments which provide contrast coming much later. Outdoor work should not be 'hoarded' for a one day, or one week, a year experience in an away place. As local study it should be a matter of routine, which blends into the normal environmental curriculum in a natural manner, not taking on the mantle of a unique learning experience to be highlighted and fussed over.

The case for out-of-the-classroom study

First-hand experience is an essential element of an environmental approach as it allows the environment to 'communicate' directly with the young learners through real people, problems and successes. Out-of-the-classroom study gives a full opportunity for this whilst it encourages pupils to develop a whole range of skills and techniques and encourages the habit of working with others. The noise and fumes of a city street, the sudden silence of the church interior, the clutter of the road signs and street furniture, the distant chug of a harvest tractor, birdsong, the landscape whitened by frost or blanketed by snow, the tree uprooted by a sudden gale, the flowers and autumn leaves of an urban park, the majestic cathedral and the homely market stall, all say more than any words from teacher in the classroom. Any learning situation which denies regular and direct experience of the environment is incomplete and without it an understanding of inter-relationships, awareness of change and an appreciation of place cannot be developed. The surroundings provide the teaching resources, it is up to the teacher to exploit them. From such exploitation pupils will, by use of the world around them, learn about their world and formulate a code of behaviour towards it. Curiosity, keenness, interest, imagination and concern are parts of the make up of every primary age child. Studies away from the classroom will foster this innate alertness and encourage a moral area of learning so that progression in its development will help the future citizen to reconcile the vested interests of self, nature, people and posterity. Much of this progression is gained from simple and diverse experiences of various environments in the early years at school.

Emphasis has already been placed on the need to structure environmental education so that learning experiences progress and continue throughout the primary school and beyond. It is essential that such a programme encompasses learning out of the classroom. The teacher should see it as a strategy for teaching across the curriculum (figure 7.1) and a method to extend pupil experience in a way which is meaningful to them. It is a way which involves the active participation of each member of the learning group. The fact that outdoor activity can be flexible and respond to opportunism, is a benefit and not a hindrance. In other words the teacher should respond to the sudden chance interest and profit from it, rather than, as in the classroom, rebuke such a diversion from the task in hand. It is the development of awareness and understanding which gives out-of-classroom experience its cutting edge. It acts as a stimulus for imaginative involvement for children of the whole range of ability; indeed the discovery that the slow learner in the classroom is the keenest observer 'in the wild' is one of the rewards for the extra teacher effort which is inevitable when the security of the classroom has been left behind.

Inter-relationship is an essential concept within environmental education. Since it is impossible to compartmentalise outdoor study in any rigid way the appreciation of this concept is a consequence of most observations, whether of the natural world or of that created by people. The reality of an 'issue-chain' can be brought within the understanding of even the youngest pupil. For example, with the natural world, an investigation into why a plant is drooping can lead to an issue chain of:

Drooping plant – greenfly infestation – ladybird predation – use of pesticide – pollution

For the created world the natural example can be matched by an observation of new foundations dug for a building on a derelict site:

Digging foundations – excavation machinery – building material – disturbance of archaeological remains – preservation versus progress

At their own level of achievement pupils can carry out extended studies which investigate matters to depths unlikely within the

TEACHING DECISIONS	PREPARATORY ACTIVITIES	FOCUS	FOLLOW-UP ACTIVITIES	REVIEW
S P E C I F I C • How will you introduce the activity? • How will you find out what the children already know? • How will you involve the children in the planning		• What activities will children do? • Will there be opportunities for talking, listening, reading and writing – for different purposes?	• How will the activities be organised in the classroom? • What range of outcomes will be produced: – written – spoken – artefacts – in other media?	• How will the children's experiences and achievements be recorded and shared? • How will the pupils' knowledge and understanding be extended?
GENERAL Checking LEA policy and school policy on: • equal opportunities • cross-curricular issues • pupils groupings • use of resources • use of time • use of information technology • opportunities for drama • opportunities for work on the media • special educational needs	Listen to and discuss with visiting expert in pairs, share expectations about visit in groups, plan the visit and share out responsibilites: • write letters to place of visit • collect on tape/in writing impressions of place of visit – from parents, older children etc • find appropriate information – using resources—books, maps, artefacts, newspapers, photographs, films etc • plan a data base • discuss how experiences will be recorded and shared • decide who is going to do what during the visit	**VISIT** Collect evidence and record impressions by: • taping, listening, questioning • observing and sensing • taking photographs/video • drawing, sketching, note-taking • collecting things, information	In pairs (not regular partners) talk about the visit. As a class, share perceptions of the visit in groups, think about ways of preparing for a presentation about the unit. This might include: • model making • dramatic representation • tape/slide sequence • edited video • visual display of writings, diagrams, maps, drawings • additional information gleaned from research • simple experiments carried out after visit • a data base Make a presentation to an invited audience such as: • original visiting expert • parents • another class • whole school	Teachers and children might ask the following questions: *Presentation* • how successful were the chosen methods? • how appropriate? • how suitable *Learning* What has been learned? • about the topic? • about ways of finding out? • about working together? What might be followed up in the future? *Development* How does this work fit into the term/year's programme? What evidence of development is there in the learning of individual children?

Figure 7.1   *An example of the way that English work may be integrated into a class visit taken from "English Key Stage 1. Non-Statutory Guidance" published by the National Curriculum Council.*

classroom. Being away from the usual work area is a stimulus in itself, even if it becomes a matter of normal routine. It is a venture into the 'real' world every time.

A plan for out-of-the-classroom work

Occasionally, the need to go out will arise spontaneously from the work in hand, but this will not be usual. Of all aspects of environmental work the case for a proper plan cannot be stronger than with 'field work', the traditional term for outdoor study (a term which can still bring a sense of academic discipline to what others may see as a waste of time and an unnecessary diversion from structured lessons within the classroom).

Plans must begin with the establishment of

- the need for outside study within the parameters of the current curriculum content,
- the activity and location to be involved,
- the objective(s) for the study,
- the outcome.

The need
Outdoor study for its own sake is not sufficient reason for the venture. Unless the activity makes a unique contribution to the overall study, or provides an alternative, relevant approach which excites and stimulates, it should not go beyond the stage of contemplation. 'Can I do this study in any other way?' must be a primary question to answer before further plans are made. Now is the time to consult with the school's co-ordinator for environmental education, now is the time to discuss the matter with the headteacher. The complexity of the activity will condition the depth and extent of this consultation process, and if it is obviously acceptable within the policy of the school, such preliminaries may be unnecessary. Individual circumstances alone can dictate this.

The activity and its location
Several alternatives, both by way of the content of the contemplated activity, and the location where it is possible to conduct the activity, are usually possible. The decision as to which 'way' to go will depend on factors which involve consideration of:

1 Adult supervision
2 Time – time of the day, time available, time restriction (eg observation of the sun at noon)

Figure 7.2   *A group of pupils about to embark on a prepared environmental trail. The organisational problem of out-of-the-classroom situations is well exemplified by the use of worksheets. Such handouts have the advantage of focusing participants' attention on the task in hand, but they also restrict individual initiative and observation. A great deal of thought needs to be given to the design and use of worksheets.*

3   Safety
4   Accessibility
5   Interference – by the school group with others and vice versa
6   Group size – both for working and overall
7   Study activities to be followed
8   Domestic arrangements and other administration – refreshments, toilets, clothing (Such factors will be considered separately later.)

As with much environmental education the teacher has a basic problem with outdoor study. S/he has to walk the tightrope between too much guidance on the one hand and insufficient direction on the other. Time must be given for the child to observe and think about what is to be seen but at the same time it is essential that the intervention of the teacher is carefully placed so that the skills, ideas and developing values of the individual are not suppressed. The real skill of the teacher is to know when and how to intervene between the pupil and the environment concerned (figure 7.2).

The objectives
Paramount in a plan for out of the classroom study, as with any educational pursuit, may be the compilation of objectives. Unless what is to be achieved is established at the outset little benefit will be gained from the activity. One important objective in the early years is to give young learners the experience of going out of the classroom in an orderly way, to encourage the positive attitudes required for outside study. This will be of benefit to their own capacity to learn and to colleagues who will teach them later in their educational life. An objective which stipulates 'enjoyment' of the outside world is not to be rejected as an unnecessary frill. Mystery and delight are concepts to be fostered not stifled. Specific objectives will be particular to the study in hand and reflect the locality being used. Broad objectives have been listed in many published works. The 1988 Kent Curriculum Statement included these objectives for Outside the Classroom work:

a)   Developing the skills of enquiry and exploration in both local and contrasting environments.
b)   Developing communication skills, particularly through discussion and debate, leading towards practice of decision making and value judgements.
c)   Developing the pupil's self reliance and ability to organise work programmes in the school and in the field, with an increasing degree of responsibility for their own learning.
d)   Building an understanding of place, time, change and relationships, using concrete phenomena that pupils can perceive and relate to.

In some cases more direct guidance as to the objectives and other aspects of local outdoor study is given. Wolverhampton adopted a ten-point Guideline[2] to indicate some idea of the approach schools are asked to consider when planning outdoor study. The concept that a school project should be of some value to the local community is an interesting one, emphasising the social, political and economic links engendered by an environmental education programme.

The Wolverhampton Guideline

The following ten-point Guideline gives some idea of the approach schools are asked to consider:

1 The Study (Topic or Theme) should be based on the immediate school surroundings, the local neighbourhood or town.
2 The Study should focus on particular features and areas and on local issues and problems that affect the quality of life of the community.
3 The Study should be directly related to the basic aims of Environmental Education.
4 When possible, the Study should be a local educational experience that may be related to a national or international environmental problem or issue.
5 Pupils should be involved in direct personal exploration of their locality and town and be required to make first hand observations.
6 The work should improve the pupil's understandings of the processes and people that plan, manage and change our surroundings.
7 The Study should involve local agencies such as Environmental and Technical Services, Parks and Gardens, Architects, Planners and Safety Officers.
8 The Study should encourage pupil's appreciation of the importance of involvement in maintaining and improving the quality of the built environment.
9 The Study should teach specific skills, techniques and concepts and encourage the operational use of basic skills especially in language.
10 The work should reflect the overall Environmental Education policy of the school.

It also suggests that school projects have some value to the local community by achieving at least ONE of the following:

a)   A specific contribution to a particular debate within the local community eg use of land, conservation proposals, play area design.
b)   The creation of resources for the future use of the local community eg trails, photographs, historical records.
c)   The physical improvements of an aspect of the local environment, including school grounds and gardens.

The outcome
A decision must be made on what is to be the end product for this plan. Is it to be a classroom display, a study file for each individual or any of the ways well established in primary schools? In many instances this part of the plan will undergo extensive alterations as the study progresses but this does not detract from the need to set an initial target.

The immediate locality
The local environment is a sensible and appropriate place for these first-hand experiences to begin. It may be to state the obvious but it is necessary for individuals to be familiar with their neighbourhood before it is possible to appreciate that other places are different. It is in the locality where they should learn to observe, record and care for both the animate and the inanimate world around them. It is here, too, that they should be introduced to the debate which surrounds environmental problems, leading on to a concern for broad environmental issues. For example the inevitable problem of litter can be their first-hand experience for the wider issue of waste disposal and recycling of finite resources (see *The Good, the Bad and the Ugly*[3]). It could be said that until the young learner has developed a sense of place locally it will be impossible to comprehend other places. To answer questions such as *What is this locality like? Would I like to change it? What do I really feel about this place?* is an essential pre-requisite for broader environmental appreciation. Some will claim that the particular environment of a particular school can offer less stimulation and educational potential than that of others elsewhere. No school is in a totally sterile situation and even the most 'deprived' establishment in terms of local resources has access to:

- weather
- local activities and people
- transport, roads and paths
- natural intrusion (if only weeds in a wall or birds and insects, however 'common')
- buildings and building materials
- energy – the sun must be in evidence sometimes!
- some space where plant containers can be installed

in fact, a considerable list can be drawn up for any site.

Further afield
The local area provides the basics for out-of-the-classroom study, particularly an insight into the skills and concepts needed to carry

out such study: inevitably, however, the familiar cannot provide an unfamiliar contrast. Town cannot be country, factory cannot be farm, city street cannot be rural lane and a 1950s chapel cannot be a Gothic cathedral. It is necessary, certainly at the upper end of the primary stage, to build contrast into the outdoor programme. The use of no more than half a day of school time should provide many environmental contrasts for it will be an unusual school which is set in a uniform environment which extends for a full hour away in any direction.

Transport problems arise, to be resolved by individual circumstances. For some, the buses which bring youngsters to school may be available during school hours; for others public transport will be plentiful; for some even a short distance to be covered will be too costly in financial terms especially in the confines of Local Management of Schools (LMS). Again it is up to the enterprise of the environmental education co-ordinator to plan an overall programme which will provide a range of contrasts within accessible limits.

It will be apparent that some experiences lie further away and involve a longer journey time. Before a decision is made to use any venue, due consideration must be given to this – often wasted – time; observation exercises can be designed for the journey although they are not always compatible with the main purpose of the travel. Generally it is not sensible to spend more than a third of the time available on the journeys; otherwise, by the time a meal break has been taken and the embarkation and disembarkation routines accomplished, little study time is left. Far better to build such visits into a residential programme.

Local environmental study centres
Many LEAs provide environmental study centres which are available to their schools. The types of programme offered in such centres are varied and are often planned to augment the type of environmental activity available elsewhere in the council area. Usually transport costs are met by the LEA, the main difficulty is to match the provision to the demand, as the latter mostly outstrips the availability of space on the programme. Nonetheless it is useful to have at least one group from a school involved so that they can act as an 'in-service' training facility for others in the school (see Environmental Study Centres, Chapter 8).

Out-of-season activity
An inherent weakness in out-of-classroom learning which involves an extended visit, is that most take place in the summer term. Yet a visit, for example, to York Minster in November is such a contrast in terms of visitor numbers, to one in June, that it might be supposed

that the venues were different. The longer daylight and the increased possibility of better weather apart – important but not of paramount importance – there is no good reason for summer 'outings', other than that of tradition. Away from the summer, traffic is less heavy, pressure on the resident education staff and resources is diminished and the demand from other schools is reduced, even transport can be cheaper with a wider choice. It is also true that it is valuable to present young learners with the various seasonal aspects of nature. Local visits can be planned to enable comprehension of the similarities and contrasts of different times of the year. The emphasis must be on progression and continuity and not on 'dip stick' experiences of unconnected samples here, there and everywhere.

Heritage education

Reference to York Minster is a reminder of one of the specialised aspects of out-of-the-classroom study, namely that of *heritage education*. Visits which involve the school crocodile following a (uniformed) guide through space after space of castle, palace, noble house or place of worship are mostly things of the past. Efforts are now made to make such experiences more attractive and educationally valuable. Many heritage properties provide Living History sessions (see figures 7.3 and 7.4) and the National Trust has its own Young National Trust Youth Theatre company which stimulates role enactment and participation.

Role play is a useful method of introducing children to the historical 'feel' of times past, but it is only one method. Too much role play is as bad as too little; certainly care must be taken to ensure that gender stereotypes are not reinforced in the recreation of the duties of housemaid and footman, and of housekeeper and butler. Yet much can be gained from the stimulation of the child's imagination: 'I forgot it was now and thought it was then!' is an actual comment from an eleven-year-old after one 'live' experience.

It is not necessary to see visits to heritage properties as the sole prerogative of the historical side of environmental education (figure 7.5). The historic house is probably set in a present-day economic unit of farm, garden centre, leisure park as well as being an established tourist attraction in its own right. Economic considerations are an often neglected aspect of environmental education.

The Sandford Award for Heritage Education is a recognition of worthwhile educational provision by heritage properties and certain museums. It is made to any heritage property where the provision for the reception of school or educational groups is deemed to meet the criteria laid down. The award is not competitive. The criteria are:

	10.00	11.00	12.00	12.30	13.00	13.30	14.30	15.15	
Group A 6 children	Cheese making and Marchpane in Brewhouse	Florentine canvas and Hessian embroidery in Attic				Mathematical Garden Work in Formal Garden	Tour of House by all groups		
Group B 7 children	Butter making and Fruit Drink in Stable	Quill making and Writing in Hall	Games in Orchard and Farmyard	Lunch Tastings in Barn	Music and Dancing in Barn	Drama (acting out the story of Charles II visit to Moseley)	"		
Group C 6 children	Pomanders and Pot Pourri in Parlour	Mathematical Garden Work in Formal Garden					"		
Group D 7 children	Rushlight making and Polishing in Hall	Pike Drill in Orchard				Pomanders and Pot Pourri in Parlour	"		

Figure 7.3 Possible timetable for a class of 10 and 11-year-olds participating in a 'Living History' programme at Moseley Old Hall (owned by the National Trust).

Figure 7.4 *Butter making in a 'Living History' session at Croxteth.*

1 Evidence of good liaison between the historic property, LEAs and teachers.
2 The imaginative way in which the full educational potential of the property is realised.
3 The good design of education materials and facilities.
4 Attention given to adequate preparation, good management during the visit and effective follow up.

Figure 7.5 *A visit to a heritage property does not necessarily mean 'history'. The formal garden at Moseley Old Hall can be used for a variety of mathematical, design, horticulture and art work.*

5   The way in which a visit is designed to kindle a lasting interest in a particular topic relating to the property.

The Award Scheme was administered originally by the Council for Environmental Education. It is now run by the Heritage Education Trust. Since its inception in 1978 many properties have received Sandford Awards, which take the form of a commemorative plaque and recognition in the *Historic Houses, Gardens and Castles* magazine. The award winners are listed in Appendix I, and are to be recommended as places which ensure a worthwhile school visit.

Outdoor study skills

The DES document *The Curriculum 5–16*, groups skills into eight areas. They are:

1   Communication
2   Observation
3   Study
4   Problem solving

5 Physical and practical
6 Creative and imaginative
7 Numerical
8 Personal and social

Some of these areas lend themselves more obviously to outside study than others. However, it would be difficult to put up a case to exclude any of these categories from out-of-the classroom study, particularly if it involved a residential element when the personal and social skills would come to the fore. A simpler pattern was adopted by the Environmental Education Task Group as we considered in Chapter 2.

Particular skills to be developed through outdoor study, according to *The Curriculum 5–16*, include the ability to:

● extract or collect information about the environment from ... first-hand experience
● analyse, interpret and evaluate information and evidence ...
● define questions for investigation
● identify the causes and consequences of particular environmental problems...
● participate in discussion and debate in relation to environmental issues
● make and act on personal decisions relating to the environment
● participate in group decision making.

It is essential to remind ourselves that skills acquisition needs to progress and it is up to the teacher to ensure that such progression occurs with out-of-the-classroom study. It is as necessary to think through the basic progressions in outdoor study as it is with any work inside the classroom. It is not good enough to give young learners first-hand experience unless it is part of a fundamental outline plan. In other words, work away from the classroom needs as much consideration as any other. Let us re-emphasise that to go outside as a fulfilment of a basic requirement for environmental education for its own sake is not good enough.

Organisation

It has already been stated that there are several criteria to be considered when assessing the location to be used for out-of-the-classroom work. These need to be examined in greater detail as part of the consideration of the organisation of work based out of the classroom.

In recent years the high level of publicity given to several unfortunate tragedies which involved school groups has highlighted the need for sound organisation. All Local Education Authorities had some guidelines, however limited, for the conduct of parties which move away from school. These have been updated and it is essential that every teacher is aware of their contents and no breach of any aspect of the rules is contemplated – or occurs through negligence. As much emphasis on sound organisation as can be delivered by the printed word has been made.

Central Government has prepared guidelines with regard to safety in the DES publication *Safety in Schools*.[4] Outside organisations have also produced helpful guidelines, in particular the NAEE's *Organisation of Outdoor Studies and Visits*.[5]

Yet despite the detail contained in all of these guidelines, it is essential to recognise that individual circumstances create individual needs. Although the conclusion reached may be that LEA guidelines are adequate, experience has shown that in most cases some local emphasis is required.

Adult supervision
The ratio of teachers to pupils will often determine the choice of outdoor study. However much it limits the activity, adherence to the maximum ratio is essential. It may be tempting to break the rule on a single occasion, but inevitably, that one time will be the occasion when something adverse happens. Other adult supervision may be available but, in legal terms, no-one can take over teacher responsibility. Each assistant – parent, student or other helper – needs firm direction, given well before the activity.

Time
Adequate time needs to be allowed for the activity and plans must compensate for the fact that procedures always take longer with a large group. Time of day and time of year are important considerations and often dictate the content of the planned activity.

Comment has been made on the fact that there are many advantages in out-of-season work, particularly to places of popular interest. Certainly an enquiry into less popular times is worthwhile if it results in a less pressured and more pleasurable visit.

It is necessary to make a preparatory visit at a similar time to that of the planned activity. Differences in conditions between one time and another may cause considerable problems, but this is often overlooked. Although advance preparation is essential, a planning visit made too far ahead may miss something recently established; at the very least a confirmatory visit as near to the actual visit as possible is desirable.

Safety
Adequate preparation (figure 7.6), adherence to the local regulations and, on the day, refusal to be persuaded away from the planned itinerary, is the best that can be done to prevent accidents occurring. This is not the place to go into lengthy details on the various aspects of safety (refer to the DES book *Safety in Schools*[4]), but it is the place to emphasise that in the final analysis the teacher is the person with the ultimate responsibility during the activity. It is the duty of the Head Teacher to ensure that selected leaders are competent to take pupils out of the classroom. The person who lacks control in the classroom will not suddenly change when in charge outside!

Accessibility
Sufficient attention must be given to access to the particular sites of interest. This may be seen in terms of convenience, finance and safety. It may be necessary to scale down the extent of the planned study

Figure 7.6 *Safety 'in the field'. This group is well protected against the inclement weather. It is small enough to be controlled by one person, the equipment is being carried sensibly and the party is keeping to the side of the field.*

to compensate for some unacceptable accessibility factor. Compromise is a strength and not a sign of weakness in planning out-of-the-classroom work.

Interference

Sufficient attention is usually given to the difficulties to be encountered from outside influences. For example it is obvious that a visit to a place of historic interest at a peak time in high summer will have to contend with crowd pressure from the general public. However, insufficient appreciation is generally paid to the effect of a school group on the rightful enjoyment of others. The point is not to be laboured, nevertheless due attention needs to be given to this.

Group size

The regulations which apply to the size of groups working outside the classroom are usually based on safety aspects. Whereas a ratio of 1 adult to 10 pupils may be adequate for supervisory purposes it may result in too large a working group. Groups may need to be smaller if they are to be educationally effective. The experience gained from the repetition of an environmental project over the years will help determine the ideal size for a learning group compatible with educational, and not just safety, considerations.

The wide range of study activities is such that it is not possible to formulate them here. The material detailed in our case studies suggests a whole range of activities which depend in no uncertain way on the individual circumstances of the school. Invention of new activities is commendable although the adaptation of the activities of others is far more likely – and this is no bad thing!

Domestic arrangements and other administration

The NAEE booklet[5] goes into considerable detail on the essential aspects of the various administrative arrangements which may be necessary for out-of-the-classroom activities other than those of a very local nature. It is surprising how easy it is to overlook an obvious requirement and even the most experienced of leaders will generally use some sort of checklist. Particular attention needs to be paid to emergency procedures to cope with delay and accident. Much distress can be avoided by the appropriate release of information in a controlled manner.

If, in spite of adequate preparation, the unforeseen happens it may well be that the thorough planning will help to minimise the impact.

Around the school

The immediate neighbourhood of the school and the area within accessible distance, that is the area where it is unnecessary to make special transport arrangements, is the most important environmental resource of all. The character of this locality will determine the content of a programme of environmental education. It will also determine the choice of distant or special-purpose environments to be studied. A plan for the environmental programme as a whole should be based on an assessment of the locality as a potential resource.

Co-operation with the local community has been advocated elsewhere but it cannot be over-emphasised how much value is to be gained through close liaison with the departments of the local council, and in particular the local planning department. The organisation of this may best be carried out through the local environmental education advisory service.

For the majority of schools, based as they are in an urban, suburban or semi-urban setting, the development of urban studies over the past few years has been an important one, still to be taken further. It must not be forgotten that environmental education is rooted in the natural world as expressed generally, but certainly not necessarily, in studies of the countryside. Too much emphasis on the local built environment is as bad as too little. The investigation of houses, shops, places of worship, police and fire stations, public buildings, streets and trans-port is worthwhile – but even in the urban locality river and canal sides, derelict land and other open spaces provide sites for natural study. No area can provide all that is needed, but the creation of 'missing' natural resources may be possible. The use of school grounds and their development have been considered previously. It is enough to say here that the apparent lack of resources offered by the school site and its surrounds is a challenge rather than an excuse for inaction.

Our next case study indicates how one inner urban school rises to such a challenge by looking at the opportunity for outdoor work created by derelict land and redevelopment areas. It points the way to what can be done environmentally even in what may, at first sight, seem to be a place of limited local resources. Not only is the place exploited for environmental education, so too are the people.

Case study 6 Room for change

Merridale School, Wolverhampton

Starting point
The school neighbourhood

The area around the school has changed considerably over the years, and is still in the process of change. From the 19th century it developed as an industrial area with factories, workshops and streets of terraced houses for the workers. As the industries declined much of this building has been demolished. Demolition sites are scattered throughout the area. In a continuous process of change these spaces fill up with new buildings or are left open for recreational use.

Aims
For the children (age range 10/11) to develop personal perception of changes in the urban neighbourhood of the school over the past years, particularly since the Second World War. By analysing and interpreting these perceptions it is hoped that children will increase their aesthetic awareness, understand their own feelings towards the changing environment and develop their powers of judgement and appreciation of community needs.

Objectives
1 For the children to discover and record, through observation and drawing, the development within spaces created in our local environment.
2 For the children to develop an aesthetic awareness of urban development.
3 For the children to develop powers of critical appraisal through comparison, discussion and analysing personal responses to the design of buildings. This will take into account factors such as:
   * position
   * size
   * shape
   * materials
   * surrounding space
   * the way in which new buildings relate to surrounding existing buildings
4 For the children to be aware of the purpose, ie use, of new buildings in relation to the community.
5 For them to question the purpose of the building in terms of:

- Does it meet the needs of the people in the community?
- Does it serve a particular group within the community or the whole community?
- Does it duplicate existing facilities?
- Is it adequate in terms of size and facilities to serve the need it is intended for?
- Is it in the best position for its purpose?

6   Having recorded, observed and made a critical response to new development, the children will then try to make their own judgements about future use of remaining spaces.

Outline of project
Introduction Brief explanation and discussion to assess children's existing awareness of new development in the local environment.

Fieldwork Children taken out to draw:

- new development and adjacent buildings;
- spaces that have not yet been developed.

Display of work Organisation to be decided. Discussion of findings.

Conclusions and plans for future development.

The project could be developed by:

- researching the history of the area in terms of urban development;
- contacting planners and architects to find out what plans are being made for future development in the area.

Room for change – work undertaken (described by the class teacher)
We worked on the project for one afternoon per week for nine weeks of the summer term.

Week 1 Our first afternoon was spent discussing the community and the various groups of people that exist within it. After a whole class discussion to introduce the idea the children were divided into groups. They then took one element of the community per group eg old people, and discussed and recorded which facilities would be useful to those people. We completed the session with each group telling the whole class about their ideas and we tried to list all the existing facilities in the area to identify those which are missing.

Week 2 We went out into the area of study with worksheets. These sheets comprised a series of paired spaces: one long section for a rough drawing of empty spaces and one smaller section for recording

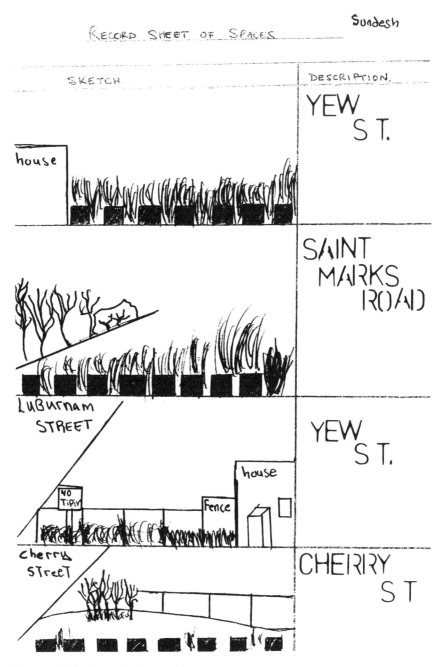

Figure 7.7   *Record sheet of spaces.*

the location of the space, eg street names. The children sketched the space and adjcent buildings in the long section and wrote other information in the smaller space (figure 7.7).

Week 3 We all went out and made careful and detailed drawings of the spaces we had identified and adjacent buildings. This involved a very close study of spaces and new additions over a longer period of time.

Week 4 The children went out with street maps and long pieces of squared paper to draw transects of the streets. On returning to school they compared their findings with maps drawn in 1962 and coloured in the spaces that exist now. In this way they could see which buildings had been knocked down.

Week 5 We looked at all the information we had gathered and talked about the spaces we had found. We also identified new facilities that had been built and linked this to our earlier discussions and community needs.

Weeks 6, 7 and 8 The children then began work on their own ideas for utilising the space. These included:

* leisure centres
* nurseries
* a library
* a veterinary centre
* old people's home
* parks

They drew pictures of their ideas, then made plans of them (figure 7.8) and finally wrote about their ideas (figure 7.9).

Presentation
A display of work was exhibited in the school hall.

Week 9 The school caretaker, who has lived in our area all his life, gave a talk to the children about the buildings that had existed before and how the way of life in the area has changed. We followed this up with a question and answer session and then the children wrote their impressions of the area in the past (figure 7.10).

Evaluation
Obviously in the time available we have not covered all the ideas in our initial plan and there is plenty of scope for extending the project. We did, however, feel that during the nine weeks we had covered areas which formed a cohesive whole.

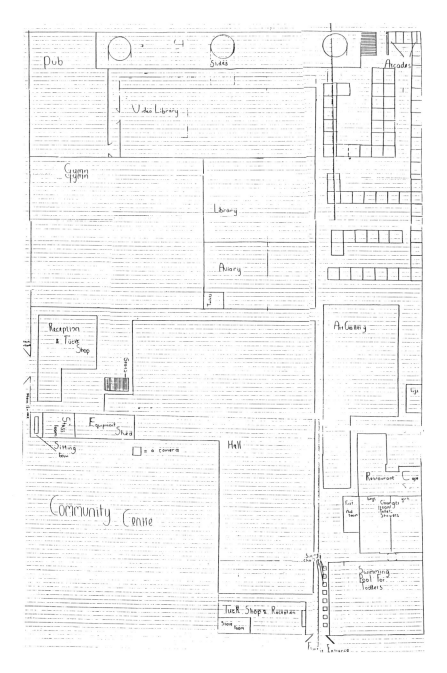

Figure 7.8 *Plan for the utilisation of derelict space.*

Old People's Centre.

I want to build an Old People's Centre because there are a lot of old people who stay at home by them selves until some one comes home. The Old People's Centre would be built on the other side of the Community Centre. It would be built there because it is a quiet place. In the Old People's Centre there would be a first aid room for people who get hurt. It will also have a sitting room for the people to sit in. It will have a cafe for the people to have a drink and something to eat. It will also have a Library for the people to read some books, and it will have men's and lady's toilets. It will be open seven day's a week from nine o'clock am to eight o'clock pm.

by
Satpal.

Figure 7.9 *A pupil's written work on the plan to utilise derelict space for an Old People's Centre.*

Items achieved
Skills

Question and answer
Research

* use of maps and plans
* interpretation of pictures

Observation and records
Process of information
Communications

* verbally
* pictorially
* written

Wednesday 21ᵗʰ June   Raibinder.

Our Area

Mr Wood is our caretaker. He has been here for many years. Mr Wood came into our class and we asked him how the merridale area looked before when he was a little boy. We talked about Fir Grove, Aspen way, Oak street and Elm street. Mr Wood told us that before Fir Grove was built there it useto be allotments. Mr Wood said to us that before Merridale primary school was built there used to be a farm. The school was built in 1973 and opened in 1976. When the school used to be the farm Mr Wood told us that he used to slap the pigs when they came by him. When Mr Wood was a little boy people used to go to work when they were the age of four teen. The field in Aspen way has always been a field but was once called the hay field. At (that) the end of Kimbery street here was a cycle spares shop which used to sell spares for bikes, cars and motor bikes but all that has been knocked down and in that place there is a Y.T.S. work shop.

By Raibinder Randhawa

Figure 7.10 *Pupil's written work on 'Our Area', based on listening to a local resident.*

		1	2	3	4	5	6	7	8	9	10	11	12
Level	5 A	√							√	√			
	5 B									√			
	6 A									√			√
	6 B	√								√			√

Figure 7.11   *Points of contact with the National Curriculum: a summary of attainment targets and levels of attainment in mathematics.*

Social

● discussion
● co-operation in a group

Solution of problems

Attitudes and values

Empathy towards environment
Development of inquisitive mind, curiosity
Open-mindedness to issues – assessment of other people's needs
Critical approach
Co-operation
Personal qualities
Environmental awareness
Care – tolerance

Concepts

Cause and effect
Interdependence
Continuity and change
Conflict and consensus
Decision making
Size and form

8 Environmental study centres in the United Kingdom

Teachers in the UK are fortunate to be able to take advantage of a whole range of specially-resourced centres directed towards study away from the classroom. A recent count put their number at over 4000. Some are establishments of LEAs, others are provided by national organisations, some belong to individual schools or colleges and the rest are the result of private, usually commercial, interests.

Such centres have been variously titled 'Field Study Centres', 'Outdoor Study/Pursuits Centres', 'Urban Study Centres', 'Farm Study Centres' and so on. The all-embracing 'Environmental Study Centre' is now more common as a title as it aptly encompasses the whole range of activities which take place.

Centres can be divided into those which provide residential facilities and those which cater for day visitors. The same centre may be set up for both. Most are staffed by qualified teachers. Whether the centre staff conduct the whole of the teaching or only part, which then leaves the class teacher to follow his/her own initiative, depends on individual circumstances. There are advantages in either system.

The finances involved in attendance at a study centre are individual and often depend on the attitude of the LEA and the headteacher of the participant school. The cost of any out-of-school visit is made up of transport, admission, resource material and equipment, and subsistence. In times past it has been usual for some combination to occur of contributions from parents, school and LEA. The latter were particularly involved in support of those families who were in financial stress. For some visits the LEA also paid for the cost of transport, especially to their own centres.

Recent legislation with regard to charging for extra-curricular activities, under which heading many visits to study centres will be listed, has raised many issues which have yet to be resolved. As always with legislation, there is a need for test cases to be assessed and this takes time. Meanwhile no school which recognises the value to the pupil of a visit to a study centre will remain restricted for long. In the main, parents are as keen as ever for their children to gain as much benefit from school visits as they can – in some way or another their money-raising efforts an direct contribution to a school fund will provide headteachers with the necessary flexibility of choice. Perhaps the greater concern is how much changes in Local Management of Schools will affect the finances and staff establishment of LEA centres. Individual interpretations by local council committees will also reflect the value placed on first-hand experiences out of the classroom.

Residential centres

In addition to whatever environmental experiences are provided by a centre, those which have residential facilities also contribute to social education. How much residential experience pupils of primary age should undertake and for how long, as with so much of environmental education, will be determined by the individual circumstances of the school. The DES Curriculum Matters 13: *Environmental Education from 5–16*[1] suggests that all pupils by age 12 should have had the opportunity to have participated in a residential situation away from home, independent of their family. It may well be that week long or further extended visits are best left to the secondary stage, with older primary pupils participating only in visits of two or three nights duration. Nevertheless, with proper preparation and adequate adult supervision, even an overnight stay with infant children can be remarkably successful. The golden rule of adequate adult supervision applies to all residential work. The idea that such a visit is a vacation for the teacher must be stillborn. The stresses and strains of 24 hour responsibility for other people's children has to be experienced to be believed. What is absolutely certain is that if preparation for out-of-the-classroom study has to be thorough, that for residential visits has to be doubly so. Although there may be a warden and other centre staff, the ultimate responsibility is that of the accompanying teacher(s). Preliminary visits are essential.

From a work point of view a residential centre gives an opportunity for environmental study to be undertaken in depth and for the various aspects of it to be followed, if not at leisure, at least with adequate time available for completion. Although the centre will inevitably provide study opportunities on its own site the whole purpose will be to give the young learners the chance to experience and study an environment which contrasts with their own neighbourhood. To spend time, money and effort for a residential visit only to carry out exercises, for instance 'tree recognition' or 'bark rubbing', which can be organised in the school locality, is to fritter away a golden opportunity. It comes an an unpleasant surprise to us that this goes on regularly.

The basis for much stimulating work back at school, as a follow-up to the residential study, is to compare and contrast the 'home' and the 'away' situation. This is adequately illustrated in *The Good, the Bad and the Ugly*, published by the Geographical Association.

Day centres

The majority of environmental work carried out at study centres will be at those catering for non-residential groups. In order to fit in with the school day, most centres will provide for visitors in two or four hour sessions, particularly those run by LEAs. Others, such as those based in 'tourist' attractions, are able to offer shorter sessions accompanied by other activities on the site, independent of the resident staff.

It is worth emphasising again that visits planned for the 'out of season' months are often more rewarding, in that pressures on the staff and facilities are usually less. Some centres attached to properties which close to the public in the winter months are often willing to open for school groups on a restricted number of days.

Invariably day visits are 'one off'. This is a pity, for most study centres present a different personality dependent on the season of the year. It is to be hoped that two or three visits at different times of the year might be possible – it does depend so much on the proximity of the centre to the school. To choose a venue which is more accessible but less exhilarating environmentally, may not be a bad thing, certainly if it results in the possibility of extra visits.

There is, however, one splendid system operated by a few day centres. It may be termed a progressive or rolling programme. With this, the same group of children attend the centre once every three or four weeks. In this way not only do the pupils learn to appreciate the importance of time on place, but they are also able to build up a relationship with the centre staff. It enables the resident teacher to see what progress is being made, to evaluate the work s/he is doing with the group and to feel a sense of identity with the school involved. If the school uses the instruction received by the participating class as a basis for in-service training, it is possible for the whole school, staff and pupils to benefit over the year. However it does not take a mathematician to work out that the number of groups which can participate in the programme has to be limited. If the centre is open for ten sessions every week and the rolling programme is monthly, only 40 groups can be involved. These are usually spread amongst 30 to 40 schools so that in an LEA of 300 primary schools the participation rate is low. Centres which have facilities and staff able to cope with more than one group at a time will be able to widen their clientele. Unfortunately experience has shown there to be few of these around.

It is of concern that with so few schools directly involved in this type of programme a full Local Management of Schools delegation of funds to individual schools may mean that they are unable to afford to participate. If the full costs of running a centre are to be carried by relatively few schools the situation will be impossible. It is hoped that LEAs will use their reserve powers to fund day centres centrally.

Local authority centres

Most local education authorities manage their own environmental study centres which provide residential and day facilities. But few, if any, LEAs appear to have an overall strategy for a complete cross-curricular coverage. The establishment of their centres seems to be based on historical accident or the patronage of some vested interest. This is not to detract from the centres which are available within council control, for all of them can be exploited by individual schools for their own curriculum purposes. Nevertheless it is often necessary for a school to look beyond local resources for a particular need, as, for example, urban study as a topic, or children with special needs as a distinct educational requirement. Some LEAs have taken advantage of the fact that the closure of some schools has enabled the setting up of study centres. This is not without merit but it does mean that the location of the centre often dictates its activities rather than a need recognition being fulfilled with the acquisition of suitable premises.

Broadly speaking, the staff of centres are employed by the LEA and their appointment and terms of reference are part of the schools' service. Heads of centres are drawn from the local teaching force or appointed as a result of national advertisement. They often move back into the school service at a senior level. In some cases teachers at centres are on secondment from their own schools. One problem for centre staff is that they work in isolation; a concerned LEA will see that they are kept 'within' the local orbit by good communication and sympathetic supervision by an environmental education adviser.

Despite comment on the lack of a strategy for the establishment of environmental study centres the overall provision is wide and there often exists an opportunity for a reciprocal use of centres between one LEA and another. This applies particularly to highly-specialised centres. Those designed for pupils with special needs usually serve a catchment zone broader than that of one council. Farm centres, too, provide a restricted programme of study compared with environmental study centres and it follows that their services are in demand from outside the one authority. It is certainly worth enquiring if any arrangements exist with neighbouring councils. This sort of organisation more commonly occurs where a centre has been sponsored by an outside body, such as a charity. For example, the Variety Club of Great Britain have a particular interest in financial facilities for disabled pupils. Industrialists have set up trusts, often funding centres reflecting their particular interest, as, for instance the backing of the Cadbury Trust of a centre dealing with dairy farming. Although it is usual for one LEA to be responsible for the teaching staff, the schools of several councils may be entitled to use the centre. A similar situation exists with field centres based on what was, until recently, land owned by the Central Electricity Generating Board. These centres are listed on page 216.

It is unfortunate that in many instances centre sites are not owned by the LEA but are leased from other bodies. Often this is a quirk of history, dating back to the time of 'city fathers' and 'benevolent benefactors'. The peppercorn rents of times past are now no longer appropriate to the modern economic climate which results in the local treasury being reluctant to pay out a substantial annual sum of money when council-owned sites are underused. There have been some cases of closure of centres and a number of threatened sites. Environmental centres develop over the years and it is not a simple or viable matter to move elsewhere however financially attractive.

One positive move of recent years has been for the local leisure and amenity service, responsible for the art galleries, museums, parks and other special facilities of an area, to become involved in the provision of study bases for school groups. They have provided the physical site and the education committee have put in the staff. This has applied to museums, botanical gardens, nature centres, parks and art galleries. Each area has its local examples.

Despite the breadth and the variety of provision of local centres it is unlikely that individual pupils at the end of their school careers will have attended such centres for anything more than one or two days. This is an area of environmental education where much more resourcing and structured planning is required. The splendid experiences gained by children at local centres cannot be measured in economic terms alone.

Field Studies Council

The Field Studies Council has nine residential centres and two day centres located throughout England and Wales (figure 8.1) Even the residential centres are often available for day only visits. The resident staff are all specialists in one aspect of the environment but experienced in a whole range of outdoor activities. Courses can be taught by the centre staff or by the group's own teachers. Usually it works out to be a combination of the two. There are set courses available for all centres, as listed in the comprehensive details supplied by the centres themselves or by the Central Services at Shrewsbury. For primary groups the FSC's aim is to have them investigate the environment through discovery and observation.

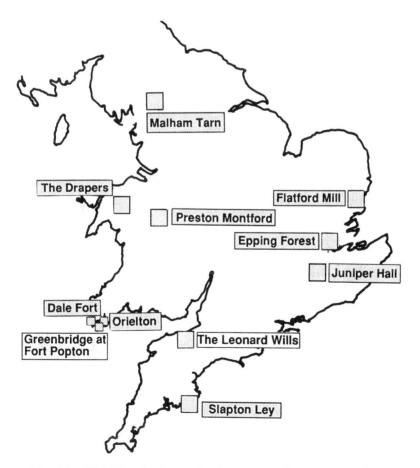

Figure 8.1 *The Field Study Council's Centres in England and Wales.*

Each centre can provide class sets of field equipment and the work-rooms and laboratories have facilities to enable experimental follow-up of investigations carried out in the field. One great advantage for school groups is that negotiated access to study sites has been obtained from landowners and the potential hazards of such sites are well known to the centre staff.

Most centres have computer facilities, usually compatible with those in the visiting school. This enables work done at the centre to be translated back into the home base. Much of the software at the centres has been developed by the FSC specifically for the range of investigations that are carried out at its centres.

Although each centre has developed particular lines of enquiry spec-ific to the area in which it is situated, for example Malham Tarn for limestone scenery or Slapton Ley for seashore study, in the case of primary school environmental study each one is able to concentrate on local study at an appropriate level. Thus most schools in England and Wales have a centre within fairly easy travelling distance. The FSC has, in fact, negotiated a special package discount rail travel service with School Rail at very competitive prices.

All this leads us to comment on cost. The use of centres out of season is reflected in the prices charged. The FSC divides its year into High and Low seasons, the high is from early March to late September with the rest of the year forming the low season. In the low season accompanying staff pay no charge at all, even for board and lodging and the charges for primary age children are reduced. Obviously it is necessary to obtain proper quotations from the centre itself.

The eleven centres are listed in Appendix C along with the address of the Central Services of the FSC.

The Field Studies Council also provides excellent facilities and courses for in-service training in environmental study activities. It is worthwhile contacting the Director of Studies of an FSC centre if there is one nearby, in order to discuss the possibilities of a special 'tailor made' course being arranged.

The case study which follows describes a project at Preston Montford Field Study Centre. This is local to schools in Shrewsbury and can be used on a day basis. Several schools have developed close links with the centre. This example is essentially a geographical investi-gation of a nearby tributary of the River Severn but, again, it encompasses many other subject areas and underlines the cross-curricular nature of environmental education. The facilities at the centre and the equipment available, coupled with the cooperation of expert advice, enabled St George's School to achieve results beyond those to be anticipated from a purely school-based enquiry. This study is an important indication of what can be achieved if resources near a school are professionally exploited.

The arguments advanced for history in our first case study are equally valid for geography. Similar reservations have been expressed by HMI and by the chairman of the Geography group of the National Curriculum Council, concerning the fact that the subject is not taught discernibly in the primary phase. As with history, it is necessary for any environmental theme or project to identify both the content and the progression where geography is concerned. This case study illustrates the way in which separate subject disciplines, including geography, need to be built into the planning and fulfilment of what is essentially a local study – but with ramifications that extend concentrically outward. The use of globe and atlas are as much an essential element of such studies as are the large scale maps and plans of the local area. This particular study, part of the ongoing theme of 'Water', placed great emphasis on scientific method and geographical understanding, including an awareness of time and place and links with the wider world.

Case Study 7   Study of a stream, using the facilities of a Field Study Centre

St George's Junior School, Shrewsbury

Starting point
Use of day visit to Field Study Centre to study a local stream, the River Perry.

Introduction
This was an environmental study designed to integrate cross-curriculum work in the core subjects of the National Curriculum, together with History, Geography, Art, Craft, RE, Music and Drama. Objectively it studies a stream as an ecosystem in itself, whilst looking at the wider aspects of water in the environment and fostering care and responsibility towards it.

Age range 9–10

This study is part of an on-going investigation using the theme of 'Water'. It was carried out by a class of 35 third-year juniors (age range 9–10) in a suburban school of a moderately sized country town. It follows on from work done by the same class when second year juniors in the previous summer (figure 8.2). At that time the study

Environmental Education Project

THEME – WATER (2nd year)

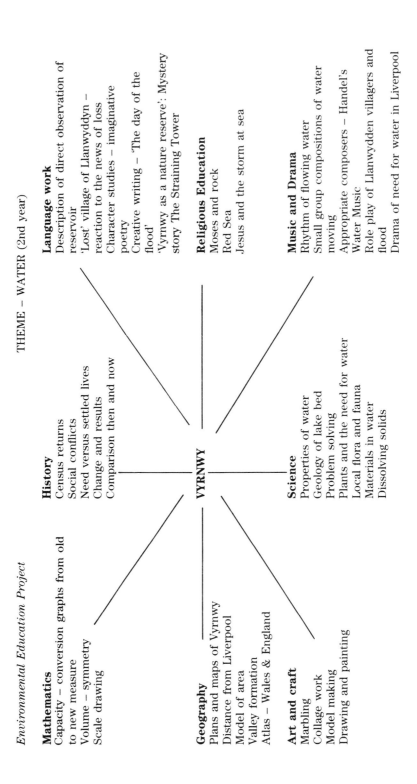

Mathematics
Capacity – conversion graphs from old to new measure
Volume – symmetry
Scale drawing

History
Census returns
Social conflicts
Need versus settled lives
Change and results
Comparison then and now

Language work
Description of direct observation of reservoir
'Lost' village of Llanwyddyn – reaction to the news of loss
Character studies – imaginative poetry
Creative writing – 'The day of the flood'
'Vyrnwy as a nature reserve': Mystery story The Straining Tower

Religious Education
Moses and rock
Red Sea
Jesus and the storm at sea

Geography
Plans and maps of Vyrnwy
Distance from Liverpool
Model of area
Valley formation
Atlas – Wales & England

Science
Properties of water
Geology of lake bed
Problem solving
Plants and the need for water
Local flora and fauna
Materials in water
Dissolving solids

Music and Drama
Rhythm of flowing water
Small group compositions of water moving
Appropriate composers – Handel's Water Music
Role play of Llanwydden villagers and flood
Drama of need for water in Liverpool

Art and craft
Marbling
Collage work
Model making
Drawing and painting

VYRNWY

Figure 8.2 *2nd year subject web on the theme of 'Water'.*

focused on a day visit to Lake Vyrnwy. The details of the study are summarised in figure 8.3. It is intended that the theme will continue into the fourth year, with a study of the River Severn (into which the Perry flows), possibly based on a visit to a local water treatment works, and to the River Severn itself which conveniently flows through a local public space where it is even possible to hire boats. Details of the possible lines of enquiry to be followed are shown in figure 8.4.

Aims

- To continue the pupil's study of the environment based on the theme of 'Water'.
- To lay the foundation for further study during the pupil's time in the final year of the junior school.
- To use the study to integrate cross-curricular work in Science, English, Mathematics, Geography, History, Art/Craft, Religious Education, Music and Drama.
- To evaluate the ways in which the proposed Attainment Targets of the subjects of the National Curriculum for Key Stage 2 can be achieved in a cross-curriculum environmental study.

Objectives

1 To introduce a stream as a special and diverse ecosystem.
2 To familiarise the children with techniques of stream mapping, sampling and collecting.
3 To identify and classify plants and creatures adapted to life in freshwater.
4 To foster care for the environment, a social responsibility towards conservation and the value of freshwater life.
5 To recognise and experiment with some of the properties of water.

Preparation and planning
The choice of an environmental study at a field study centre was based on the wish to:

- give pupils the experience of a specialist base which contained professional resources with expert staff;
- use a fieldwork location which was well known to the centre staff as being accessible, safe and suitable for the project;
- have extra professional supervisory staff available for the field work;
- have extra minibus transport available with accredited drivers.

Environmental Education Project

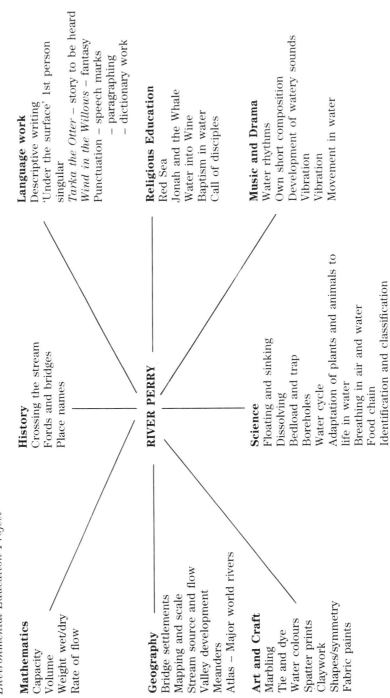

Mathematics
Capacity
Volume
Weight wet/dry
Rate of flow

History
Crossing the stream
Fords and bridges
Place names

Language work
Descriptive writing
'Under the surface' 1st person
singular
Tarka the Otter – story to be heard
Wind in the Willows – fantasy
Punctuation – speech marks
               – paragraphing
               – dictionary work

Geography
Bridge settlements
Mapping and scale
Stream source and flow
Valley development
Meanders
Atlas – Major world rivers

RIVER PERRY

Religious Education
Red Sea
Jonah and the Whale
Water into Wine
Baptism in water
Call of disciples

Art and Craft
Marbling
Tie and dye
Water colours
Spatter prints
Claywork
Shapes/symmetry
Fabric paints

Science
Floating and sinking
Dissolving
Bedload and trap
Boreholes
Water cycle
Adaptation of plants and animals to
life in water
Breathing in air and water
Food chain
Identification and classification

Music and Drama
Water rhythms
Own short composition
Development of watery sounds
Vibration
Vibration
Movement in water

Figure 8.3   *3rd year subject web on the theme of 'Water'.*

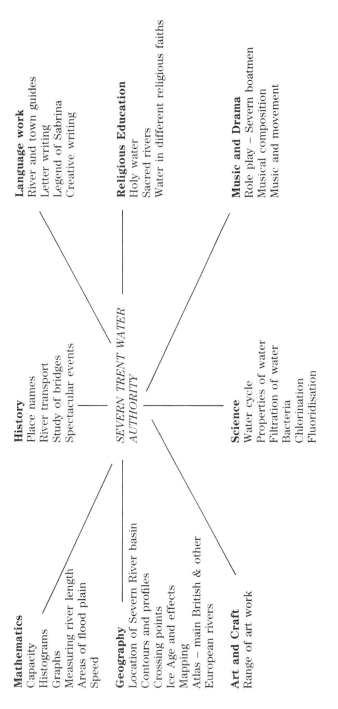

Mathematics
Capacity
Histograms
Graphs
Measuring river length
Areas of flood plain
Speed

Geography
Location of Severn River basin
Contours and profiles
Crossing points
Ice Age and effects
Mapping
Atlas – main British & other
European rivers

Art and Craft
Range of art work

History
Place names
River transport
Study of bridges
Spectacular events

Science
Water cycle
Properties of water
Filtration of water
Bacteria
Chlorination
Fluoridisation

Language work
River and town guides
Letter writing
Legend of Sabrina
Creative writing

Religious Education
Holy water
Sacred rivers
Water in different religious faiths

Music and Drama
Role play – Severn boatmen
Musical composition
Music and movement

*SEVERN TRENT WATER
AUTHORITY*

Figure 8.4   *4th year subject web on the theme of 'Water'.*

The use of the centre out of season meant that accommodation, staff and equipment were readily to hand and costs were kept to a minimum. The fact that the work had to be carried out on a day in January incurred the risk of adverse weather conditions although in the event the day was dry and relatively mild; the water, though cold, was fordable in places and low in level. Conditions for a follow-up visit in the summer were far worse with a full survey being impossible to mount.

The January date had the added advantage that postponement was possible as the centre and the transport would have been available on other days. With the follow-up visit the planned day had to be adhered to or cancelled because of summer pressures on resources.

The choice of the environmental study of a small stretch of freshwater was deliberate. It afforded the class an opportunity to learn and investigate the skills and experiences planned in the Term Web (figure 8.3) and the three Core Curriculum Subject Webs (figure 8.6). Preparation for the day's activities involved

1   The centre and the centre staff
2   The pupils
3   Preliminary visits to the field work site.

	Level	1	2	3	4	5	6	7	8	9	10	11	12	13
	3	√	√											
English	4	√	√	√										
	5		√	√										
	3												√	
Mathematics	4	√							√				√	√
	5													√
	3	√	√	√	√	√	√	√		√	√		√	√
Science	4	√	√	√	√	√	√	√		√	√		√	√
	5		√	√										

Figure 8.5 *Summary of Attainment Targets in the core subjects of the National Curriculum, addressed at the levels indicated in the River Perry project.*

1 The centre and the centre staff

Arrangements to use the centre and its staff were made by telephone. A good relationship had built up between the centre and the school over the years. In particular the Field Centre Warden was amenable to working with local schools. For the study itself, initial preparation involved a full afternoon visit to the centre and onto the site by the class teacher, and a final year student on teaching practice. They met the Warden and another staff member.

The topic was discussed and the idea to use the chosen site for the objectives of the study were explored. At the site practical matters were discussed with special emphasis placed on safety and welfare. Various possibilities for work connected with Science, Mathematics and Language were assessed and agreed. The use of centre facilities, particularly the use of a laboratory and equipment for stream investigation and classification study were negotiated. Detailed arrangements for transport were agreed.

2 The pupils

In the lead-up time to the field visit, class discussions took place on river and pond life, on the river system itself, slow and fast water, and the preparation of identification sheets for plants and creatures likely to be seen or caught. For the fauna, clues for identification were decided, such as:

- What shape is it?
- How many legs?
- How many body sections does it have?
- What all over colour is it?
- Was it caught in slow/fast moving water?

Similar questions were raised for the plants and the sort of river characteristics to be observed and the measurements to be taken were established. Considerable time was given to organisational details, particularly to safe behaviour; this enabled discussion to focus on water safety conduct generally.

3 Preliminary visits to the field work site

In addition to the site visit with the centre staff, the class teacher returned to the site on other occasions and in particular the evening before the visit. The area was checked for any change to the water level or hindrance of any kind that would make it dangerous or impossible for the children to work where it had been planned. The positive relationship between the centre and the local farmer ensured

Figure 8.6 *Someone has to get wet to ford the river.*

that the access field would be free of livestock or dangerous machinery. In the event, as has been said, the day was as perfect as it could be for a January day but at the summer follow-up excessive rain in the uplands had resulted in the usually friendly stream becoming a dangerous torrent.

School procedures and Local Authority regulations were all observed in preparation for the visit.

The field work visit
The day was divided into two sections:

1 Work on the River Perry at the site.
2 Observation and the start of classification in the laboratory.

1 The River Perry
The river is a tributary of the Upper Severn and the section studied is close to the village of Fitz near Montford Bridge, Shropshire. 100 square metres was measured, 10 metres along the bank and 10 across the river over to the other bank. The river was recognised to have flats and riffles. The water was deep and had a slow flow in the flats. Someone had to get quite wet to ford the river at this point (figure 8.6). Every metre across was marked with a stick and, with the use of nets, a catch was made at each point. Plant life was observed and noted. The invertebrates and vertebrate creatures were placed in

sample trays. A similar technique was used downstream in the riffles. This section consisted of a faster flow of water with a shallow rocky bed. The children could wade quite easily in this area and use nets as well as hands to upturn rocks. The catch, equipment, children and staff all returned to the field centre. Audio records and photographs were taken of the work on site. It was not possible to make a video film although this might have been desirable.

2 At the Field Centre

In the laboratory the children worked with naked eye, hand lenses and microscopes in order to identify and classify their trophies. It soon became evident that some water creatures inhabited only the deep or the shallow water and had a lifestyle to match, others were capable of life in both, so the development of sets was possible as an obvious mathematical aid to selection.

There was time for the children to sketch *in situ* and the previously planned identification sheets were invaluable as the children were able to help themselves until staff could aid their observations and identification.

Pupils were also expected to return the equipment to its allotted storage in as good a condition as when loaned. Arrangements were made for the catch to be returned to its place of capture. It was also possible for the children to be shown the centre's permanent station for water flow and sediment load at the minor streams on site (figure 8.7) and to record their observations.

Figure 8.7 *Measuring a minor stream.*

John
Hutchinson

Measuring The Depth Of The Stream.

In order to measure the depth of the stream we began by measuring 10 metres along the bank of the stream. Mr Bailey then attached measuring-tapes to sticks at the 0 metre mark, the 6 metre mark and the 10 metre mark. With the first tape-measure he waded into the water and attached it to a stick at the opposite side. He then did the same with the other two tape-measures. All these tape-measures were marked off in metres.

Using a long stick marked off in centimetres Paul Minton measured how deep the water was at every metre along the first measuring-tape. Melanie Lee measured how deep the water was at every metre along the second measuring-tape and Matthew S measured how deep the water was at every metre along the third measuring tape.

1. There are no readings the same in '2'.
2. At 10 centimetres deep there are two the same and at 20 centimetres deep there are two the same.
3. The pattern was down and then up and then down.

Figure 8.8 *Pupil's description of investigative field work.*

Follow up work

The immediate task of creating a record in a permanent fashion by spoken and written word and picture was undertaken in a systematic way with the production of a work folder by each child (figures 8.8,

I am a minnow. I have an
enemy he is the pike. He
gets the minnows and I
hide under a rock. He
cannot get me. He cannot
get in the gap. When it is
safe I come out and
sometimes people do net
dipping and one caught me
and I pretended that I was
dead. They put me in the
River Perry. I swam the
opposite way and they
went. The pike was caught
he could find nowhere to
hide. I lived for a another
adventure.

Nathan

Figure 8.9a *Imaginative writing by a pupil, using a word processor.*

8.9, 8.10). Beyond this initial task the rest of the term's work was
based on the stimulation provided by the fieldwork. Many of the
topics undertaken are listed on the theme web (see figure 8.4). To
describe the full range of work undertaken would involve a book in
itself; it is possible here to give a detailed example of only one piece
of follow-up work. In music the class composed a rondo utilising a
theme tune to link individual contributions. Enjoyment of the tale of
The Wind in the Willows led to The Water Rat's Day being taken as
the subject. The class not only listened to the tale read to them by
their teacher but had been able to see a performance of the play by
Theatre Clwyd. The individual parts were based on

Rat waking
Rat swimming across the Perry
Rat running through the harvest field
Rat visiting town
Rat sleeping

Access to the school's musical instruments was limited to one hour
a week but it was possible to carry some of them to the (open plan) class
area, with the inevitable disturbance of others. Much interest was

Figure 8.9b *A three-dimensional collage picture created to illustrate imaginative writing.*

shown in the creation of 'watery sounds' of a vibratory nature with the use of a whole variety of official and unofficial instruments. A tape of the finished product was available for open evening.

Presentation of the term's work
Individual folders were produced and pupils participated in class and group discussions. Work accomplished was the basis for a classroom

Robbie Blackledge

It was Winter
In the River Perry
A watery sun in the sky
Like a pale moon
I dart about the stones
Skulling like a boat
Then something happens ....
Its a heron
I see my freinds being gobbled up!
First it's a dragon-fly the a Mayfly
Then a whole mouthgull of fish
It's dreadful!
I swim under the stones
To get away from the horrible menace
It pokes it's great beak to feel around for
me
He finds me and picks me up
I struggle feroicously
Then he swallows me
I feel myself going down
Into .... DOOM!

Figure 8.10 *Empathic poem of 'watery ideas'.*

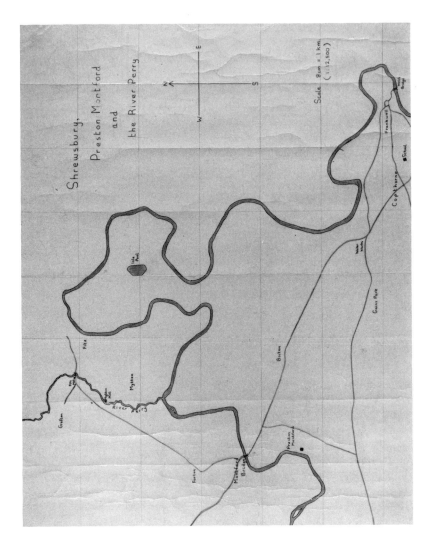

Figure 8.11 *Map of the Severn and Perry (group work).*

wall display which grew to fill the space available before term end. As part of the overall school policy some of the work appeared in corridor displays throughout the term (figures 8.11 and 8.12).

The music was heard on open evening and limited drama presentations were made to other classes. Some of the display material was made available for use at the Field Centre.

Any visitor to the class area could not help but be impressed with the extent, variety and high quality of the work emanating from the environment.

Evaluation (in the words of the teacher involved)

> This is a good theme for Environmental work and a great number of skills can be learned and absorbed. Choose a sensible stretch of water and let the children *safely wade* and explore. Do not direct their 'finding out' too vigorously. Much discovery is made there and then – if possible make tapes of oral conversations on the spot – all this helps recall. Photographs are essential and we took a vast number. Tangible objects to have and to hold always afford excitement and interest in children and this study carried us easily through a term.
>
> It is pleasing that many of the National Curriculum skills can be applied in the core subjects to this particular vehicle of Direct Experience and the webs show how we incorporated quite a few of them.
>
> From the study we certainly began to appreciate fresh water and our mapping aspects took us into the formation of tributaries and where they enter a river. We thought of pollution problems and our responsibilities to prevent these. In fact one small area of fresh water taught us all about another world of life and its inter-relationships and diversities.
>
> Possibly we became over-absorbed and like Rupert Brooke we echoed the wishes of all fish,
> 'And in the heaven of their wish
> There shall be no more land, say fish'.

Summary
The starting point for this piece of environmental work was the close proximity of a field centre with a co-operative warden. The school was willing to use it out of season and by so doing gained all of the benefits in short supply in the more amenable times of the year. The topic chosen tied in both with the needs of the school and the skills of the centre. Few schools are far from some type of environmental study centre, be it one of those supported by the Local Authority or one privately run. What is necessary is the commitment of the school to be flexible about timings and to be prepared to spend time and

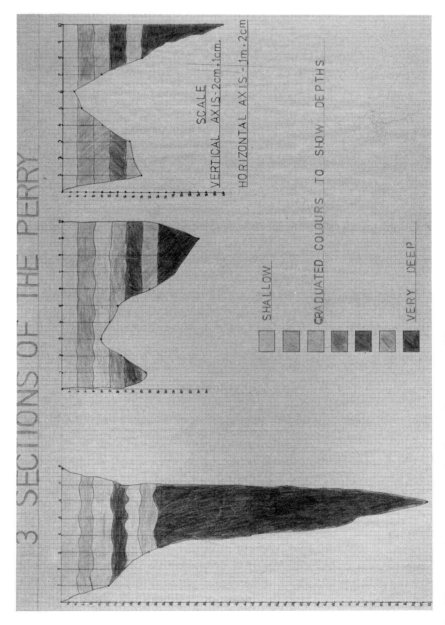

Figure 8.12 *Three sections across the Perry (group work).*

effort in building up a favourable relationship. This project exemplifies all of these in a splendid way.

Urban Study Centres

Environmental study centres aimed almost exclusively at urban studies exist in several areas. Many of those so designated do not provide day centre facilities but act only as a resource base for teachers and provide in-service training. A certain number do enable school parties to visit them and to utilise the centre neighbourhood for field study. For schools based in an urban area it is useful to capitalise on the expertise of these centres and then to translate this into studies of the school neighbourhood.

The journal *Streetwise*, published by the National Association for Urban Studies, keeps teachers up-to-date with these developments. A list of Urban Study Centres is published in Appendix D.

Youth Hostels Association

The Youth Hostels Association is no longer an organisation solely providing inexpensive holiday board and lodging. Although this is still the mainstay of its existence many of its hostels have provision for both day and residential environmental study visits. The new YHA International Centre, in a converted port warehouse overlooking the City Docks in Bristol, points the way. Its many facilities provide for urban studies in particular and it is equipped for both day and residential groups. The Scottish YHA and the YHA of Northern Ireland administer their own centres. Details of these and other centre facilities are listed in Appendix E.

Other national organisations

Several national organisations provide environmental study facilities which often go beyond their own 'vested' interest. The Royal Society for the Prevention of Cruelty to Animals (RSPCA) for example, has a splendid study centre near Hastings called the Mallydams Centre. It is the local base for the RSPCA and to it are brought creatures in physical distress. For schools, however, it is the wooded habitat and the well-equipped laboratories and classroom which, together with the education staff, provide the attraction.

The Royal Society for the Protection of Birds (RSPB) has Nature Centres and Countryside Classrooms at selected reserves where teaching facilities are available for visiting school parties. These educational centres, listed in Appendix F, provide the opportunity for teachers and children to gain first-hand experience of birds and other wildlife in the field. The teaching emphasises the ecology of the habitats on the reserve and such aspects as food chains and adaptations of plants and animals. Incidentally, these centres are open to the general public at weekends so could be used by young people's groups other than schools. On occasion the RSPB run temporary visiting schemes at times of peak interest at certain reserves and other wildlife areas. Involvement in teacher training is another related aspect of the educational provision of the RSPB.

City Farms are increasing in number and in educational value. Locational details may be obtained from the National Federation of City Farms (see Useful Addresses). Established working farms increasingly have educational facilities particularly under the 'Set Aside' schemes now in operation. The National Farmers' Union or the Association of Agriculture can supply details of these. The list of national organisations that provide study facilities is not endless but it is too long to continue to give examples. The list of useful addresses at the end of this book will remind readers of possible providers.

Many national institutions are based on a single special location. For example, the Slimbridge Wildfowl Trust near Gloucester has its own education officer and facilities for school groups. Not far away from there, the Cotswold Farm Park concentrates on rare breed survival again employing an education officer with classroom facilities. The Chatterley Mining Museum, near Stoke on Trent, may be thought of as a study centre rather than a museum in the accepted use of the word. It has excellent study facilities, and education staff and a whole range of practical experiences to impart to the young visitor. To mention these examples and not to mention the Domestic Fowl Trust near Evesham, the Acton Scott Farm near Craven Arms, the Centre for Alternative Technology set in a former slate quarry near Machynlleth in mid Wales and a host of other splendid opportunities for environmental study centre work, is to be selective on the grounds of a limitation on space and for no other reason. Several publications from the Tourist Boards list these centres and they advertise regularly in the professional educational journals. How fortunate we are in the UK to have such a wide choice.

Heritage properties

The very useful annual publication *Historic Houses, Castles and Gardens*, and its sister volume *Museums and Galleries*[2] provide a valuable mine of information on heritage properties, usually associated with history as a subject, but of equal importance to those pursuing broader environmental education. Names, addresses, opening times and what is on offer are shown as well as information as to educational facilities available. It is quite common now for such properties to pay as much educational attention to the surrounding estate, with its woodlands, wild areas, fields and farms, as is given to the house and its artefacts. Many of these properties are in the care of the National Trust but the majority are still in private ownership.

Private properties

Environmental study facilities exist at an increasing number of private castles, mansions and smaller houses. The largest have education staff and various other aids to study. For example Blenheim Palace, visited by thousands of children every year, has a classroom in the stable block and its own education staff. Canterbury Cathedral and York Minster are among the ecclesiastical buildings which have a full range of study centre facilities.

For no reason other than that it is well known to the writers, let Harewood House near Leeds be used to give greater detail of a typical heritage study centre. School groups have access to an audio-visual projection room with taped presentations, to several 'hands on' display rooms, to a workshop and to the large classroom. Apart from the house itself, there is a rainforest display, a bird garden, and access to the rest of the estate. An education officer and staff are to hand to provide a direct input or to supplement the teacher contribution. A whole range of option activities are available, as is teacher resource material. As with any study centre a prior on-site investigation by the teacher is essential. This is always a free visit by arrangement. Special role play events can be organised and Harewood, as with most others, is keen to co-operate with the school for, say, Christmas celebrations.

The National Trust (and the National Trust for Scotland)

Properties owned by the National Trust have the advantage of regional and national education advisers and many estates and gardens have a resident education staff. Certainly those with study centre facilities have education specialists on site. Each region of the National Trust publishes a list of its properties where study facilities are available. For example, the Yorkshire Region produces a *Welcome Schools* leaflet which lists the educational facilities at 14 sites. Four of them have an indoor study base. Ravenscar, overlooking Robin Hood's Bay near Scarborough, is unique in that a whole range of activities have been designed for school visitors, although there is no physical study centre. Based on the fact that Ravenscar is a 'Town that Never Was' the opportunities for environmental study are enormous, unique and wonderfully exciting for the young visitor. For most NT properties advanced booking is essential, preliminary visits by the teacher are highly desirable and group size and the ratio of adults to children is plainly stipulated.

In South Wales an interesting educational development has taken place at Stackpole where the NT has established a residential study centre on a 1000 hectare estate. It contains a vast range of habitats from ponds and dunes to woods and cliffs.

Schools able to make use of NT properties on a regular basis are advised to look into the advantages, not least of which is financial, of taking out Corporate Membership of the NT. This can be done, to the great advantage of individual schools, on a local education authority basis.

English Heritage

English Heritage now looks after the 350+ properties originally in the care of the Department of the Environment. From Dover Castle to Hadrian's Wall there are many study centre provisions for school parties.

In Wales a similar role to English Heritage is carried out by CADW, whilst in Scotland it is the Historic Buildings and Monuments section of the Scottish Development Department. In Northern Ireland the Department of the Environment for Northern Ireland should be contacted. Appendix G gives more details.

The Electricity Generating Boards

Whatever else a power station may provide in negative environmental terms there is no doubt that it can make a positive contribution to environmental education, not least in terms of releasing part of the site as an environmental study centre. Many such have been established. In Warwickshire the Hams Hall Environmental Studies Centre has been created on the site of the power station of that name. This is a splendid site beside the River Tame with extensive classroom and field facilities for countryside studies. At Rugeley Power Station in Staffordshire another excellent environmental study centre has been set up. It too is local to stretches of water and provides a whole range of nature studies for the schools of that county. It has adequate indoor rooms for preparatory and follow-up work, to augment that carried out in the local area.

Power Stations with environmental study centres are listed in Appendix H.

The National Parks in England and Wales

The eleven national parks of England and Wales stretch from Northumberland in the north to Dartmoor in the south. There are day visit centres, residential centres, study bases, lecture rooms and information centres although not every park has the full range. Most of the parks produce an education leaflet outlining their general services and their service for schools in particular. The residential centres at Losehill Hall in the Peak District near Sheffield and that at Plas Tan y Bwlch in Snowdonia near Blaenau Ffestiniog, are worth a particular mention. Again, for the more general purpose of primary environmental education any one of the areas will provide opportunities for outdoor study. Appendix I lists the facilities and addresses of each park.

Individual schools

It is not uncommon for individual schools or groups of schools to own or lease premises which are used for environmental education purposes amongst other things. It is not the case that such initiatives are only associated with schools in areas of economic affluence. More usually it reflects the attitude of staff and parents to the obvious advantages of having access to a centre all year round.

It is unusual for primary schools to be in the fortunate position of having their own centre, but it is quite common for the catchment primary schools to have some access to the centre owned by the secondary school which they 'feed'. Indeed, with some, the links formed in this way are an important part of primary/secondary school liaison.

It is also true that many schools, primary included, have their own minibus. This also enables a freedom of activity to take place without the restrictions of LEA involvement.

Inevitably the ownership of centre, or of transport, places a great responsibility upon the school with regard to matters of safety, legal requirements and insurance. There are many myths concerning such matters which can inhibit individual initiatives. It is possible to be independent, but it does require cool consideration, advice from experts and money-raising skills. Determination helps as well!

Private individuals or companies

Advertisements in any of the educational journals and the incoming school mail will reveal that there are many private initiatives in the provision of study centres. Many of them are excellent, usually an attempt to utilise spare accommodation at times in the year away from the popular holiday months. Such can be used with confidence but only after prior inspection and, where possible, consultation with an officer of the LEA in whose area the centre is located. The national reputation of some of the companies involved in these centres is a general proof of 'respectability' but not always a proof of competence in the educational field. It must be repeated – prior inspection is essential. There are, however, many excellent examples of individual initiatives, for example, making a local farm available for school parties to visit. In this particular instance such bodies as the Association of Agriculture can often give advice. Successful use of this type of centre usually comes from experience built up over a number of years.

More formally there are several school travel companies who are involved in environmental study and have a list of centres on their books. Reputable companies will not be afraid to pass on the names of schools who have used their services in the past. It is then possible to base a decision on the use of the company on the experience of colleagues in the profession.

Zoos

Zoos, nature centres, aquaria, bird gardens, and other places where wild creatures are kept in captivity may not be considered as ideal sites for environmental study. A decision to use them or not is the prerogative of the school involved. What must be said is that many zoos have excellent day visit facilities, not least of which is London Zoo. Many zoos have education staff who offer special option programmes rather than the previous general 'wander and look' excursion of school groups. Twycross, Chester, Dudley, Windsor Safari Park and others have good facilities and varied programmes of study for the day visitor.

Private arrangements

Many schools make individual arrangements with private institutions, in particular with farms. The fact that one school has a site all to itself is not without great appeal and such field study can work very well. Most often this type of visit is non-commercial and relies on goodwill on both sides. But there are hazards to be avoided; do ensure that the LEA accepts such a visit as within its regulations which insure teachers against third party claims. Make sure, too, that the 'host' is well aware of the inquisitive nature of young children and that any items or places of potential danger are secured against their attentions. Thorough briefing on both sides is essential. Nevertheless an ongoing association between a school and a private venue can be most rewarding and flexible from an organisational viewpoint.

9 Help, advice and resources

It has already been emphasised that resource material for environmental education is abundant, for the greatest resource of all is our own neighbourhood. The assessment and exploitation of its potential has been discussed in relation to the task of the school co-ordinator for environmental education. It is, perhaps, valuable to remind readers of the help and resource material to be gathered from an LEA's advisory team for environmental education and/or primary schools who will know of many of the opportunities for help in the local area. The museum and library services are more and more geared to support environmental projects and many have a strong local studies section. Reproductions of archive material are a particularly useful adjunct to the more common learning aids.

An increasing number of local authorities are providing information technology links between the centre and schools, between schools, and between schools and local commercial and industrial companies. The final case study details an individual project which was part of a cross-county venture which followed on from an INSET course on computer links, in particular the use of the Modem and the Times Network Systems.

The study is a splendid example of how a school has made meaningful links with industry in the local area. In National Curriculum terms, both environmental education and education for economic and industrial understanding are cross-curricular themes. Integration of the two is obviously desirable and worthwhile in terms of promoting permeation of cross-curricular matters with core and foundation subjects. A survey (*Evaluation of Primary School/Industry Links 1986–89*,[1] funded by the Department of Trade and Industry) suggests that the number of primary schools which have established links with local companies has doubled in the three-year period of the survey. Some 60 percent of authorities have a policy for primary education and industry and a similar percentage have developed mini-enterprise schemes. Certainly firms are demonstrating an increased enthusiasm for working with primary schools – reflected in an increased number of visits to companies by schools, and the promotion of consultancy roles in which industrialists provide staff who may advise on the establishment of mini-enterprises or help with opportunities for both school pupils and staff to gain first-hand experiences of industry. Also, a number of LEAs have taken sound initiatives to involve local industry in the development of curriculum materials for primary schools.

Case Study 8 Producing a school newspaper

Introduction
This study was an industrial awareness project based on using the Modem Computer Link to produce an edition of the *Hope Post*.

By setting up an editorial board, by using a computer link with the local *Shropshire Star* newspaper and by study visits to appropriate newspaper offices and printing works the project aimed to make pupils (age range 10–11) aware of the complexity of newspaper production and by so doing introduce them to our industrial society. Objectively the study was geared to several of the attainment targets of the core subjects of the National Curriculum and to general curriculum objectives in Art, Music and Drama. The enhancement of personal relationships and working as a team contributed towards the pupils' Personal and Social development.

Starting point
Link with local industry

A local newspaper is a rich source of information on community events. In a rural area it plays a vital communication and co-ordination role. It reflects the views and news of the neighbourhood and, as such, impinges as much on the local school as anywhere else. With the introduction of a computer link between schools compatible with that used by the local newspaper, pupils in one LEA were able to have direct access to news and press agencies. This enabled them to publish a local newspaper based on real resources.

The study
Aim to produce a newspaper for distribution to parents and friends of the school on a stipulated date.

Objectives
For the school:

- to promote the use of language through the written, spoken and heard word;
- to secure links with local industry.

For the children:

- to be aware of the skill and effort which goes into the production of a newspaper;
- to participate in decision making;
- to understand and practise prioritisation;
- to practise design skills;
- to evaluate the importance of international, national and local events to the local community;
- to assess the careers potential of newspaper work;
- to participate in business management;
- to practise financial management.

Preparation and planning

It was necessary for the pupil participants to become competent in the use of

- a computer and the Times Network System;
- a photocopier and other reprographic equipment;
- a polaroid camera;
- the photograph library of the local newspaper;
- Teletex;
- a word processor.

Representatives of the local paper visited the school and use was made of a video programme on newspaper production. The pupils visited the newspaper offices and printing works. They practised creative writing based on information gathered from witnesses and interviewees. Techniques for the composition of headlines from a news report were investigated.

Project details

An editorial board of six pupils was selected, with the rest of the class designated as researchers, reporters and administrators. Ideas for local articles were submitted and those considered to be of merit were further researched. Other aspects of the project are indicated in the planning diagram (figure 9.1).

It was possible to produce several of the pages of the paper before the publication date. This involved the composition of feature articles, research into the TV and radio programmes for publication day, the production of a sports page and the collection and setting of advertisements.

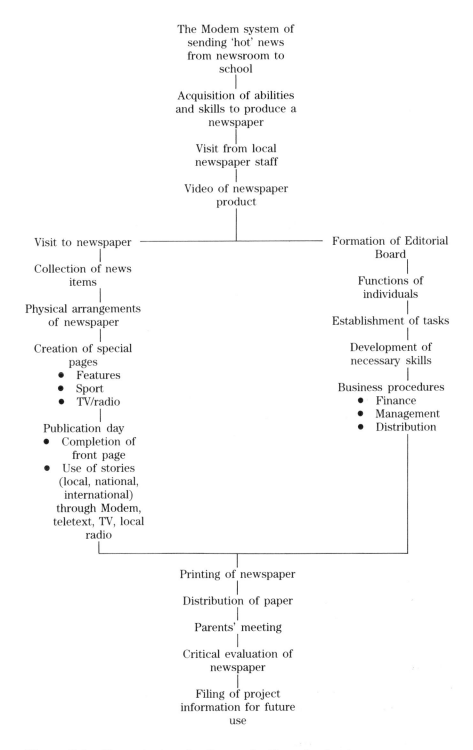

Figure 9.1   *Network plan for the production of a local newspaper.*

The editorial board planned the day-to-day activities and made the necessary arrangements for interviews and visits. A strict budget control was placed on the expenditure of individuals.

Page layouts had to be planned and proofs set up and copied for critical comment from the whole class. The final selection of front page and other current material was made as late as possible before publication day. Inevitably, as in the real world, last-minute problems had to be resolved in order to meet the deadline date.

Presentation of the project

The culmination of this environmental study was the publication itself (figure 9.2). It was duly presented to the meeting of parents and distributed locally at a cover price of 10p. It became an item of news itself in the real local paper (figure 9.3).

Follow up

The study could be completed only by drawing up a financial statement and by an evaluation of the quality of the publication. Consideration was given to improvements which could have been made in project procedures.

Curriculum aspects

The production of the newspaper was seen as an example of a cross-curricular approach to environmental education. Nevertheless it was necessary to list the objectives and outline content for the National Curriculum.

Mathematics
Objectives

1   To develop awareness of the importance of size/area
2   To give practice in working out costs
3   To discuss the practice of capital, the necessity for profit and covering ones financial outlay
4   To give practice in sorting and setting
5   To organise and display data
6   To use measurement

Content

1   Measuring size of pages in centimetres. Division of papers between set columns – how many words – length/width. Area taken up by photographs/advertisements. Symmetry
2   Advertisements – how many, cost; receipts for customers, comparison of prices to size – number of words

HOPE POST

March 3 1989   Hope Edition   10p

RUSHDIE HIDING IN SWITZERLAND

Salman Rushdie, author of The Satanic Verses, is believed to be in hiding in Switzerland, a Zurich weekly said today. The weekly Zuri-Woche said information that the author has fled to Switzerland had leaked out from literary circles close to Rushdie.

A RATS TALE

TOKYO, Friday — Two fugitive rats have given themselves up after grounding a Japan Airlines 747 for 30 hours by hiding in the cargo hold, a JAL spokesman said today. The pair were among 25 laboratory rats imported from New York who ran away after their cage broke open aboard the jumbo jet shortly after it arrived at Tokyo's Narita airport on Wednesday night. Frantic searches by airline officials failed to uncover the rodent hideout, but eventually they came out by themselves. The plane was scheduled to return to New York immediately, but had to be grounded until the two were found, causing a six-hour delay for more than 300 passengers.

THE NEEDLE NUISANCE.

A motorcycle courier was responsible for the M6 chaos when thousands of hypodermic needles were strewn across the motorway near Walsall, police revealed today.

More than 100 motorists were stranded with punctures, and the M6 was littered with breakdowns from Walsall through Staffordshire and into Cheshire.

Police are still trying to trace the rider. Drivers were stranded on the hard shoulders for hours as they waited for rescue services to reach them, and the full cost of the damage is estimated at around £10,000.

The only people who did not mind the mayhem were the tyre companies who had a real blow-out bonanza yesterday afternoon.

Mr. Chris Tenn, Corr. manager of Kwik-Fit in Stafford Street, Walsall, said motorists were hopping mad, but they were happy to handle nearly thirty punctures.

At Tyreways in Littleton Street West, Walsall, where business doubled, manager Mr. Tony Rees said: "The tyres were just like porcupines. They were covered in needles".

At Motorway Tyres in Wednesbury Road, Walsall, Mr. Euan Edwardson said business was also booming:"You would have thought we had all got together and planned it," he said.

West Midlands police said at least 66 motorists had reported punctures to them, and in Staffordshire another 50 cases were reported after the incident.

LOCAL CHILDREN PRODUCE PAPER.

Seven school across Shropshire were today (Friday) busy producing their own newspaper with the help of the Shropshire Star.

Idsall and Phoenix secondary schools, Brookside and Stirchley middle schools, Hope and Crovedale primary schools and Wombridge County Infants were all taking part in the project.

Stories will be sent to the schools from the Shropshire Star via the Times Network System in London and it will be up to the schools to choose which to use in their paper.

Some schools have been preparing for the project by writing features and some have even persuaded local businesses to advertise.

The project has been arranged jointly by Mr. John Ravenscroft from Shropshire County Council's education department and the Shropshire Star.

Mr. Ravenscroft said: "It is very real to the children. They are making the decisions and it will be their newspaper at the end of the day."

"The children become so absorbed with producing the paper that they use the computer as a tool."

Reported Accident

A pedestrian was treated for shock after being involved in a collision with a securicor van in Shrewsbury. Mrs. Pat Burke of Pulrose Walk, Shrewsbury was taken by ambulance to the Royal Shrewsbury, but not detained. The accident happened yesterday afternoon in Castle Street.

Securicor van driver, Mr. Albert Cottey, of Solway Drive, Sutton Heights, Telford, was unhurt.

Figure 9.2 *The 'local paper' that was finally produced.*

Figure 9.3   *The 'real' local newspaper reported the pupils' work, and photographed them interviewing the village postmistress.*

3   Building a collection of shapes through number of words, pages and sentences
4   Timing run of an edition – 24 hour clock. Cut-off time
5   Computation. Frequency of words. Number bonds. Football leagues. Crosswords, black and white squares. Percentages – advertisements to text. Fractions – size of content.

Language
Objectives

1   To develop writing and interviewing skills
2   To develop the techniques of collaborative talk, writing and selection
3   To introduce the concept of sequential reporting
4   To practise listening to other people and the use of recall
5   To develop word-processing skills
6   To write for a particular audience
7   To create opportunities for individual and collective creative writing

Content

1   Recording written and taped experiences
2   Establishing a pattern of writing for journalistic purposes – dramatic vocabulary, short sentences, notemaking
3   Hearing and reforming interviews
4   Discussion, making and taking decisions

Reading
Objectives

1   To read everyday experiences critically
2   To introduce scanning as a technique
3   To use reference material
4   To emphasise the relevance of rechecking

Content

1   Collection of words and use of captions
2   Critical reading of articles written by themselves
3   Recognising and commenting on the quality of the content and layout of real newspaper items

Art, Design and Technology
Objectives

1   To continue to develop observational and creative skills
2   To introduce new techniques in the use of colour and shape
3   To work collaboratively

Content

1   Using lines to create shapes
2   Pattern and colour tones
3   Screen printing

Music and Drama
Objectives

1   To build on skills in percussion work
2   To create opportunities for role play
3   To express feelings through movement

Content

1   Interviewing; role play; narration; dramatic presentation
2   Interpreting the sound of the presses in the print room
3   Interpreting the movement of the paper through its processes of unrolling, lying flat and coming together in a pile

Summary
This environmental study was directed towards a specific target, that of the production of a newspaper. It involved many skills and concepts which had a wider environmental application and which could be developed in other situations. Those of primary importance include:

- teamwork
- industry/school links
- contact and communication with the outside world
- interview techniques
- diary commitment
- reprographic techniques
- use of computer and word processor
- photography
- deadlines
- information selection and précis
- prioritisation
- budget control
- design
- critical analysis – both given and received
- parental involvement
- interpretation of environmental problems and issues
- job satisfaction

Conclusion

This programme of study proved to be an excellent example of the cross-curricular nature of environmental education in the primary school with its essential elements of preparation, planning and continuity. The achievement of good personal relationships and teamwork contributed to the pupils' personal and social development.

National and international sources

Having emphasised the use to be made of neighbourhood assistance the rest of this section will attempt to direct attention to the help available from national and international sources, whose addresses are to be found in the *Useful address* section (page 220). Inevitably there is no room here to include every organisation, because of space and clearly, others must exist of which the authors have no knowledge. Generally information on the vast amount of valuable help and resource material available from manufacturing and other businesses has been omitted.

The Council for Environmental Education

The leading source of environmental education information is the Council for Environmental Education based at Reading University. Most LEAs subscribe to CEE and, as a result, their monthly newsletter should reach every staffroom. If this does not happen check that a subscription is paid by your LEA. It is worth pressing for your LEA to take out a subscription for the newsletter contents are invaluable as a source of information on courses, publications and happenings in the environmental education world. The Council has a computerised resource centre and a wide collection of publications, many available for loan. It publishes several booklets and a series of helpful, inexpensive resource leaflets. Although personal visits are welcomed their location limits such an opportunity for most teachers. If the information officer is unable to give a direct answer to a query there will be a response which suggests where further assistance may be obtained, especially if one of the 60 plus organisations affiliated to the CEE are involved. Important as the information service is, perhaps the work which CEE does to improve the status of environmental education is of most help to teachers. For example, the Council has taken a major role in presenting the views of its membership on the cross-curriculum role of environmental education in the national curriculum. It has lobbied the government on its policy for the charging of out-of-school visits, a particular bone of contention with teachers active in out-of-the-classroom work. Through its Schools and Colleges Committee the CEE keeps before it the views of individual schools and teachers. It welcomes expressions of opinion or concern. This is of particular help where a local problem may pressage its spread to other areas.

The National Association for Environmental Education

The National Association for Environmental Education is a founder member of the CEE and has provided its main teacher input. The association is made up of individual and institutional members (schools, colleges, libraries) and of groups of environmental educationalists in local areas. Some 25 local corporate associations exist and an enquiry to the offices of the NAEE in the West Midlands will locate the nearest to you. Each local group has its own full programme of activity directed towards furthering environmental learning in its own locality. The NAEE's prime concern is to help and encourage teachers to provide environmental awareness opportunities amongst the rising generation. It, too, provides an information service with the emphasis on initial and in-service training, teaching methods and learning materials. Although it receives many enquiries its main task does not include providing information on environmental issues and problems directly.

One of the NAEE's main objectives is to act as a forum for the exchange of teaching ideas and it does this in several ways. The termly journal *Environmental Education*[2] contains articles by practising teachers and others, on examples of learning situations as well as descriptions of the broader aspects of this curriculum area. The journal contains a News and Views supplement which attempts to keep the membership up-to-date with courses, events and publications. Details of courses organised by the association are given, including those of its annual weekend event. Reviews of publications and a summary of relevant HMI reports are included. More detailed teaching help is given in the NAEE's series of practical guides,[3] as for example the *Traffic Study and Surveys* and *An Incubator in the Classroom*. Occasional papers record important topics which have been presented to meetings of the association and also the result of research carried out on its behalf.

The NAEE will help with particular problems, such as, for example, the proposed closure of a local field centre. Its national recognition enables it to make direct contact with the Department of Education and Science, the Department of the Environment and other influential bodies both in the UK and overseas. It does, in fact, have many overseas environmentalists in membership.

The Conservation Trust

Another useful source of information and resource material is the Conservation Trust. It has its base in Reading. Details of its very wide range of activities are available on request. It publishes a news bulletin and many other booklets and pamphlets useful to teachers. It has a series of leaflets which give information on environmental problems. It, too, has a computerised information service and a well-stocked resource centre open to personal callers.

The Worldwide Fund for Nature

The Worldwide Fund for Nature (until recently the World Wildlife Fund) is probably the leading national and international organisation concerned about the environmental issues and problems of the natural world. Their campaigns are well known and receive support from schools regularly. At the same time the WWF produces a whole range of learning materials and publications. Imaginative projects to interest young people in the environment are typified by the 'opera' Yanamamo, which portrays the difficulties faced by a tribe of Brazilian Indians who live in the Amazon rainforest.

The WWF operates an education service which is most helpful to enquirers. A catalogue of its publications can be obtained which includes details of appropriate classroom posters.

The Nature Conservancy Council

The Nature Conservancy Council's main role is associated with the protection of the natural environment in the UK. It has an education department which not only anwers enquiries but also produces a whole range of publications, including pamphlets describing the main environmental problems of the world, each of which contains a helpful bibliography. In addition the NCC encourages schools to create their own natural areas in the school grounds. They are prepared to give grants of money to serious schemes – many schools have benefited from such grants in the past.

The RSPB and the RSPCA

In their own particular field of environmental concern the Royal Society for the Protection of Birds and the Royal Society for the Prevention of Cruelty to Animals produce a large range of publications for schools. Details of their study centres are given elsewhere. Both have junior membership schemes to which schools can belong, membership entitles the subscriber to receive regular bulletins and printed matter. The RSPB's *Focus on Birds* is a well known poster/bulletin to be seen on many a classroom wall. Of late it has undergone some change in presentation which may limit its direct display usefulness. Both organisations provide material which is very useful as a starting point for topic work. Their representatives are more than willing to visit schools to give both talks and demonstrations. The same applies to their attendance at in-service training courses. Both these societies provide opportunities for parents to become involved in a school environmental activity.

The Royal Society for Nature Conservation

WATCH is the young people's section of the Royal Society for Nature Conservation and can provide much of great help to the teacher of environmental education. Schools which enrol as members receive the stimulating 'newspaper' *Watchword*. WATCH involves children in serious research. Acid rain, lichens, ponds, and ozone levels are but some of the investigative projects. Descriptions and directions are provided as to what needs to be done and when. Research kits are supplied which, when their usefulness for the task in hand has been completed, can be used for further study later on. WATCH has a staff of helpful education officers who also organise local and regional events appropriate to their particular interest. A number of schools can combine to make use of this service. Like the Young Ornithologists Club run by the RSPB, WATCH is an extremely good 'after school' activity which can involve the whole age range.

Groundwork Trusts

Groundwork Trusts are operative in a number of areas (reference to the local telephone directory will provide the necessary information). They work in different ways in various locations but all of them can provide useful back-up help for environmental projects. Although they might be considered as a local resource it is possible to use them beyond their immediate neighbourhood. Direct enquiry will elicit their potential as an assisting agency.

The Urban Wildlife Group

The Urban Wildlife Group is very active in promoting environmental education in urban areas; it produces several publications which contain practical guidance. Where the teacher is interested in an urban project with a natural world context it is well worth finding out what the UWG has to offer.

The National Trust

The National Trust is extending its involvement with schools beyond that of acting as 'hosts' to groups visiting historic properties. It is trying to develop the potential of the many hectares of countryside and estate grounds which it controls. Although there is a central education service headed by an education officer, you will find that the Trust's basic organisation is devolved to the regions. Again, reference to the Yellow Pages of the telephone directory or a call to the nearest National Trust property will reveal the regional office of the local area. Most regions have staff with particular responsibility for school activities and their advice will be invaluable. Considering the wide range of land type which the National Trust controls which contain farms, sheep, cattle and deer, woodlands and sea shore, the choice for a teacher is immense. The Trust now produces a regular news, information and general interest pamphlet for children. Schools can add their name to the mailing list. It is worth repeating that corporate membership of the National Trust brings many advantages to the enrolled school, and for an active 'out of the classroom' school, saves money!

The Royal Town Planning Institute

In our experience many teachers find that planning an urban project is far more daunting than organising one which is based on nature. If it is to be more than just an enquiry and observation exercise, the task is even more difficult to organise. The Royal Town Planning Institute is active in the field of environmental education, wishing to promote knowledge of planning and its procedures. The RTPI is organised regionally and some regions have environmental education groups. Nationally and regionally the RTPI, through its members, is eager to help teachers. In particular they will know of the right contact for teachers in their own locality. Some of the regions have produced guides which contain useful addresses of people and organisations able to help with urban studies. The West Midlands Region of the RTPI, for example, has produced a book for each of the counties within its area, which list an enormous quantity of helpful people and institutions. Though the addresses in such publications tend to become dated they still provide a point of contact for the busy teacher. The same region organises an annual conference for sixth form students which, though obviously beyond the remit of this volume, does indicate the lengths to which the members of the RTPI will go to aid environmental awareness amongst the young. Perhaps the concept of urban and other planning may be thought to go beyond the interest of primary school pupils. Our modern world is regulated by the rules and regulations of national and local government departments. It cannot be too early to stimulate interest in such an important aspect of citizenship, in as simple a way as is necessary.

Campaigning organisations

There are numerous UK and international campaigning organisations associated with environmental issues. Of these many produce resources (magazines, newsletters, books, pictures, charts and videos) which are informative and useful in schools. But they do come from people supportive of a particular viewpoint and cannot be clear of bias. It is essential to recognise this and to take positive steps to bring in the 'other side' of all these organisations. Greenpeace and Friends of the Earth stand out as being of major importance. Both are active campaigners, with Greenpeace being the most aggressive in its actions. They produce useful information on global problems and will respond to particular enquiries. Friends of the Earth have a UK environmental education officer. Local members of these groups will visit schools to present their points of view. At the same time 'establishment' institutions will provide resources and speakers to present the opposing viewpoint, so that the teacher can offer a balanced view of the question in hand. The Electricity Council, British Nuclear Fuels Ltd, British Coal, The Game Conservancy, the British Association for Shooting and Conservation, and the National Farmers Union are typical of these organisations. Most have educational sections.

Publishers and publications
There are some commercial publications and publishers which are worth a mention in this chapter. (Possibly there are others some may consider to be valuable sources of resource material. We can only record those which we have found to be of use.) Pictorial Charts offer a wide range of classroom posters at a reasonable cost. Some are more suitable than others for primary use but a scrutiny of the company's comprehensive catalogues will soon clarify the situation. The International Centre for Conservation Education (ICCE) produces audio/visual material. Their slide packs are useful as an aid to teaching in themselves, although most as a unit are better suited for older students; but each pack contains a wealth of individual pictures which can be used to illustrate personal presentations. Focal Point also provide a good source of coloured slides.

Some publishers contain helpful titles in their series of books on environmental matters. Batsford, Franklin Watts, Hodder and Stoughton and Wayland all have useful publications for individual interest, general reading or group work.

Without doubt the environmental education teacher is well served by the monthly publications *Child Education* (up to 7 years of age) and *Junior Education* (for the rest of the primary age range). Their Project or Topic Files, included in each issue, are valuable sources of information or teaching material. Both magazines are full of practical ideas, nearly all based on actual examples of classroom practice.

Since each announces the topics which they are to cover well in advance, it is possible for the class teacher to 'shadow' the magazine activity with one of her/his own. What has been said about the co-ordinator setting up a well-indexed resource centre in the school is worth a reminder where these two journals are concerned. For instance, projects which involve frogs, flights or forests do not date and the material of five years ago is equally valid now, provided it is known to exist, has been filed and, most importantly, returned after the last time it was used!

The organisations we have mentioned, and many others beside, are inundated with letters of request from pupils, students and teachers. How many contain a stamped addressed envelope for reply? Certainly it is less than one in ten. Few of these institutions are well endowed with money – their splendid titles often mask a struggle to make ends meet. If they are prepared to give time to answering requests it does seem a small thing to ask for reciprocal help to be given by covering the costs of a reply. If an enquiry is to be made it is essential that it is specific. 'I am preparing for a project on mining. Are you able to let me have the addresses of organisations who may be able to assist me'? can be answered – 'I am starting a project on the environment in two weeks time. Please send me all you have on it' cannot. (Incidentally these are actual examples of letters received by one organisation we have mentioned.) It is nice to give children the chance to write off for their own information, and it is good for them to learn the courtesy of the SAE enclosure. Again it is good for them to learn to be specific in their request. What does seem to the authors to be inexcusable is to have several members of the same class write to the same address, often with identical letters. No doubt the benefits of letter writing are valuable but these are real letters to real places where reaction will be (understandably) hostile. Our plea must be for the teacher to:

- ensure that the organisation is the right sort to deal with the request
- realise that the enquiry will be one of many received in the same post
- foot the postage bill. All of which will lead to a rich return for the trouble taken to enquire.

Appendices

Appendix A and Appendix B Environmental education and the national curriculum

Appendices A and B are extracts from the consultation papers produced by the Environmental Education Task Group of the Interim Whole Curriculum Committee of the National Curriculum Council which were distributed to interested individuals and groups for response. The final Task Group papers were later submitted to the IWCC, who, in turn, reported to the NCC and on to the Secretary of State for Education and Science. These final papers had not been published by the time this book was produced. Generally the final papers submitted to the IWCC reflected the statements made at the consultation stage.

Appendix A Knowledge & understanding in relation to the environment

All of the following material should be presented to pupils from the point of view of helping them to understand the issues related to the environment, and to appreciate the different viewpoints to these issues conscientiously held by different people. The areas of knowledge and understanding outlined represent those areas of environmental education which relate directly to awareness of environmental issues. It is at the same time clearly recognised that there are whole areas of education, not included here, which relate to learning *about* the environment, such as basic ecological principals or aspects of physical geography. These also should, quite properly, form part of the National Curriculum; they are recognised as important and promote knowledge of the environment which supports understanding of environmental issues. Further, there are aspects of learning *in* a direct environmental context and which relate to the development of a broad range of understanding and abilities; these too have not been included and should be part of the experience of all children within the National Curriculum. Such experiences are also an important component of environmental education since they are likely to contribute significantly to general awareness of the environment and the issues involved.

The outline of Knowledge and Understanding in relation to the environment addresses key stages 1–2 and 3–4. It is felt that it will be necessary to include, at a later stage, how the material should be divided appropriately for the separate stages i.e. 1, 2, 3 and 4.

The section related to aesthetic aspects should be interpreted in terms of the aesthetic knowledge and understanding that exists in relation to the environment. By this is meant design, poetry, music, literature etc., which already exists and which draws from the environment. The idea of children using drama, art, poetry or music etc. to explore ideas or express feelings about the environment is also recognised as important although not included in this section. The expectation will be that these will form part of the *approach* to Environmental Education across all of the areas given in the outline of essential knowledge and understanding.

The outline was developed with reference to published materials relating to core subjects in the National Curriculum, the NAEE Statement of Aims, the HMI Discussion Document of 1979, the HMI Curriculum Matters Document of 1989 and recent discussion with groups of practising teacher.

Area	Key Stages *(Key stages 3 and 4 have been omitted)*	Knowledge and Understanding
From global to local considerations	1–2	Experience orientation within the local and national environment. Learn the use of local and world maps. Understand that the world is an entity, i.e. although the world consists of many separate nations there is a close relationship between countries in terms of space, resources and the effects of their activities on each other which transcends boundaries.
Climate and factors affecting climate	1–2	Can describe and measure simple climatic factors in the local environment. Can identify the major climatic and vegetative patterns of the world. Understand the effect of climate on agriculture, both locally and in remote environments.
Soils, rocks and minerals	1–2	Know something of the soil and rock types that make up the earth. Understand that an important part of soil composition consists of living things and their role in decomposition. Know about a range of different mineral resources and where they are to be found; understand that these resources are limited e.g. oil, coal and minerals such as tin.
Water and water supplies	1–2	Know about the necessity of water for life and its importance as a natural resource. Know about the water cycle and water pollution, be aware of

		simple practical water conservation measures. Know about sewage disposal.
Fuels and energy	1–2	Investigate the range of fuels and sources of energy used in a domestic context and locally; understand where the fuels and sources of energy come from, including the role of the sun in energy production, the economy of the earth and the origin of fossil fuels. Understand about energy conservation particularly in a domestic and local context and know that many fuels are a limited resource.
Living things	1–2	Know from first-hand experience and investigation a variety of plants and animals in their local environment. Appreciate the inter-dependence among soil, atmosphere, plants and animals. Be aware of some endangered species and some measures taken for conservation. Understand the contribution of destruction to natural habitats, such as forests, to species removal. To know and experience some simple conservation measures that they can practise in their own local environment.
Human populations	1–2	Recognise variety and similarity among people and populations. Know how people live in and use different environments. Be aware of population changes and patterns in different parts of the world and the effects of this on life styles and the environment.
The built environment, industrialisation and waste	1–2	Recognise different buildings and functional areas in the locality eg residential, shopping, industrial, leisure; also the requirement for services, transportation and communication. Understand the implications of human activity, especially on communities in terms of waste production, types of waste and ways of coping with waste.
Aesthetic aspects	1–2	Consider aesthetic aspects of the environment, use written, oral, drama, visual art and music to describe and interpret different environments. To be aware of art and design factors in the made environment.
Historical aspects	1–2	To develop a historical perspective to the environment in which there is an appreciation of the way in which human activity has brought about change.

| Controls and decision making | 1–2 | Understand the importance of individual and group responsibility in relation to the environment. Experience at first hand a group activity in which responsibility for an aspect of environmental improvement or conservation is taken. Recognise different agencies working on environmental problems and the need for cooperation nationally and internationally. |

Appendix B The environmental context for the linking of skills with knowledge and understanding

KEY STAGES 1 and 2

1st order skills.

Using the knowledge and understanding which they possess, children communicate ideas at their level of understanding and at that level are able to express their ideas through the appropriate medium.

2nd order skills.

At this stage children investigate new ideas and learn to share those ideas with others. Throughout this process knowledge and understanding is increasing and being referenced back to their previous knowledge bank.

3rd order skills.

Having refined and improved their store of knowledge and understanding children will investigate approaches to problem solving. This attempt at problem solving will increase their level of understanding and awareness.

4th order skills.

Children begin to make decisions which are based on the development of their own current knowledge and understanding. This now becomes part of their own action knowledge.

EXAMPLES

KEY STAGE ONE.

Litter.

The children express their feelings about the litter in their own playground, by discussing it with the teacher and through drawing pictures or simple writing. (1) They then undertake an investigation of the actual litter and record their findings in the form of graphs, pictographs or other appropriate ways. They discuss the range and variety of litter and consider how much of it is a direct result of their actions. (2) They investigate ways of disposing of the litter and how some is harder to get rid of than others. They then try to see how they could improve the look of the playground and keep down the litter. This could involve a survey of bin positions, the emptying programme or the type of food sold in school. (3) Based on the above they may decide to make suggestions for the improvement of the situation and write, draw or talk about the effect of making changes. (4)

KEY STAGE 2.

Environmental change.

Children express their ideas in writing and through speaking about a change that is proposed should take place in their own environment. (1) They find out about the reasons for the change and the possible effect this will have on the local community. They investigate the views of other children and adults regarding this proposal and discover whether there may be a conflict between groups. (2) They understand the way that problems are dealt with in environmental change and discuss a range of actions that could be taken. (3) They come to a personal decision regarding the proposal and weigh their views against the views of others. (4)

Appendix C Field Studies Council Study Centres

Field Studies Council
The Director
Central Services
Field Studies Council
Preston Montford
Montford Bridge
Shrewsbury SY4 1HW
Tel 0743 850674

Dale Fort Field Centre
Dale
Haverfordwest
Dyfed SA62 3RD
Tel 06465 205
Dale fort is situated on the clifftop at the tip of a narrow peninsula at the approach to Milford Haven, South Wales. Magnificent folded and faulted rocks exposed in cliff sections. Variety of coastal habitats and marine biology. The centre operates an ex-RNLI lifeboat so that access is available to the offshore islands.

Flatford Mill Field Centre
East Bergholt
Colchester
Essex CO7 6UL
Tel 0206 298283
Flatford Mill comprises the historic mill, Willy Lott's cottage, and Valley Farm. A most historic setting in 'Constable Country'. A variety of natural and created habitats. A rich agricultural area. Local villages provide interesting architecture. An area full of historic interest.

Juniper Hall Field Centre
Dorking
Surrey RH5 6DA
Tel 0306 883849
Juniper Hall is a large country house in a dry valley of the North Downs near Box Hill. Chalk scenery and other landscapes. A suitable base for studying the effects of the urban sprawl, new towns (Crawley) and transport problems.

Leonard Wills Field Centre
Nettlecombe Court
Williton
Taunton
Somerset TA4 4HT
Tel 0984 40320
The Leonard Wills Centre is a country mansion on the eastern edge of Exmoor about half an hour from Taunton. Close by are marine and freshwater habitats as well as heather moorland. Porlock Bay and the Bristol Channel are nearby.

Preston Montford Field Centre
Montford Bridge
Shrewsbury SY4 1DX
Tel 0743 850380

Preston Montford is a country house set in 12 hectares of grassland bordering the River Severn. It encompasses its own stream and two large ponds. The hills of the Welsh borderlands are close by including the Longmynd with its Carding Mill Valley. Shrewsbury and other historic towns are close to hand as are Ironbridge Industrial Museum and the Acton Scott Farm Museum.

Orielton Field Centre
Pembroke
Dyfed
South Wales SA71 5EZ
Tel 064681 225
Orielton is a Georgian Mansion set in 60 hectares of woodland. Similar field study area to Dale Fort.

Slapton Ley Field Centre
Slapton
Kingsbridge
Devon TQ7 2QP
Tel 0548 580466
Slapton Ley has purpose built accommodation on the Devon coast near Totnes. Sea shore studies are the centre's speciality within the Slapton Ley Nature Reserve. Dartmoor is near to the centre.

Epping Forest Conservation Centre
High Beach
Loughton
Essex IG10 4AF
Tel 081 508 7714
Epping Forest Centre is a day centre managed by the FSC. As the crow flies it is only 12 miles from St Paul's Cathedral in London. Woodland and urban studies

with the intense agriculture of the Lea and Roding valleys. Harlow New Town is close by.

The Drapers' Field Centre
Rhyd-y-creuau
Betwys-y-coed
Gwynedd LL24 0HB
Tel 06902 494
Drapers' Field Centre is situated in the Conwy Valley on the eastern edge of Snowdonia. All of the spectacular landscapes of North Wales are within the environs of Rhyd-y-creuau. Anglesey and the North Wales coast are accessible to the centre. The area is full of historical interest.

Malham Tarn Field Centre
Settle
North Yorkshire BD24 9PU
Tel 07293 331
The centre lies on the north shore of Malham Tarn, part of the limestone plateau of the Yorkshire Dales National Park. Glaciated scenery and features of Karst landscape are its particular speciality. Hill sheep farming and tourism are important local activities.

Fort Popton Field Centre
Angle Bay
Pembroke SA71 3BD
Tel 0646 641404
This centre is a research station directed towards studies of oil pollution. Although it does put on specialist courses it is not intended for school use. It is close to Orielton and Dale Fort if schools wish to visit the area.

Appendix D Urban study centres (source *Streetwise Directory* autumn 1989)

Bath
Huntingdon Centre
Countess of Huntingdon's Chapel
The Vineyards
The Paragon
Bath BA1 5NA
Tel 0225 333895

Brighton
Lewis Cohen Urban Studies Centre
Brighton Polytechnic
68 Grand Parade
Brighton BN2 2JY
Tel 0273 673416

Bristol
Bristol Urban Studies Centre
1 All Saints Court
Bristol BS1 1JN
Tel 0272 277454

Bristol Youth Hostel Association
International Centre
Hayman House
64 Prince Street
Bristol BS1 4HU
Tel 0272 253136

Canterbury
Canterbury Urban Studies Centre
82 Alphege Lane
Canterbury
Kent CT1 2EB
Tel 0227 457009

Chester
St Mary's Centre
St Mary's Hill
Chester CH1 2DW
Tel 0244 603321

Edinburgh
Environment Centre
Drummond High School
Cochran Terrace
Edinburgh EH7 4QP
Tel 031 557 2135

Gillingham
Gillingham Urban Heritage Centre
Byron CP School
Byron Road
Gillingham
Kent
Tel 0634 52981

Glasgow
Bellarmine   Environmental   Resource
Centre
Bellarmine Secondary School
42 Cowglen Road
Pollok
Glasgow
Tel 041 880 7630

Harlow
Harlow Study & Visitors' Centre
Nettleswellbury Farm
Harlow
Essex
Tel 0279 446744

London
Bromley Urban Studies Centre
Kent House Road
Penge
London SE20
Tel 081 676 8560

Hammersmith & Fulham Urban Studies
Centre
1–15 King Street
London W6 9HR
Tel 081 741 7138

Holy Trinity Urban Centre
Carlisle Road
London SE1 7LG
Tel 071 928 5447

Nottingdale Urban Studies Centre
189 Freston Road
London W10 6TH
Tel 081 969 8942

The Urban Studies Centre
Tower Hamlets and Newham
Hayward House
55–58 East India Dock Road
Limehouse
Poplar
London E14 6JE
Tel 091 987 3864

Willowbrook Urban Studies Centre
48 Willowbrook Road
London SW15 6BW
Tel 071 732 8856

Manchester
Manchester Urban Studies Centre
328–330 Deansgate
Manchester M3 4FN
Tel 061 832 5599

Milton Keynes
City Discovery Centre
106 Tanners Drive
Blakelands
Milton Keynes MK14 5BP
Tel 0908 618751

Newcastle on Tyne
Newcastle Architectural Workshop Ltd
6 Higham Place
Newcastle on Tyne NE1 8AF
Tel 091 232 8183

Rhondda
Glyncornel Environmental Centre
Nant-y-Gwyddon Road
Llwynypia
Rhondda CF40 2JF
Tel 0443 431727

Stevenage
Stevenage Urban Studies Centre
Lonsdale Road
Stevenage
Hertfordshire SG1 5DQ
Tel 0438 316102

Swindon
Swindon Urban Studies Centre
North Wilts Centre for the Curriculum
Drove Road
Swindon SN1 3QQ
Tel 0793 616054

Warrington
North Cheshire Urban Studies Centre
New Town House
Buttermarket Street
Warrington WA1 2LF
Tel 0925 51144

Appendix E Youth Hostels with Field Study Centres or Classrooms (England & Wales)

The *Data Pack* for Group Leaders details the facilities at all hostels. Contact YHA, Trevelyan House, St Stephen's Hill, St Albans, Hertfordshire, AL1 2DY. Tel 0727 55215

Hostels with Field Study Centres
Bristol
International Centre
Hayman House
64 Prince Street
Bristol BS1 4HU

Cornwall
Golant YH
Penquite House
Fowey PL23 1LA

Devon
Instow YH
Worlington House
Instow
Bideford EX39 4LW

Somerset
Crowcombe Heathfield YH
Denzel House
Crowcombe Heathfield
Taunton TA4 4BT

Dorset
Swanage YH
Cluny
Cluny Crescent
Swanage BH19 2BS

Suffolk
Blaxhall YH
Heath Walk
Blaxhall
Woodbridge IP12 2EA

Norfolk
Sheringham YH
1 Cremers Drift
Sheringham NR26 8HX

Oxford
Charlbury YH
The Laurels
The Slade
Charlbury OX7 3SJ

Gloucester
Duntisbourne Abbots YH
Cirencester GL7 7JN

Slimbridge YH
Shepherd's Patch
Slimbridge GL2 7BP

Shropshire
Ironbridge Gorge YH
Coalbrookdale Institute
Paradise
Coalbrookdale
Telford

Wilderhope Manor YH
Easthope
Much Wenlock TF13 6EG

Derbyshire
Ilam Hall YH
Nr Ashbourne DE6 2AZ

Hartington YH
Hartington
Buxton SK17 0AT

Eyam YH
The Edge
Eyam S30 1QP

Northumberland
Rock Hall YH
Alnwick NE66 3SB

Teesside
Saltburn YH
Victoria Road
Saltburn by Sea
Cleveland TS12 1JD

Cumbria
High Close YH
Loughrigg
Ambleside LA22 0EU

Hawkshead YH
Esthwaite Lodge
Hawkshead
Ambleside LA22 0QD

Lancashire
Arnside YH
Oakfield Lodge
Redhills Road
Arnside
Carnforth LA5 0AT

Yorkshire
Grinton Lodge YH
Grinton
Richmond DL11 6HS

Boggle Hole YH
Whitby
North Yorks YO22 4UQ

North Wales
Bryn Gwynant
Caernafon LL55 4NP

Llangollen YH
Tyndwr Hall
Tyndwr Road
Llangollen LL20 8AR

Lledr Valley YH
Lledr House
Pont-y-Pant
Dolwwyddelan LL25 0DQ

South Wales
Borth YH
Morlais
Borth SY24 5JS

Llwynypia YH
Glyncornel
Llwynypia
Mid Glamorgan CF40 2JF

Broad Haven YH
Haverfordwest
Dyfed SA62 3JH

Hostels with Classrooms
Devon
Exeter YH
47 Countess Wear Road
Exeter EX2 6LR

Kent
Kemsing YH
Cleves
Pilgrim's Way
Kemsing
Sevenoaks TN15 6LT

Suffolk
Brandon YH
Heath House
Bury Road
Brandon IP27 0BU

Colchester YH
East Bay House
18 East Bay
Colchester CO1 2UE

Essex
Castle Hedingham YH
7 Falcon Square
Halstead CO9 3BU

Norfolk
Norwich YH
112 Tumer Road
Norwich NR2 4HB

Oxford
Ridgeway YH
Court Hill
Wantage

Derbyshire
Edale YH
Rowland Cote
Nether Booth
Edale
Sheffield S30 2ZH

Ravenstor YH
Miller's Dale
Buxton SK17 8SS

Yorkshire
Osmotherley YH
Northallerton
N. Yorks DL6 3AH

Cumbria
Eskdale YH
Boot
Holmrock CA19 1TH

North Wales
Bala YH
Plas Rhiwaedog
Rhos y Gwaliau
Bala LL23 7EU

South Wales
Chepstow YH
Mounton Road
Chepstow NP6 6AA

The Scottish Youth Hostel Association
Scottish YHA
7 Glebe Crescent
Stirling FK8 2JA
Tel 0786 50198

There are 11 'conference centre' hostels in Scotland which will provide field study facilities as for instance at the Loch Lomond Youth Conference Centre. The scheme is operated under the 'Rent A Hostel' title – full details are available from SYHA headquarters.

Youth Hostels Association of Northern Ireland
YHA of Northern Ireland
56 Bradbury Place
Belfast BT7 1RU
Tel 0232 324733

Irish Youth Hostels Association
Irish YHA – An Oige
39 Mountjoy Square
Dublin 1
Tel 001 363111

Many other hostels will allow the use of the dining room as a classroom at times when it is free.

Appendix F RSPB Nature Centres/ Countryside Classrooms

The Lodge The Lodge is also the RSPB headquarters
Sandy
Bedfordshire SG19 2DL
Tel 0767 80551

Lochwinnoch Nature Centre
Largs Road
Lochwinnoch
Renfrewshire
Tel 0505 842663

Vane Farm Nature Centre
Kinross DY13 7LX
Tel 0577 62355

Sandwell Valley Nature Centre
20 Tan House Avenue
Great Barr
Birmingham B43 5AG

Rye House Marsh Countryside Classroom
4 Cecil Road
Rye Park
Hoddesdon
Hertfordshire
Tel 09924 60031

Eastwood Countryside Classroom
12 Fir Tree Crescent
Dukinfield SK16 5EH
Tel 061 303 7449

Fairburn Ings Information Centre
Fairburn
Knottingly
West Yorkshire
Tel 0977 83257

Appendix G　Educational visits to historic sites

Wales
Cadw,
Welsh Historic Monuments
9th Floor
Brunel House
2 Fitzalan Road
Cardiff
CF2 1UY

Scotland
Historic Buildings & Monuments
20 Brandon Street
Edinburgh
EH3 5RA

England
English Heritage
Thames House South
Millbank
London
SW1P 4QJ

Northern Ireland
Department of the Environment for
Northern Ireland
Parliament Building
Stormont
Belfast
BT4 3SS

Royal Palaces
Education Services
Hampton Court Palace
East Molesey
Surrey KT8 9AU

Appendix H　Study Centres at Electricity Generating Power Stations in England and Wales

(Formerly under the control of the Central Electricity Generating Board. Listings based on information from Powergen Public Relations June 1990)

Powergen Centres
Kingsnorth Power Station
Hoo, St Werburgh
Rochester
Kent ME3 9NQ
A wildlife reserve

Hams Hall E S Centre
Hams Hall Power Station
Lea Marston
Sutton Coldfield
West Midlands
Full centre complex, Woodland; ponds;
17th century farm labourer's cottage

Drakelow Field Study Centre
Drakelow Power Station
Near Burton on Trent
Staffordshire DE15 9TZ
Small classroom; 5 hectares of woodland

Rheidol Centre
Rheidol Power Station
Capel Bangor
Aberystwyth
Dyfed SY2 3NB
Field study classroom, $2\frac{1}{2}$ mile trail around reservoir

National Grid
Amersham FS Centre
Mop End
Amersham
Buckinghamshire
(arrangements to
County Adviser for Middle Years

Bucks CC
County Hall
Aylesbury HP20 1UX)
Centre and trail in 30 hectares of woodland

Bishops Wood Educational Study Area
Stourport on Severn
Worcestershire
(arrangements to
Arden Transmission Office
202 Waterloo Road
Yardley
Birmingham B25 8LD
Fully-equipped field classroom; woodland

Bramley Frith Wood Trail
Sub station
Bramley
Basingstoke
(arrangements to
District Manager
Thames District
617 London Road
Reading RG6 1AX)
33 hectares of woodland

Canterbury FS Centre
Ex Broadoak Substation
Broadoak Road
Canterbury
Kent
Study centre in 10 hectares of old gravel workings

Ninfield Study Centre
Potman's Lane
Ninfield
Sussex
(arrangements to
ES Adviser
East Sussex CC
PO Box 4
County Hall
St Annes Crescent
Lewes B77 1SG)
Centre in 22 hectares of woods & meadows

Pelham FS Centre
Pelham Substation
Stocking Pelham
Buntingford
Hertfordshire

Study centre on 20 hectare site of ponds, spinneys & hedges

Penwortham FS Centre
Penwortham Substation
Preston)
(arrangements to
c/o Hothersall Lodge
Longridge
Preston)
Wood, pond & fields beside study centre

National Power
Didcot Power Station
Oxfordshire
(arrangements to
Headteacher
Sutton Courtenay Primary School
Didcot
Oxfordshire
Centre in 18 hectares of regenerated land

Rugeley ES Centre
Rugeley Power Station
Armitage Road
Rugeley
Staffordshire WS15 1PR
Classroom beside lake; woodland; butterfly garden

Thorpe Marsh Nature Reserve
Thorpe Marsh Power Station
(arrangements to
Yorkshire Wildlife Trust
43 Princes Street
Doncaster
South Yorkshire)
25 hectares of nature reserve

Nuclear Electric
Teesmouth FS Centre
Tees Road
Hartlepool
Cleveland
Centre on estuary of Tees

Trawsfynydd Nature Trail
Trawsfynydd Power Station
Trawsfynydd
Blaenau Ffestiniog
Gwynedd LL41 4DT
Trail beside lake and nuclear power station

Appendix I The National Parks of England and Wales

Brecon Beacons
Danywenallt residential centre at Talybont on Usk. Day centres at the mountain centre near Brecon and at Craig-y-nos Country Park in the Upper Swansea Valley.
Brecon Beacons National Park
7 Glamorgan Street
Brecon
Powys LD3 7DP
Tel 0874 4437

The Broads
It was only in 1989 that The Broads was established as an area similarly protected as the other national parks. There are several information centres. Facilities for schools are being developed.
The Broads Authority
Thomas Harvey House
18 Colegate
Norwich
Tel 0603 610734

Dartmoor
There is a schools guided walks service.
Dartmoor National Park
Parke
Haytor Road
Bovey Tracey
Devon TQ13 9JQ
Tel 0626 832093

Exmoor
There is a lecture room at Exmoor House, several field centres which can be used for day visits and some camp sites.
Exmoor National Park
Exmoor House
Dulverton
Somerset TA22 9HL
Tel 0398 23665

Lake District
Residential facilities at Blencathra Centre, Threkeld with day visit bases at Brockhole, Windermere and Seatoller, Borrowdale.

Lake District National Park
National Park Visitor Centre
Brockhole
Windermere
Cumbria LA23 1LJ
Tel 09662 3467

Northumberland
Study bases are to be found at the information centres. Guided walks and fieldwork available.
Northumberland National Park
Eastburn
South Park
Hexham
Northumberland NE46 1BS
Tel 0434 605555

North York Moors
Activities based at the educational visits centre at Danby.
North York Moors National Park
The Moors Centre
Danby
Whitby
North Yorkshire YO21 2NB
Tel 0287 60540

Peak District
Residential centre at Losehill Hall, Castleton with day visit bases at Bakewell, Ilam and Edale.
Peak Park National Park
Losehill Hall
Castleton
Derbyshire S30 2WB
Tel 0433 20373

Pembrokeshire Coast
Residential or day visits at Broad Haven. Day visits at Kilgetty.
Pembrokeshire Coast National Park
County Offices
Haverfordwest
Pembrokeshire
Dyfed SA61 1QZ
Tel 0437 4591

Snowdonia
Residential centre at Plas Tan y Bwlch,
Maentwrog.
Snowdonia National Park
Penrhyndeudraeth
Gwynedd LL48 6LS
Tel 0766 770274

Yorkshire Dales
Day or residential bases at Malham, Cla-
pham and Whernside.
Yorkshire Dales National Park
Colvend
Hebden Road
Grassington
Skipton BD23 5LB
Tel 0756 752748

Appendix J Sandford award winners

AVONCROFT MUSEUM OF
BUILDINGS, Bromsgrove, Worcs (1988)
BEAULIEU ABBEY, Nr Lyndhurst,
Hampshire (1978) (1986)
BEDE MONASTERY MUSEUM, Jarrow,
Tyne and Wear (1988)
BICKLEIGH CASTLE, Nr Tiverton,
Devon (1983) (1988)
BLENHEIM PALACE, Woodstock,
Oxfordshire (1982) (1987)
BOLLING HALL, Bradford, West
Yorkshire (1978) (1987)
THE BOAT MUSEUM, Ellesmere Port,
South Wirral (1986)
BOUGHTON HOUSE, Kettering,
Northants (1988)
BUCKFAST ABBEY, Buckfastleigh,
Devon (1985)
CANTERBURY CATHEDRAL,
Canterbury, Kent (1988)
CASTLE MUSEUM, York (1987)
CASTLE WARD, County Down,
Northern Ireland (1980) (1987)
CATHEDRAL & ABBEY CHURCH OF
ST ALBAN, St Albans, Herts (1986)
CECIL HIGGINS ART GALLERY &
BEDFORD MUSEUM, Bedford (1989)
CHATTERLEY WHITFIELD MINING
MUSEUM, Tunstall, Stoke-on-Trent
(1988)
COLDHARBOUR MILL (1989)
COMBE SYDENHAM, Nr Taunton,
Somerset (1984) (1989)
CROXTETH HALL & COUNTRY PARK,
Liverpool, Merseyside (1980) (1989)
CULZEAN CASTLE & COUNTRY
PARK, Ayrshire, Scotland (1984) (1989)
DODDINGTON HALL, Doddington,
Lincolnshire (1978) (1986)

DRUMLANRIG CASTLE & COUNTRY
PARK, Dumfries (1989)
GAINSBOROUGH OLD HALL,
Gainsborough, Lincolnshire (1988)
GEORGIAN HOUSE, Edinburgh,
Lothian Region (1978)
HAGLEY HALL, Nr Stourbridge, West
Midlands (1981)
HAREWOOD HOUSE, Leeds, West
Yorkshire (1979) (1989)
HOLDENBY HOUSE, Northampton,
Northamptonshire (1985)
HOLKER HALL, Cart in Cartmel,
Cumbria (1982) (1988)
HOPETOUN HOUSE, South
Queensferry, Lothian Region (1983)
HORNSEA MUSEUM, North
Humberside (1987)
IXWORTH ABBEY, Nr Bury St
Edmunds, Suffolk (1982)
LAMPORT HALL, Northampton,
Northamptonshire (1985)
LEIGHTON HALL, Carnforth,
Lancashire (1982)
MACCLESFIELD MUSEUMS,
Macclesfield (1988)
MARGAM PARK, Nr Port Talbot, West
Glamorgan (1981) (1986)
MOSELEY OLD HALL, Wolverhampton,
West Midlands (1983) (1989)
OAKWELL HALL COUNTRY PARK,
Birstall, West Yorkshire (1988)
PENHOW CASTLE, Nr Newport, Gwent
(1980) (1986)
QUARRY BANK MILL, Styal, Cheshire
(1987)
RANGER'S HOUSE, Blackheath,
London (1979) (1987)

ROCKINGHAM CASTLE, Nr Corby, Northamptonshire (1980) (1987)
SHELDON MANOR, Wiltshire (1985)
THE SHUGBOROUGH ESTATE, Stafford (1987)
TATTON PARK, Knutsford, Cheshire (1979) (1987)

TOWER OF LONDON, Tower Bridge, London (1978) (1986)
WIGAN PIER, Lancashire (1987)
WIGHTWICK MANOR, Wolverhampton, West Midlands (1986)
WIMPOLE HALL, Nr Cambridge (1988)
YORK MINSTER, York (1984) (1989)

Useful addresses

Association of Agriculture
Victoria Chambers
16–20 Strutton Ground
London SW1P 2HP
071 222 6115

Civic Trust
17 Carlton House Terrace
London SW1Y 5AW
071 930 0914

The Conservation Trust
George Palmer Site
Northumberland Avenue
Reading
Berkshire RG2 7PW
0734 868442

Council for Environmental Education
School of Education
University of Reading
London Road
Reading
Berkshire RG1 5AQ
0734 317921

National Association for Environmental Education
(NAEE)
Wolverhampton Polytechnic
Walsall Campus
Gorway
Walsall
West Midlands WS1 3BD
0922 31200

Nature Conservancy Council
North Minster House
Peterborough
Cambridgeshire PE1 1UA
0733 40345

Tidy Britain Group
The Pier
Wigan
Greater Manchester WN3 4EX
0942 824620

United Nations Environment Programme
PO Box 30552
Nairobi
Kenya
East Africa
010 2542 333930

Watch
The Green
Witham Park
Lincoln LN5 7JR
0522 544400

World Wild Fund for Nature (UK)
Panda House
Weyside Park
Godalming
Surrey GU17 1XR
0483 426444

References

Chapter 1

1 UNESCO 1977. Conference Proceedings. Environmental Education in the UK. Papers prepared as part of the UK delegation's contribution to the UNESCO inter-governmental conference, Tbilisi USSR

2 Carson S McB (Ed) 1978 *Environmental Education – Principles and Practice* London, Edward Arnold

3 Carson R 1962 *Silent Spring* Penguin

4 International Union for the Conservation of Nature and Natural Resources (IUCN) 1970. Final report *International Working Meeting on Environmental Education in the School Curriculum* IUCN

5 DES 1967 *Children and their Primary Schools* (The Plowden Report), HMSO

6 UNESCO 1977 *The International Workshop on Environmental Education Belgrade October 1975 Final Report*

7 IUCN 1980 *The World Conservation Strategy*

8 *The Conservation and Development Programme for the UK (a response to the World Conservation Strategy)* 1983 Kogan Paul

9 UNESCO 1980 *Environmental Education in the light of the Tbilisi Conference. Education on the Move* UNESCO

10 Booth R 1987 *Thoughts after Moscow* Annual Review of Environmental Education. Council for Environmental Education

11 UNESCO 1975 *Trends in Environmental Education* (based on working documents for the Belgrade Conference)

12 National Association for Environmental Education 1982 *A Statement of Aims* NAEE publication

13 CEE 1987 *Introducing Environmental Education* Book 2. Schools: Educating for Life CEE

14 Schools Council 1974 *Project Environment* Longmans

15 Scottish Education Department 1974 *Environmental Education A report by HM Inspectors of Schools (Scotland)* HMSO Scotland

16 Schools Council 1972 Environmental Studies Project (5–13) Rupert Hart-Davies Educational

17 DES 1985 *Quality in Schools: Evaluation and Appraisal* HMSO

18 DES 1984 *Learning and Teaching: The Environment and Primary School Curriculum* HMSO Scotland

19 DES 1985 *The Curriculum from 5–16* Curriculum Matters 2 HMSO

20 DES 1989 *Environmental Education from 5–16* Curriculum Matters 13 HMSO

21 City of Birmingham Education Department 1980 *Curriculum Guidelines*

22 Kent County Council 1988 *An Education for Life. Kent Curriculum Statement Children aged 5–16* Kent CC

23 Hertfordshire County Council 1978 *Environmental Education Guidelines for the Primary and Middle Years*

24 City of Birmingham Education Committee 1980 *Further developments in the Primary Curriculum Environmental Education*

25 Palmer 1977 *Progress and continuity in skill acquisition through Environmental Education in the Primary School* Volume 6 1977 *Environmental Education* NAEE

26 Neal 1982 *Environmental Education. It must start early* Times Educational Supplement

27 DES 1986 *Geography from 5–16* Curriculum Matters 7 HMSO

Chapter 2

1 DES 1987 *The National Curriculum 5–16 A consultation document* HMSO
2 CEE 1989 (Unpublished response to National Curriculum documentation)
3 Letter to NAEE October 1988
4 World Commission on Environmental Development 1987 *Our Common Future* The Brundtland Report OUP
5 DES 1989 *Environmental Education from 5–16* Curriculum Matters 13 HMSO

Chapter 3

1 The Conservation and Development Programme for the UK (a response to the World Conservation Strategy) 1983, Kogan Paul
2 National Curriculum Council 1989 *A Framework for the Primary Curriculum* Curriculum Guidance 1 NCC
3 City of Sheffield 1989 *Curriculum Policy Statement* City of Sheffield Council
4 Norfolk County Council 1989 *A Statement of Policy for the Curriculum 5–16* and *Environmental Education Primary Guidelines. An Agenda for Action* Norfolk CC
5 Wiltshire County Council 1989 *The Wiltshire Curriculum Policy 5–16* Wiltshire CC
6 Kent County Council 1988 *Kent Curriculum Statement: Children aged 5–16* Kent CC
7 Scottish Environmental Education Council 1987 *Curriculum Guidelines for Environmental Education* SEEC
8 UNESCO/UNEP Environmental Education newsletter 'Connect' volume XIV no 3 September 1989. A fuller presentation and development can be found in the UNESCO/UNEP International Environmental Education Programme (IEEP) publication no 22 in the Environmental Education series *Procedures for Developing an Environmental Education Curriculum*
9 DES 1985 *The Curriculum from 5–16* Curriculum Matters 2 HMSO
10 New South Wales Department of Education 1989 *Environmental Education guidelines* New South Wales Australia
11 Nature Conservancy Council 1988 *Nature Areas and the Primary Curriculum* Conservation Education Matters 2 NCC

Chapter 4

1 NCC 1989 unpublished submission by the Environmental Task Group
2 DES 1988 Curriculum Matters Series HMSO
3 Science 5–13 Macdonald Educational Schools Council 1972

Chapter 5

1 Morrison 1989 *Assessment, Environmental Education and the National Curriculum* NAEE conference paper Durham 1989
2 Environmental Education Task Group 1989 *Environmental Education as a cross curricular component of the national curriculum – towards a rationale* Consultation document CEE
3 Morrison 1989 *Assessing Skills Progression in Environmental Studies Curricula* NAEE Occasional Paper 12

Chapter 6

1 *The Conservation and Development Programme for the UK (a response to the World Conservation Strategy* 1983 Kogan Paul

2 DES 1989 *Environmental Education from 5–16* Curriculum Matters 13 HMSO

Chapter 7

1 Kent County Council 1988 *An Education for Life. Kent Curriculum Statement Children aged 5 to 16* Kent CC
2 Wolverhampton Borough Council Environmental Awareness Unit
3 Palmer and Wise 1982 *The Good, the Bad and the Ugly* Geographical Association
4 DES 1989 *Safety in Schools* HMSO
5 NAEE 1988 *Organisation of Outdoor Studies and Visits* Practical Guide 2 NAEE

Chapter 8

1 DES 1989 *Environmental Education from 5 to 16* Curriculum Matters 13 HMSO
2 *Historic Houses, Castles and Gardens* and *Museums and Galleries* published annually by British Leisure Publications

Chapter 9

1 DTI 1989 *Evaluation of Primary School Industry Links 1986–89* DTI
2 NAEE *Environmental Education* published termly NAEE
3 NAEE *Incubator in the Classroom* and *Traffic Study and Surveys*

The following publications are also useful:
DES 1981 *Environmental Education – a Review* HMSO

DES 1983 *A survey of environmental education in some Derbyshire Primary Schools* Report by HM Inspectors 5910/7017 143/83 DS 19/82 DES

DES 1985 *History in the Primary and Secondary Years. An HMI view* HMSO

DES 1989 *Aspects of Primary Education. The teaching and learning of History and Geography* HMSO

Mays 1985 *Teaching Children through the Environment* Hodder & Stoughton

Taylor 1980 *Towards a school policy in environmental education* Scottish Committee for Environmental Education

Smyth 1987 *Tbilisi plus ten* Annual Review of Environmental Education CEE

McLeish 1987 *The National Curriculum 5–16 Threat or Promise* AREE CEE

Essex County Council *Essex assessment initiatives. Primary and Secondary* Essex CC (30 or more local authorities have also published assessment resources)

Bennett 1985 *Evaluating Environmental Education in Schools* UNESCO – UNEP Environmental Education series 12

Lange *Environmental Education Needs Assessment and Evaluation Manual* (Two volumes) Denver CO: Colorado Department of Education 1980 (Order nos ED 199 093, ED 199 094)

Environmental Education Program Evaluation ERIC/SMEAC Environmental Education Fact Sheet No 1. Available from: ERIC Document Reproduction Service, PO Box 190, Arlington, VA 22210, United States of America

The Journal of Environmental Education Special issue – Evaluating Environmental Education Programs Volume 13 No 4 (Summer 1982) Published in the United States. Contains a number of useful case-studies in environmental education evaluation.

A Guide to Teacher Assessment 1990 School Examinations & Assessment Council

Munby 1989 *Assessing and Recording Achievement* Blackwell Education

Morrison and Ridley 1988 *Curriculum Planning and the Primary School* Paul Chapman Publishing Company

Tann 1988 *Developing Topic Work in the Primary School* Falmer Press

Northamptonshire Association for Environmental Education *School Grounds Resource List* NAEE

National Association for Environmental Education selected publications:

Practical guides:
1 Incubator in the classroom
2 Organisation of Outdoor Studies and Visits
4 Using the School Greenhouse
5 An Aviary in School
6 An Aquarium in School
7 Heritage Education
8 Using Maps 5–16
9 Traffic Study and Surveys
10 Amphibians and Reptiles
11 Developing a School Nature Reserve
12 Creating and maintaining a Garden to Attract Butterflies
13 Using Invertebrates in the Classroom

Occasional papers:
2 Environmental Education – Its Future Role
9 Planners and Environmental Education
13 The National Curriculum – The Location of Environmental Education as a Cross Curricula Issue

Other publications:
Using the Environment in Early Education NAEE

Environmental Education The termly journal of the NAEE

Annual Review of Environmental Education Annual journal of the CEE

Index